# Exploring the Labyrinth

For Anna

# EXPLORING THE LABYRINTH

## *Making Sense of the New Spirituality*

Nevill Drury

CONTINUUM • NEW YORK

1999
The Continuum Publishing Company
370 Lexington Avenue
New York, NY 10017

Printed in the United States of America

*Library of Congress Cataloging-in-Publication Data*

Drury, Nevill, 1947—
    Exploring the labyrinth : making sense of the new spirituality /
Nevill Drury.
        p. cm.
    Includes bibliographical references and index.
    ISBN 0—8264—1182—7
    1. New Age movement.    2. Christianity and other religions— New Age
movement.    I. Title.
BP605.N48D78    1999
299'.93— dc21                                                          99-13593
                                                                          CIP

# Contents

# Acknowledgements

Many people have assisted me in the preparation of this book, both directly and indirectly. As a result of my involvement with various transpersonal conferences over almost two decades, and also 'through my role as editor of the holistic health magazine *Nature & Health* for six years during the 1980s, I have been privileged to meet a number of very special people who have been instrumental in shaping the New Spirituality of the 1990s. They include Stanislav Grof, Michael Harner, Jean Houston and her husband Robert Masters, Timothy Leary, John Lilly, Joan Halifax, Starhawk, Charles Tart, Ralph Metzner, James Fadiman, Kenneth Ring, Robert Monroe and Terence McKenna, and I thank them all for sharing their perspectives with me. Other influential figures like Mircea Eliade, Joseph Campbell, Alan Watts, Carlos Castaneda, Ken Wilber, Ram Dass, David Spangler, Elisabeth Kubler-Ross, Jean Shinoda Bolen and Fritjof Capra I know only through their writings and published interviews, but they too have had a major impact on my own perspectives. To all of these people I owe an enormous debt of thanks.

For their helpful editorial suggestions I would like to thank Jane Gleeson-White, Emma Cotter and Patrick Gallagher of Allen & Unwin. And, most importantly of all, I would like to thank my wife Anna Voigt, for her encouragement and support— and for helping me to revitalise my own creative endeavours over the last few years. This book owes as much to her as anyone.

# Introduction

Any book on spirituality must remain, on one level or another, highly personal. Personal in terms of the particular points of emphasis one brings to the text and personal also in terms of the process of reflective thought which accompanies the writing itself. The book becomes a journey and helps to clarify issues which arise as one seeks to assemble strands of data into a meaningful sequence of ideas. Writing also helps to bring into focus issues which may have lain dormant or unresolved for many years. Writing this particular book was very much like this for me.

My wife Anna and I very much enjoy strolling along the sandy coastline near our home, exploring the play of the waves as they flow up onto the beach, and watching intently as the sea crests against the jagged rock formations that are part of the terrain. Recently, while I was walking along the beach, I realised for the first time that the flow of the sea onto the sand could teach me almost everything I really needed to know about my spiritual identity and my life upon this earth. I reflected on the beauty and distinctiveness of an arched wave—that exquisite moment when an individual wave seems poised in the air before crashing into formlessness—and it reminded me that all forms have their special moment of uniqueness before dissolving into a greater, more all encompassing domain. It seems to me that not only individual lives but also religious teachings and ideas are like that too. They have their time and currency in history but eventually yield to the tides of change, as more expansive perspectives take their place, or as new modifications transform the original vision into a form more relevant to the times.

I also noticed all the intersecting eddies in the water, running at odds with each other and then being forced by the prevailing potency of the current to resolve themselves in a unified direction. At present the world seems beset by an enormous number of political and social difficulties, many of them the consequence of a clash of wills in the struggle for power or dominance. But the eddies in the sea suggested to me that while in all circumstances interactions produce outcomes, beneath the torrents of individual lives in conflict life itself continues. The planet and the cosmos are far bigger than all of us, and will be here in one form or another long after we are gone. In this context our individual struggles and concerns are essentially ephemeral and transient, however significant they seem at the time.

This last point was brought home to me by the insubstantiality of the foam upon the sand. Each bubble had its moment of light and brilliance, reflecting the sun in its brief life upon the beach. But each small bubble soon dissolved and was gone, absorbed within the tidal ebb and flow of successive waves upon the sand.

Familiar as it is as an image from eastern mysticism, the idea of the ocean as a symbol for the vastness of life and spirit seems entirely appropriate to me. And I feel that contemporary spirituality reflects something of this too. There is now a call for an approach to spirituality unfettered by the limitations of belief and doctrine, attuned to the natural rhythms of the earth and cosmos. There is a call for us to appreciate what the philosopher Gregory Bateson called 'the pattern that connects'—the flow of intersecting, intermingling spiritual eddies and ideas which constitutes the tide of human consciousness itself. A call to recognise the spiritual dimensions of life which unite us—rather than be preoccupied with forces that divide us from one another.

For many years I have been interested in the nature of mystical and visionary consciousness but until I worked on this book I hadn't really resolved for myself how I really felt about the new spiritual undercurrents emerging in our society, and their relationship to orthodox religion. We live in times of widespread social upheaval and confusion amidst the turbulent pace of technological change. Some people have responded by clinging to their religious beliefs like a type of fixed point within the midst of all this change—and for me this helps explain the rise of Christian and Islamic fundamentalism. But others are keen to see where the tides of change will take them. For these people, the limits of personal belief are yet another challenge to be overcome.

I must make an admission right away. Although this book is subtitled *Making Sense of the New Spirituality* it is really about the New Age or, more specifically, about those aspects of the New Age that I consider both valuable and useful. For the most part, though, I would prefer not to use the term *New Age*, and in this book I am calling it instead the *New Spirituality*. I feel that this can easily be justified. For many, the expression 'New Age' has become debased, if not totally discredited. It is widely employed in the popular media to connote a type of faddish contemporary 'religion' that focuses on the individual and is therefore narcissistic and hedonistic. It is also associated with baby-boomer materialism and with an extraordinary array of alternative therapies, metaphysical products and self-help gimmicks, and is rarely taken seriously. So I am proposing the alternative in an attempt to be heard in the first instance, rather than be dismissed without a second thought. I am also using this approach because I believe that the New Spirituality, despite its many flaws, offers a potentially revolutionary expansion beyond the constrictions of formal religious doctrine and practice whilst also avoiding the pitfalls of reductionist scepticism.

It also seems to me that the issue of *religious belief* itself is one we must consider, because once we delineate belief we propose boundaries, and the New Spirituality is all about pushing boundaries—if not dissolving them altogether. So, basically I am opting to use the expression *New Spirituality* because I think there are some major issues involved, and they are well worth considering if we are to retain our sanity and our authenticity in the 1990s. These issues are essentially what this book is all about.

Another point must be made right away, and it is one which has already been affirmed by a number of commentators in this field: *many elements within the New Spirituality of the 1990s are not especially 'new'*. If the New Spirituality draws substantially on the wisdom traditions and health modalities of the East, as will become clear, so too does it also ground itself within the mystical and metaphysical traditions of the West. Indeed, many of its themes have existed for centuries in one form or another. It is by fusing ancient mystical thought with the more recent perspectives of depth psychology, experiential consciousness research and a certain egalitarianism of spiritual belief and practice, that it has acquired its distinctive characteristics today.

However, while as I have said, certain elements within the media and also within the Church have hastened to present the New Age as a somewhat faddish phenomenon associated primarily with self-gratification and narcissistic indulgence, it seems to me that something potentially much more significant is taking place. In my view we are dealing here with the development of a broad-based spiritual perspective which may well consolidate with time into a quite different type of public awareness—different from most forms of institutionalised religion, for reasons which will be explained later, and also different from the secular humanism which for many has replaced adherence to religious faith altogether. It may well be that the New Spirituality enters this divide mid-way, moving away from conventional religious patterns on the one hand but also acknowledging spirituality as an innate dimension of the human condition on the other. We may, indeed, come close to the mark if we consider the New Spirituality as a type of *spiritual humanism*—a form of humanism which finds a sacred or spiritual dimension at the deepest level of human experience and which acknowledges this dimension as one which transcends the limitations of formal religious allegiance.

In more recent times I have felt the need—as many others have—to differentiate between religion and spirituality. For me, religion implies adherence to a specific doctrine or belief system and this in turn brings with it the need for conceptual boundaries—because one is necessarily excluding other religious teachings through the very act of personal allegiance. Spirituality on the other hand seems to me to be all about sacred values and qualities that remain eternally profound without being subsumed as the exclusive property of any specific belief system or institution. Spirituality can, and often does, reside within religious traditions, but is not contained by them. Neither is spirituality restricted by temporal authority—it is a timeless and transcendent dimension of our existence and knows no philosophical or cultural boundaries. Many have referred to it as the *very ground of our being*. This is how I regard it also.

This book could have been written in a number of different ways, and perhaps I should explain why I have structured it the way I have. As a starting point, I believe that a fundamental distinction can be made between following a specific belief system founded on revelation—as with Judaism, Christianity, and Islam, for example—and pursuing the more generalised eclecticism of the New Spirituality. The fundamentalist forms of the major Western faiths exclude those who are not devotees—outsiders literally have no spiritual future—whereas the New Spirituality is essentially inclusive and holistic and does not judge or damn those who fail to adhere to the dominant tenets of the faith. With this distinction in mind, I have spent some time in this book exploring the visionary origins of some of the major religious traditions in an effort to explain how the universal aspects of mystical experience could, perhaps, inspire all of us towards greater spiritual self-knowledge and religious tolerance.

Like many others who have explored contemporary spirituality I feel that religious and metaphysical concepts from both east and west inform the New Spirituality, and I have given each of these a separate chapter. However various psychological thinkers—including Freud, Jung, Maslow, Stanislav Grof and Ken Wilber—have also played a crucial role in the emergence of the new spiritual paradigm. These frameworks and ideas are introduced at different stages of the book because some of these key figures draw heavily on mystical and cosmological concepts requiring prior explanation. Neither have I shied away from giving space to some of the major 'popularisers' of the movement—the New Age gurus who have attracted considerable attention, and criticism, in the international media. Attention-seeking channellers, psychics, past-life therapists and show-biz healers have all played a part in drawing attention to some of the main ideas in the New Spirituality but in my view do not push these ideas nearly deep enough. My main objection to these individuals is not so much that they are essentially self-serving but that they so often trivialise issues that are really important. In doing this they attract ridicule from the public at large and this in turn debases the New Spirituality as a whole. Personally I believe the central themes of the New Spirituality deserve better treatment than this.

Finally, an interesting comparison may be made between the very earliest spiritual tradition on the planet—shamanism—and perspectives which have emerged from the New Physics. Both support the idea of interconnectedness, and the concept of a universe which is fundamentally *alive*. Shamanic cultures are animistic, and for them the whole world consists of *spirit*. I am not suggesting that contemporary physicists share this view specifically, but several proponents of the New Physics believe that it is increasingly difficult to distinguish between living and inert matter. And as physicist David Bohm has pointed out, consciousness may be fundamental to the very structure of the universe.

This is a challenging idea indeed, and one which no doubt will cause sceptics and materialist reductionists some concern. Nevertheless the New Spirituality itself presents us with a whole spectrum of challenges, encompassing the very nature of both life and death. The key task as I see it is to merge authentic spiritual perspectives with the findings of modern science and psychology, and in so doing to try to make sense of our lives on the planet. What could be more fundamentally important than exploring the frontiers of our spiritual awareness?

*Nevill Drury*
*Thirroul, 1998*

# 1
# The Roots of the New Spirituality

*Our dreams are a second life*
—Gerard de Nerval

*We are a more extraordinary animal than we think,*
*but also a more dangerous one;*
*We are closer to destruction and to transcendence than we*
*know,*
*In a race with the different pieces of ourselves*
—Robert Ornstein

If we are to understand the core orientation of the New Spirituality we must first consider some basic issues related to the fundamentals of religious belief, faith and experience.

In the first instance a contrast may be made between formal, institutional forms of western religion like Judaism, Christianity and Islam—the 'pillars' of the western religious tradition—and the broad-based spiritual eclecticism which characterises popular western culture in the 1990s. Sooner or later we are obliged to distinguish between those who adhere to the core doctrines of the dominant western religious belief systems—and who by definition tend to base their personal religious perspectives on the principle of a unique spiritual revelation—and those who are less interested in personal salvation than in exploring the many paths which lead towards individual and global transformation.

Those in the latter camp are likely to find illumination in diversity, exploring spiritual traditions from both East and West in the belief that, essentially, spiritual truth is where you find it. A century ago spiritual eclecticism of this sort was associated with organisations like the Theosophical Society which proposed

1

the idea of a universal wisdom tradition unhindered by cultural or historic boundaries. Within this eclectic perspective—an eclecticism which continues in the New Spirituality of the 1990s—no particular spiritual teaching can claim dominance or exclusivity, and there are many equally valid pathways associated with the human quest for spiritual grace and salvation. It seems to me that this particular distinction is still a vital one in our own times and that once again it demands resolution—for the very concept of religious tolerance depends upon it. Among the core questions are these: Can spiritual truth be found in more than one place, and in more than one religious tradition? Does adherence to one doctrine entail rejecting all others? Is one spiritual teacher more 'enlightened' or special than another?

Put simply, the New Spirituality embraces openness rather than exclusivity and favours experience over doctrine, but it is not simply a fusion of Eastern mysticism and Western esotericism served up in a new guise. It has also drawn on many of the self-help modalities and motivational perspectives derived in-itially from humanistic psychology, so we are obliged to look at the rise of psychological theory if we wish to understand the position of the New Spirituality in the 1990s. This in turn involves exploring what used to be called the human potential movement—itself an offshoot of transpersonal psychology—which developed in the early 1970s from humanistic psychology. Both owe a profound debt to Sigmund Freud and Carl Jung, and so we must consider these 'precursors' as well. As will become apparent, the New Spirituality draws concurrently on a wide number of spiritual and psychological perspectives—some of them drawn from earlier civilisations and cultures, others asso-ciated with our own era. But the fusion itself is very much of our own time, and has arisen in response to the needs of many of us living on the planet now. In this sense the New Spirituality is both old and new, a continuation of the ancient and perennial wisdom traditions combined with themes and issues that are entirely contemporary.

## THE CONTRIBUTION OF FREUD AND JUNG

Freud and Jung are both important in the development of the New Spirituality because both highlighted the inner resources of human consciousness. Freud had led the way with his extremely important work *The Interpretation of Dreams*, first published in 1900, which explained for the first time the censoring role of the ego on the unconscious mind. Dreams allowed this censor to be removed, enabling wish-fulfilments to express themselves. Here in the unconscious mind lay a reservoir of imagery, of repressed thoughts and emotions, which could potentially impinge on everyday awareness but which, through dreams, provided an 'escape valve' for pent-up psychic conflict. Freud was also challenging the somewhat smug world-view that had developed with the nineteenth century concepts of civilisation and progress. Suddenly Freud was exposing humanity's psychic underbelly by pointing out the awesome power of dream imagery and its connection with human personality and motivation. Humanity was less 'stable' than it appeared, and his new approach to therapy acknowledged the potent dynamics of the unconscious.

For Freud, the essential task of psychoanalysis, in aiding the process of self-knowledge and personal growth, was to help the patient recover and reintegrate material from the unconscious mind—and in so doing to counter psychosis and neurosis. Freud's concept of self-knowledge entailed discovering who one *is*, which in turn entailed becoming what one was not before. As Ilham Dilman, a noted interpreter of Freud, has observed: 'It is not only the shedding of screens, but also the integration of what is old, and the assimilation of what is new.'[1]

Freud was especially interested in the less familiar areas of the mind, which he termed the 'pre-conscious'—representing areas like immediate memories, readily accessible to consciousness—and the 'unconscious', that vast pool of non-conscious material including instincts and repressed memories. Early on, Freud considered erotic and physically gratifying sexual instincts and aggressive, destructive instincts to be the two main impulses of human life. He later changed his emphasis, contrasting life-supporting and life-denying instincts as unresolved polarities in human nature. He conceived of a conscious ego welling up from a formless, unorganised *id*, representing a kind of 'reservoir of energy for the whole personality'.[2] The life-instinct, or *libido*, he tended to equate with sexual energy: a support for the ego in its quest to pursue pleasure and self-preservation. Freud also formulated his idea of the super-ego as a censor to the ego, inhibiting unwelcome thoughts and providing a sense of morality or conscience. In this sense the super-ego was a restrictive overseer of voluntary actions.

According to Freud, however, the unconscious contents of the mind only remained unconscious at the expense of a considerable amount of libidinal energy. He also believed that the dramatic release of pent-up energies invariably provided a sense of 'explosive satisfaction'.[3] In making this observation, Freud influenced both Wilhelm Reich, and in turn many forms of contemporary New Age 'bodywork', which tend to regard the body's musculature as a repository of stored tension and sexual repression. Freud's insight also underlies the development of modern cathartic approaches to mind and body which help to move subjects past barriers of blocked emotion and provide a supportive setting for releasing these energies in a dramatic outpouring. These therapies are discussed in more detail later in this book, in the section dealing with alternative and holistic approaches to health and well-being.

Freud emphasised that energy could be rechannelled from essentially sexual, or aggressive, goals towards artistic, intellectual or cultural pursuits, but he believed that, in essence, human beings are not the rational creatures they think they are. Instead, he regarded them as beings driven by powerful emotional forces which were unconscious in origin—the restriction of these forces invariably leading to neurosis, suffering and pain.

Freud liked to believe in a world where, ideally, the rational ego could rise up and overcome the irrational id—he once declared, 'Where id is, there let ego be'[4]—but he also felt that there were no psychological accidents in human behaviour. Our choice of friends, locations, favourite foods, recreational pastimes—all of these, he believed, were linked to unconscious memories, and in turn provided clues towards a rationale of our conscious lives. The essential task, then, was to further self-knowledge by probing as far as possible into the contents of the unconscious mind. Freud developed psychoanalysis specifically with this purpose in mind. It was intended 'to liberate previously inaccessible unconscious materials so that they may be dealt with consciously',[5] thereby enabling people to be freed from the suffering they so often bring upon themselves.

The idea that we cause our own suffering and, by extension, that we are to blame for many of the diseases we inflict upon ourselves, is also very much a New Age belief. In a manner which blends Freud and the Hindu concept of karma, it is now

4

fashionable to emphasise that we each 'create our own reality' and that each of us in turn should take the responsibility to liberate ourselves from the shortcomings that we have unconsciously 'chosen'. This is Freud simplified to the point of a cliché, but nevertheless expressed in a manner which is easy to understand. It also aligns with Freud's notion that the practical goal of psychoanalysis is to strengthen the ego—to eliminate the unconscious blocks which cause self-destructive behaviour. The Freudian idea of personal growth is therefore to reclaim one's life-energy from the grip of the unconscious.

According to Freud, one of the most important pathways to one's unconscious energies was through analysing the contents of dreams. Dreams, he believed, provided 'the royal road to a knowledge of the unconscious'. While he had originally considered that dreams were a garbled expression of mental events, after formulating the concept of the id in 1897 he arrived at the conclusion that we all dream because the id yearns for self-expression. Sleep relaxes the ego's censoring control of the unconscious, allowing all manner of fantasies and wish-fulfilments to rise. For Freud, every dream—even a nightmare or anxiety dream—was an attempt to fulfil a wish, and these wish-fulfilments could stem as much from early childhood as from current daily events. Freud also noted that in neurotic behaviour sexuality was invariably associated with repressed or suppressed wishes. All of these patterns one could uncover through dream analysis or, as Freud termed it, 'dream-work'.

During sleep the dreamer's mind would find expression in dreams. Freud therefore developed the technique of afterwards talking his patients through their dreams, heeding their own 'free association' of ideas and memories, and then scrutinising the dream reports in detail. Basically, Freud believed that dreams help the psyche to protect and satisfy itself, channelling previously unfulfilled desires through to awareness without arousing the resting physical body. Dreams could therefore be seen as a way of playing out fantasies which could not be fulfilled during the day. It was intriguing to Freud how often dreams allowed a person to overstep the boundaries of conventional morality, but this in turn was a key to understanding their role: dreams were able to help release tension because the id made no distinction between the resolution of needs in the physical, sensory world or the dream world.

Although dreams would often appear jumbled and distorted, Freud showed that they could be unravelled and decoded.

5

However he was inclined to look for recurring motifs in dreams, with specific connotations. Freud believed that dream symbols usually represented the human body in some way—long stiff objects equating with the penis, hair-cutting with castration, boxes and chests with the womb, walking up and down steps with coitus, and so on—and he came to view such dreams as symbolic expressions of sex wishes.[6] It was here, in particular, that he would come to part company with Carl Jung, whose analysis of dreams had a quite different emphasis.

Jung acknowledged the pioneering role in dream analysis made by Freud and he said of him that 'by evaluating dreams as the most important source of information concerning the unconscious processes, he gave back to mankind a tool that had seemed irretrievably lost'.[7] Nevertheless, while Jung accepted the Freudian concept of a personal unconscious he soon began to conceive of a broader-based 'collective' unconscious which transcended the individual psyche. He also found himself increasingly dissatisfied with Freud's model of sexual repression and made the final split with him in 1912, following the publication of *Symbols of Transformation*, which rejected the sexual libido.

There was also a more profound issue at stake. Jung believed that Freud had not ventured far enough into the spiritual depths of the mind—that beyond the biographical and sexual components of the unconscious there were also mythic 'archetypes' that provided the core impetus for visionary and religious experience. According to Jung, these archetypes transcended personal and cultural variables and manifested in numerous symbolic forms around the world, always having a profound impact on those visionaries fortunate enough to enounter them first-hand through dreams, altered states of consciousness like trances or mystical visions, or through acts of creative inspiration in art, music and literature.

Jung was making a momentous point that in many ways underscores the entire ethos of the New Spirituality today: namely, that divinity is not external to humanity but lies within—that it is an aspect of our 'humanness' which we all share and can have access to. In subsequent writings Jung would increasingly emphasise that the sacred depths of the psyche provided the origin of all religious and mystical experiences, and to this extent he was continuing the Gnostic emphasis on spiritual knowledge referred to earlier. For Jung, dream-work and therapies based on 'active imagination' could open the individual systematically to archetypal awareness, opening the door literally to the 'God consciousness' within. Jung's approach also differed from the Judaeo-Christian model, for it was not a matter of believing in a 'God up There', external to human events, so much as recognising the divine potentiality within every human being. The encounter with the archetypes was not simply an act of grace bestowed by God: one could facilitate the process of spiritual awareness oneself, through dream-work and visualisation techniques, as well as through other techniques like meditation and yoga.

In rejecting Freud's view of the unconscious as too narrow, Jung increasingly recognised that the unconscious seemed to contain a vast storehouse of imagery which was much greater than the repressions of the individual. It also seemed to him that to a certain extent the unconscious appeared to act independently of the conscious mind. In addition, Jung began to move away from Freud's original approach to dream analysis, relying less on the 'free association' technique. Gradually he came to the view that to allow the patient to discuss dreams at random would entail moving away from the dream itself. For him each dream was complete within itself and 'expressed something specific that the unconscious was trying to say'. Whereas Freud invariably tended to uncover sexual motifs in dreams, Jung regarded the individual situation as foremost in solving the language of the dream, rather than attempting to identify fixed motifs like the penis or breast. Jung emphasised this point when he wrote:

> A man may dream of inserting a key in a lock, of wielding a heavy stick, or of breaking down a door with a battering ram. Each of these can be regarded as a sexual allegory. But the fact that his unconscious, for its own purposes, has chosen one of these specific images—it may be the key, the stick or the battering ram—is also of major significance. The real task is to understand why the key has been preferred to the stick, or the stick to the ram. And sometimes this might even lead one to discover that it is not the sexual act at all that is represented, but some quite different psychological point.[8]

Jung concluded that the dream had 'its own limitation' and could not be manipulated so that a symbol meant the same thing in every dream. Nevertheless the dream was not a random occurrence but intrinsically made sense, if only its meaning could be discovered. The dream was 'a specific expression of the unconscious'⁹ and the reason why it was expressed at all, said Jung, was that it was compensating for aspects of the personality which were unbalanced. An over-egotistical person would frequently have dreams about symbolically 'coming down to earth' for example.

But there were also certain motifs within dreams which did not seem to Jung to be a part of the individual psyche. It was the study of these symbols which led him to formulate the concept of the 'collective unconscious':

> There are many symbols that are not individual but collective in their nature and origin. These are chiefly religious images; their origin is so far buried in the mystery of the past that they seem to have no human source. But they are, in fact, 'collective representations' emanating from primeval dreams and creative fantasies. As such, these images are involuntary spontaneous manifestations and by no means intentional inventions.¹⁰

What Jung was saying, in effect, was that at a certain psychic level, motifs common to the whole of mankind were capable of manifesting in dreams. These motifs were a symbolic expression of 'the constantly repeated experiences of humanity'. That is to say, they were derived from observations about Nature (the sky, changes of the seasons, and so on) which had become embedded in the psychic patterns of the whole species. Jung called these primordial images 'archetypes' and gave the following example of how an archetype is formed:

> One of the commonest and at the same time most impressive experiences is the apparent movement of the sun every day. We certainly cannot discover anything of this kind in the unconscious, so far as the known physical process is concerned. What we do find, on the other hand, is the myth of the sun hero in all its countless modifications. It is this myth and *not the physical process* that forms the archetype.¹¹

Thus the archetype may take the form of an anthropomorphic rendition of a force in Nature. Its potency derives from the fact that the observation of the Sun's movement constitutes one of the universal, fundamental experiences of existence, and is something which humans cannot change, a power beyond our manipulation. The Sun becomes an object of veneration, and mystically one of a number of archetypes with which to identify in religious or ritual acts of transcendence. Naturally, different cultures would conceive of the sun-hero in a different form (for example, as Apollo–Helios in classical Rome and Greece, Ohrmazd in ancient Persia) because traditions and styles colour our various conceptions, but Jung regarded all of these as patterns on a theme—the core common to all of these specific representations being, in this instance, the archetypal sun-god himself. But apart from its universality there was another side to the archetype—its awe-inspiring vibrancy and its apparent autonomy, or ability to appear separate. As Jung notes:

> The 'primordial images', or archetypes, lead their own independent life . . . as can easily be seen in those philosophical or gnostic systems which rely on an awareness of the unconscious as the source of knowledge. The idea of angels, archangels, 'principalities and powers' in St Paul, the archons of the Gnostics, the heavenly hierarchy of Dionysius the Areopagite, all come from the perception of the relative autonomy of the archetypes.[12]

Furthermore, said Jung, an archetype contains within it a certain type of power or influence: 'It seizes hold of the psyche with a kind of primeval force'.[13]

Over the years, and especially with the development of the idea of archetypes, a clear tendency began to emerge in Jung's thinking which differentiated him markedly from Freud. Jung considered the deepest regions of the psyche to be profoundly spiritual, whereas Freud's concept of the id suggested formlessness or chaos. Increasingly, Jung came to embrace the view that the essential aim of personal growth was to move towards a state of wholeness by integrating the conflicting contents and archetypal processes of the unconscious: he called this process *individuation*.

Jung distinguished different aspects of the personality. These included the *persona*, the face we present to the world, and the *ego*, which included all the conscious contents of personal experience. However, Jung also believed that men and women should accommodate opposite gender polarities within their consciousness—he termed these the *anima* for men and the *animus* for women—and he talked of the *shadow*, an embodiment of memories and experiences repressed from consciousness altogether. The shadow would often appear in dreams and nightmares as a dark, repellent figure. Jung argued, however, that if material from the shadow was acknowledged and allowed back into consciousness, that much of its dark, frightening nature would disappear. Dealing with the dark side of the psyche remains an important aspect of all Jungian forms of psychotherapy.

Jung regarded the *self* as the totality of the personality, including all the aspects of the psyche mentioned above. He also considered the self to be a central archetype, personified symbolically by a circle or mandala, representations of wholeness. The thrust of all individual self-development was therefore towards wholeness of being. Self-realisation, or individuation, simply meant 'becoming oneself' in a true and total sense. Jung described the process of personal growth in his essay 'The Relations Between the Ego and the Unconscious' (1928):

> The more we become conscious of ourselves through self-knowledge, and act accordingly, the more the layer of the personal unconscious that is superimposed on the collective unconscious will be diminished. In this way there arises a consciousness which is no longer imprisoned in the petty, oversensitive, personal world of objective interests. This widened consciousness is no longer that touchy, egotistical bundle of personal wishes, fears, hopes and ambitions which always has to be compensated or corrected by unconscious countertendencies; instead, it is a function of relationship to the world of objects, bringing the individual into absolute, binding and indissoluble communion with the world at large.[14]

Jung's impact on the New Spirituality has been enormous—greater, perhaps, than many people realise. Jung emphasised dreams as living realities—direct communications from the psyche—and we find the idea of heeding the inner voice not only in New Age dream-workshops, but as a broad-based principle underlying the widespread resurgence of inner-directed growth and visualisation techniques in general. Jung also believed that *spontaneous* manifestations of the psyche were most important, and this is reflected in the free-form sketch drawings of psychic and spiritual states which feature so prominently in many New Age workshops. Meanwhile, Jung's idea of a collective unconscious has also encouraged many to look at myths, fables and legends for insights into the human condition, and also to relate the cycles of symbolic rebirth, found in many of the world's religions, to the process of personal individuation.

Jung's focus is undoubtedly on *individual* transformation, although obviously the individuation process broadens through relationships with other people. Nevertheless, Jung's orientation reinforces a commonly held perception among adherents of the New Spirituality that one must work on oneself first, before expanding the process of self-development to include others. Otherwise it is simply a matter of the blind leading the blind.

In the final analysis Jung is saying that we hold our spiritual destinies in our own hands—and this is a profoundly Gnostic attitude, quite different from the spiritual message which emanates from most forms of western institutional religion. According to Jung, the archetypes of the collective unconscious provide spiritual milestones along the awe-inspiring pathway which leads to the reintegration of the psyche. Where this journey takes us is really up to us.

## ABRAHAM MASLOW AND THE PSYCHOLOGY OF PERSONAL GROWTH

If Sigmund Freud and Carl Jung have clearly played a key role in helping to define the parameters of the New Spirituality, so too has Abraham Maslow. It was Maslow, together with therapist and counsellor Anthony Sutich, who would lay the basis of humanistic psychology and in turn its more holistic and spiritually oriented counterpart, transpersonal psychology. As its name suggests, transpersonal psychology deals with states of being beyond the ego, and the transpersonal perspective seeks to broaden the traditional scope of psychological enquiry, encompassing such themes as the nature of holistic well-being, peak religious and mystical experiences, the experiential psychotherapies and the wisdom traditions from both East and West.

Abraham Maslow was appointed to the Chair of Psychology at Brandeis University, Massachusetts, in 1952 and was strongly opposed to the Behaviorist frameworks which dominated most American psychology departments at that time. Two years after his appointment to Brandeis, Maslow began to develop a mailing list of other psychologists who shared his own specific concerns. He clearly felt a need to network with other psychologists who, like him, had rejected the reductionist ethos of behaviourism in favour of an approach to human psychology which placed more emphasis on intangible human qualities like creativity, love, self-actualisation and the need for personal growth and self-expression. Although such themes are now widely acknowledged in the literature of experiential psychology, Maslow found it difficult connecting with like-minded academics in other psychology departments across America: by 1957 his mailing list contained only around 125 names!

Maslow's personal orientation was quite far-reaching, drawing on cultural anthropology, neuropsychiatry and gestalt psychology. Max Wertheimer's work on productive thinking and Kurt Goldstein's focus on the organism as a unified whole were both important elements in his holistic approach and, like Jung, Maslow emphasised that the human organism should be viewed in terms of its total intellectual, emotional and spiritual potential.

One of Maslow's most significant contributions to what would later become known as transpersonal psychology was his concept of *self-actualisation*, which he defined in his book *Motivation and Personality* as 'the full use and exploitation of talents, capacities, potentialities . . .' Later he would elaborate further on this definition: 'I think of the self-actualising man not as an ordinary man with something added but rather as the ordinary man with nothing taken away. The average man is a full human being with dampened and inhibited powers and capacities.'[15] Maslow became interested in classifying the sorts of people who would be capable of self-actualisation and came to believe that they could be identified by certain personal characteristics. Such people, he maintained, would tend to be spontaneous and independent in their thinking, were given to deep interpersonal relationships, were fundamentally democratic rather than authoritarian in their character, and were essentially creative in their approach to life. He also believed that self-actualisers often had the ability to have a mystical or 'peak' experience.

While Freud had emphasised neurosis as an innate human condition, Maslow's psychological research interests focused on identifying and evaluating subjects who seemed healthy and creative, rather than those who showed clear signs of being unhealthy or neurotic. Maslow believed that studying unhealthy, psychologically unbalanced or maladjusted people would not lead to an understanding of the true potentials of human development—for him the idea of self-actualisation was closely related to personal growth. According to Maslow, it was vital that individuals committed to some path of personal development should learn to overcome both the distorting images they had of themselves and also the defence mechanisms which obscured the 'real' person inside. As Maslow later noted in his important book *The Farther Reaches of Human Nature*: 'One cannot choose wisely for a life unless he dares to listen to himself, *his own self*, at each moment in life.'[16]

Maslow was well aware that those whom he considered to be 'self-actualisers' often suffered from the same problems as other ordinary, everyday people. And in fact, some of his self-actualisers were also inclined to become so engrossed in their personal perspectives that they could appear insensitive to the needs of others. 'There are no perfect human beings,' said Maslow.

> Persons can be found who are good, very good indeed, in fact great. There do in fact exist creators, seers, sages, saints, shakers and movers. This can certainly give us hope for the future of the species even if they *are* uncommon and do *not* come by the dozen. And yet these very same people can at times be boring, irritating, petulant, selfish, angry or depressed. To avoid disillusionment with human nature, we must first give up our illusions about it.[17]

The term 'peak experience' is widely associated with Maslow's work, and for him such an experience was a moment of self-actualisation when an individual felt more self-aware and could think and respond more clearly than in routine, everday states of consciousness. There were also ways of triggering peak experiences—by acts of love, by listening to great music, and by opening oneself to the beauty of Nature. These sorts of experiences invariably had a sense of completeness about them. But Maslow also knew that the 'highest' peaks were comparatively rare—they were perhaps best exemplified by moments of poetic or mystical experience . . . 'feelings of limitless horizons opening up to the vision, the feeling of being simultaneously more powerful and also more helpless than one ever was before, the feeling of great ecstasy and awe, the loss of placing in time and space . . .'[18]

In Maslow's conception, self-actualisation could only occur after basic human needs had been met. For Maslow, neurosis was a type of 'deficiency disease' caused by the deprivation of basic needs. Any individual human being had a variety of needs. They might be physiological (hunger, sleep etc.); they might relate to safety (the need for stability and order); they might involve the need for belonging and love (associated with family and friendship) or to self-esteem (a sense of self-respect and recognition). According to Maslow, it was only after these basic needs were satisfied in a human being that the fullest development of individual capacities could occur. 'Man's higher nature rests upon man's lower nature,' he wrote in *Toward a Psychology of Being*: '. . . for the mass of mankind, man's higher nature is inconceivable without a satisfied lower nature as a base.'[19]

Maslow acknowledged, however, that when the basic needs were met in a human being, newer and 'higher' needs would then emerge. Individuals whose basic needs were met would in all likelihood develop what Maslow called 'meta-needs' or needs related to one's sense of *being* (Maslow sometimes referred to them as B-values for this reason). For Maslow, these higher, more aesthetic needs—encompassing such issues as the quest for truth, beauty, intuition and transcendence—were as important to the human organism as the more tangible physiological considerations associated with physical survival. He also felt that these meta-needs should be explored by science, and not simply relegated to the more subjective domains of art, philosophy and religion. For Maslow it was important to acknowledge scientifically that the gratification of meta-needs—or the fulfilment of B-values—provided human beings with 'the highest pleasures or happiness that we know of'. These might include such experiences as being with good friends, the joy of listening to great music, the fulfilment of having a child or the bliss of the most profound love-experiences. And this did not simply condone hedonism: '. . . at this level there is . . . no contradiction between pleasure and duty, since the highest obligations of human beings are certainly to truth, justice, beauty etc which however are also the highest pleasures that the species can experience.'[20] Maslow believed that at the highest levels of experience, the world of facts and values appear to fuse:

> At this fusion level 'love for intrinsic values' is the same as 'love of ultimate reality' . . . Contemplation of ultimate realities becomes the same as contemplation of the nature of the world . . . our attitude toward the real, or at least the reality we get glimpses of when we are at our best and when *it* is at *its* best, can no longer be only 'cool', purely cognitive, rational, logical, detached, uninvolved assent. This reality calls forth a warm and emotional response, a response of love, of devotion, of loyalty, even peak experiences. At its best, reality is not only true, lawful, orderly, integrated etc.; it is also good and beautiful and lovable as well.[21]

Maslow's spectrum is thus one which culminates in a sense of ecstatic affirmation, for it encompasses all of the aesthetic and spiritual values that imbue the world with meaning at the deepest levels of human experience. In the final analysis, however, Maslow does not regard the quest for the value-life as an act of transcendence so much as a recognition of what is innate to human nature:

> Not only is man part of Nature, and it part of him, but also he must be at least minimally isomorphic with Nature [similar to it] in order to be viable in it. It has evolved him. His communion with what transcends him therefore need not be defined as non-natural or supernatural. It may be seen as a 'biological' experience . . .

This *biological* or evolutionary version of the mystic experience or the peak experience—here perhaps no different from the spiritual or religious experience—reminds us again that we must ultimately outgrow the obsolescent usage of 'highest' as the opposite of 'lowest' or 'deepest'. Here the 'highest' experience ever described, the joyful fusion with the ultimate that we can conceive, can be seen simultaneously as the deepest experience of our ultimate personal animality and specieshood, as the acceptance of our profound biological nature as isomorphic with Nature in general.[22]

## ANTHONY SUTICH AND HUMANISTIC PSYCHOLOGY

If Maslow remains the dominant figure in the early years of the transpersonal movement and a worthy successor to Jung in helping to develop what would later be known as 'sacred psychology', it is important to also acknowledge the role played by Anthony Sutich in the development of both humanistic and transpersonal psychology in the United States. Sutich was not an academic—he would come to think of himself as a 'maverick psychotherapist'—but he brought to the new psychological perspective a profound interest in spiritual and mystical concerns. He was always interested in attending lectures by visiting Indian spiritual teachers and later became friendly with the expatriate English Zen teacher Alan Watts—who in turn would be a key figure in the American counterculture. Sutich was very much a 'bridging' person whose energy, enthusiasm and networking skills did much to build the base of the transpersonal movement, which in turn has been of such central importance to the New Spirituality as we know it today.

Born in 1907, Sutich had developed progressive rheumatoid arthritis following an accident in a baseball game when he was twelve years old. By the time he was 18 he was totally physically disabled, and the remainder of his life would be spent for the most part on a gurney—a four-wheeled stretcher fitted with a telephone, reading stand and other devices.

Nevertheless, despite his physical disability, Sutich would often talk with nursing staff about personal concerns and in due course developed a reputation as a trusted friend and counsellor. In 1938 he was asked to become a group counsellor for the Palo Alto Society for the Blind and three years later he began a full-time private practice in individual and group counselling. He also had a long-standing interest in both Western and Eastern religion. He read widely in the fields of Yoga, Vedanta, Buddhism, Theosophy and Christian Science and was familiar with the writings of Jung and Adler. But he was especially influenced by Swami Ashokananda of the San Francisco Vedanta Society, who emphasised in his lectures 'the strong case for the value and validity of scientific investigation directed toward the inner realm of human potentialities, especially the spiritual potential'.[23]

Sutich was already familiar with the works of Swami Ramakrishna and Swami Vivekananda, and after having adjustments made to his car to accommodate his physical disability was able to travel to psychology and mysticism seminars in person, including a series of lectures by Krishnamurti held at Ojai, California, in 1948. Sutich was greatly encouraged by reading Swami Akhilananda's *Hindu Psychology*, while at the same time feeling increasingly alienated by the rising wave of behavioural psychology at nearby Stanford University. As a counsellor, Sutich would often test the attitudes and expressions of his clients and he began to think very much in terms of their 'psychological growth'. However, few of his colleagues used terms like this in their practices.

In due course, Sutich came to hear of Maslow's work and decided to write to him in November 1948:

> I understand that you have recently been working in something that has been vaguely described to me as the 'extremely well-adjusted personality'; alternatively, the 'super-normal personality'. The reference to your work came up as a result of my exploration and experimental counselling work on what I call the 'growth-centred attitude' ('growth-conscious' or 'growth-minded') as the 'core' of a 'full-valued personality'.[24]

16

Maslow did not reply directly but in March 1949 Maslow was visiting Berkeley and one of Sutich's clients arranged for the two to meet. It was a friendly meeting and on Maslow's rec-ommendation Sutich submitted an article to *The Journal of Psychology* titled 'The Growth-experience and Growth-centred Attitude', which was accepted for publication.

Between 1949 and 1957 Sutich had little contact with Maslow but he did attend a lecture at Stanford University where he noted that there was strong opposition from Ernest Hilgard's Behaviorist Department of Psychology to Maslow's concept of self-actualisation. However in 1952, Sutich was introduced to Alan Watts, and this renewed his interest in mysticism and psychotherapy. Sutich later recalled:

> The more I talked with him, the more I read about mysticism. In addition to Watts' books I read everything in mysticism I could get hold of. This carried me into the works of Sri Aurobindo (1948), Besant (1897), Blavatsky (1927), the Bhagavad Gita (Isherwood, 1947), Muller (1899), the Upanishads (Radhakrishnan, 1953) and a variety of books dealing with yoga.[25]

Sutich subsequently began to instruct Watts in a variety of holistic counselling techniques and was intrigued when Watts said that he intended combining these methods with Zen Bud-dhism. Watts felt he could apply 'non-directive counselling', the main idea being 'to help those who run into certain kinds of paradoxes or contradictions'. Sutich also had detailed discussions with Watts about *satori*—the Zen concept of sudden enlighten-ment.

Mention was made earlier of Maslow's mailing list of like-minded psychologists. Sutich took a personal interest in this list and would later reflect upon it as the very basis of the new humanistic psychology. 'The mailing list,' he commented, 'was like the Committee on Correspondence that played such an important part in the history of the American Revolution.' This, by way of contrast, was a key document in the 'consciousness revolution' which would fuel the New Spirituality of the 1980s and 1990s.

Sutich observed that even though the mailing list was grow-ing, there were no substantial inroads against the Behaviorists, who still dominated the academic journals with their publi-cations. Maslow, who had recently had an article on peak experiences rejected by *Psychology Review*, urged Sutich to start a new journal which could focus on those aspects of human potential currently being ignored by mainstream psychology. The new publication was called *The Journal of Ortho-Psychology*, and in its statement of purpose it sought to identify 'human capacities and potentialities that have no systematic place either in positivistic or behavioristic theory or in classical psychoanalytic theory'. These human qualities of course included love, self-actualisation, creativity, psychological health, responsibility and transcendence. In 1959 the journal was renamed *The Journal of Humanistic Psychology* and the American Association of Humanistic Psychology and the journal were subsequently established under the auspices of Brandeis University on 21 July 1960.

Maslow and Sutich were interested to meet and cooperate with other like-minded organisations and in 1962 Maslow wrote to Sutich about a new contact he had made: Michael Murphy and his close friend Richard Price had established a centre called the Esalen Institute in Big Sur, California, south of Monterey. 'They are planning a conference centre there devoted, among other topics, to just the things you are interested in,' wrote Maslow. He added: 'By the way, I suggested you as a teacher to them . . .'[26]

Murphy later contacted Sutich and proposed inviting him to Esalen as a guest, once administrative procedures had been formulated. 'We are planning seminars and conferences for next Fall and beyond and so are gathering ideas,' wrote Murphy. 'I have written to several people already, asking them to suggest ideas and people who would be good leaders. One interest we hope to develop is the inter-disciplinary approach to human nature—getting people together who usually don't get together . . .'[27]

## THE BIRTH OF THE TRANSPERSONAL PERSPECTIVE

Esalen Institute—named after the Native American tribe that once inhabited the Big Sur coast in California—used to be known simply as Slate's Hot Springs. The land was acquired in 1910 by Henry Murphy, a doctor from Salinas, and he built the dwelling now known as the Big House as a holiday home. For some time the property languished in a state of disrepair but in 1962 Dr Murphy's son Michael and Zen enthusiast Richard Price drove down to the property to have a look at it. Together they came up with an idea which would have far-reaching consequences for the Californian counter-culture and the emerging alternative spirituality movement: the homestead and grounds could become a meeting place for different spiritual traditions and for the exploration of consciousness. Philosophers, writers, mystics and visionaries could come here to impart their knowledge and share their experiences. It could become a very special place indeed.

In one of his early information newsletters circulated at Esalen Institute in May 1965, Michael Murphy posed a question which would become central to the transpersonal perspective as a whole: 'What is the fundamental growth process which takes the human organism beyond its present situation into the yet unrealised potential of its particular future?'

Ensuing programmes at Esalen would be held to explore this important question. A seminar on 'Humanistic Theology' was held at Esalen on 7–9 January 1966 with the aim of exploring the connections between personal growth, psychology and theology, and to discuss the issue of 'spiritual evolution' as an aspect of human potential. The seminar was attended by a number of Jesuit theologians as well as notable humanistic psychologists and research scientists like James Fadiman, Willis Harman and Miles Vich. Anthony Sutich was also present. One of the lecturers at the seminar asked the Jesuits in the audience whether they had ever had a mystical experience and whether it was Church policy to encourage the attainment of that experience. To both questions they replied 'No', and Sutich recalled that he was very surprised by these answers.

Shortly after this seminar Sutich attended two further meetings at Big Sur which highlighted the limitations of humanistic psychology. Sutich began to feel that the original idea of self-actualisation was no longer comprehensive enough and he expressed these views in a letter to Maslow in August 1966, noting that a humanistic therapist could hardly avoid the issue of 'ultimate goals' and mystical experiences. Sutich argued that the therapist should also be able to assist his client in developing skills and pertinent techniques for awakening these faculties. 'Esalen and other places and processes,' he added hopefully, 'may become at least the American equivalent of Zen monastries. The Residential program that has just begun at Esalen may be a more concrete example of what may develop eventually throughout the country.'[28]

Increasingly, Sutich felt inclined to blend mysticism and humanistic psychology. He proposed a new term—'Humanisticism'

—but Maslow noted that the British biologist Julian Huxley was already using a somewhat comparable expression, 'Transhumanistic', with the same approach in mind. Meanwhile, in February 1964 Sutich suggested to Maslow that a new journal be founded, perhaps with a title like *A Journal of Transhumanism* or *Transhumanistic Psychology*.

On 14 September 1967, in an address to the San Francisco Unitarian Church titled 'The Farther Reaches of Human Nature'—later employed as the title of his final book—Maslow made the first reference to what he called the 'Fourth Force' in psychology—a school of psychology dedicated to the transformation of human life. Fond of delineating specific objectives, Sutich proposed to Maslow a more complete definition of the new school:

> Transhumanistic (or Fourth Force) Psychology is the title given to an emerging force in the psychology field by a group of psychologists and professional men and women from other fields who are interested in those ultimate human capacities and potentialities and their actualisation that have no systematic place in either the First Force (classical psychoanalytical theory), Second Force (positivistic or behavioristic theory), or Third Force (humanistic psychology, which deals with such concepts as creativity, love, growth, basic need-gratification, psychological health, self-actualisation etc.) The emerging 'Fourth Force' is specifically concerned with the study, understanding, and responsible implementation of such states as being, becoming, self-actualisation, expression and actualisation of meta-needs (individual and 'species-wide'), ultimate values, self-transcendence, unitive consciousness, peak experiences, ecstasy, mystical experience, awe, wonder, ultimate meaning, transformation of the self, spirit, species-wide transformation, oneness, cosmic awareness, maximal sensory responsiveness, cosmic play, individual and species-wide synergy, optimal or maximal relevant interpersonal encounter, realisation, and expression of transpersonal and transcendental potentialities, and related concepts, experiences and activities.[29]

Sutich and Maslow continued to correspond and in November 1967 Maslow wrote suggesting that the word 'transpersonal' might be the most appropriate term to define the focus of the new psychological movement. 'The more I think of it,' he noted, 'the more this word says what we are all trying to say, that is, beyond individuality, beyond the development of the individual person into something which is more inclusive than the individual person, or which is bigger than he is.'[30]

Interestingly, the term 'transpersonal' had been used two months earlier by the Czechoslovakian psychiatrist Dr Stanislav Grof during a lecture at Berkeley, California. During the lecture Grof had used the word with reference to the terms 'Supra-individual' and the 'Death and Rebirth of the Ego'. Grof himself was a specialist in altered states of consciousness and prior to arriving in the United States had spent many years researching LSD and its effects on human consciousness. Sutich later had a lengthy discussion with Grof at the Esalen Institute about his research and later read Grof's then unpublished manuscript on LSD—which would later be released as *Realms of the Human Unconscious*.

The important thing at this stage was that a new term—*transpersonal*—had emerged as the best word for the new movement. Maslow reaffirmed the need for scientific research into transpersonal states of consciousness, and in Fall 1969 the first issue of *The Journal of Transpersonal Psychology* was released. It included the text of Maslow's 1967 San Francisco lecture, 'The Farther Reaches of Human Nature', and as Sutich later recalled, 'It was a marvellous experience for the staff to be able to hand Maslow one of the first copies.' Maslow himself was in poor health, having suffered a heart attack in January 1968, and he died from a subsequent heart attack on 8 June 1970. Following Maslow's death, Sutich became increasingly involved with the Transpersonal Institute and, in the ensuing years, gave much of his time to documenting his personal involvement with both humanistic and transpersonal psychology. His doctorate was conferred by the Humanistic Psychology Institute of San Francisco on 9 April 1976, and Sutich died the following day.

Maslow's concepts of self-actualisation and 'meta-needs', and Sutich's personal focus on the spiritual aspects of personal growth, remain central to transpersonal thought and have permeated through the human potential movement to a central place in the New Spirituality. However, Maslow himself emphasised in his later writings that self-actualisation—the idea of optimal, efficient, healthy and integrated functioning—was not in itself enough. Beyond such self-fulfilment, one must always strive for self-transcendence. Maslow believed that even the most personally fulfilled, self-actualising individual must inevitably pass beyond the boundaries of familiar everyday experience, beyond personal and social integration and basic physiological and emotional needs, to the transpersonal levels of consciousness. These, said Maslow, would present themselves as '. . . the happiest moments of life . . . experiences of ecstasy, rapture, bliss, of the greatest joy'.[31]

## COUNTER-CULTURE SPIRITUALITY

It goes without saying that the eclecticism of the New Spirituality in the 1990s has a direct counterpart in the hybrid spiritual mix that emerged in the so-called 'counterculture' of the 1960s and 1970s. The 'psychedelic era'—a spontaneous and often reckless period of hallucinogenic drug-taking—is associated with the empassioned pursuit of altered states of consciousness and with charismatic figures like Timothy Leary and Ken Kesey. As an underground movement, challenging the perceived received values of the day, it gained substantial impetus from the psychedelic writings of Aldous Huxley and from members of the Beat movement like Allen Ginsberg and Gary Snyder. As with the Beats, many counter-culture devotees were fascinated by exotic Eastern religions, and were intrigued by the possibility of directly experiencing mystical consciousness—of tapping into the Universal Godhead that was both 'out there' and also within. Not surprisingly, some of the earliest debates about mystical consciousness focused on what was 'authentic' and what was 'artificial' in the pursuit of 'chemical ecstasy'.

The debate had been triggered initially by the publication in 1954 of Aldous Huxley's *The Doors of Perception*. Huxley had taken his title from William Blake's pronouncement that 'if the doors of perception were cleansed, everything would appear to man as it is, infinite'. Huxley's book would later inspire the poet and singer Jim Morrison to name his band The Doors by way of tribute.

Huxley related how in May 1953 he had swallowed four-tenths of a gram of mescalin dissolved in a glass of water and sat down to wait for results. For Huxley, mescalin brought revelation: his 'I' became 'Not-Self' and the everyday objects around him—flowers, books and furniture—seemed to radiate jewel-like colours and profound significance. Here, he felt, was 'contemplation at its height'. Huxley later conceded that mescalin could plunge some people into hell rather than lifting them into heaven, but on balance he decided that it could certainly serve as a catalyst to mystical awareness—especially for rational or 'verbal' intellectuals like himself who felt 'compelled to take an occasional trip through some chemical Door in the Wall into the world of transcendental experience'. Later, in 1958, in *The Saturday Evening Post*, Huxley emphasised the mystical relevance of both mescalin and the more recently discovered psychedelic, LSD (lysergic acid diethylamide). Of LSD he wrote:

> It lowers the barrier between conscious and subconscious and permits the patient to look more deeply and understandingly into the recesses of his own mind. The deepening of self-knowledge takes place against a background of visionary and even mystical experience.[32]

Alan Watts, meanwhile, was now teaching at the School of Asian Studies in San Francisco after working as an Anglican counsellor at Northwestern University. Watts had rejected Christianity as his chosen spiritual path and would also, somewhat controversially, come to endorse Huxley's view of psychedelics. Watts had come to the view that Christianity did not trust humanity's natural urges—that it was always downplaying the flesh in favour of the spirit—and that it had inherited this dualism from the ancient Greeks. Watts wrote:

> It has often been said that the human being is a combination of angel and animal, a spirit imprisoned in flesh, a descent of divinity into materiality, charged with the duty of transforming the gross elements of the lower world into the image of God . . . Not to cherish both the angel and the animal, both the spirit and the flesh, is to renounce the whole interest and greatness of being human.[33]

Watts also felt that in the Christian context this distinction between body and spirit was projected as a burden onto women, and this meant that they could not adequately express themselves sexually within their relationships. He was keen to explore ways in which men and women could interrelate more positively, and found helpful insights in gestalt psychology and encounter therapy, both of which would later play a prominent role in the human potential movement.

Watts had been fascinated for many years by Zen Buddhism, especially in its role in helping alienated and lonely people find spiritual 'release'. Watts was also a friend of the Beat poet Gary Snyder, who had spent over a decade in Zen temples in Kyoto, and knew a number of the other Beats—including Jack Kerouac,

Lawrence Ferlinghetti and Allen Ginsberg—who were already very familiar with Zen Buddhism and the concept of *satori*, or direct enlightenment. Together, Watts, Snyder and Kerouac denounced bourgeois suburban values, and Watts took up residence on an old ferry boat called the *Vallejo*, moored in Sausalito, across the bay from San Francisco. A skilled teacher and radio broadcaster, Watts became a frequent visitor to college campuses across the country. In 1961 he addressed students and academics at Columbia, Cornell, Chicago, Harvard and Yale Medical School, and also held seminars on the *Vallejo*. Watts talked about everything—sexuality, sensuality, mind-expanding drugs, food and popular lifestyles—everything which at the time was considered risqué in conventional middle-class society. He had taken LSD on a number of occasions and believed, like Aldous Huxley, that psychedelics could be used meaningfully as spiritual sacraments rather than for recreational 'kicks'. In like fashion, Snyder believed that Zen meditators who had previously experienced LSD would find it easier to practise *zazen* in their quest for *dhyana*, or ultimate enlightenment.

Watts also knew Dr Timothy Leary, the controversial psychologist, formerly of Harvard University, who had been experimenting with psychedelics. Leary and his colleagues Ralph Metzner and Richard Alpert had written a book outlining how the *Tibetan Book of the Dead* could be used as a spiritual-rebirth framework for the psychedelic experience. Leary at this time was advocating that if enough people took LSD, society could be transformed by their collective spiritual vision. Watts and Leary both believed in the transformative potential of psychedelics and both had been attracted to Buddhist frameworks of consciousness expansion.

As mentioned earlier, Abraham Maslow argued that the pursuit of higher states consciousness depended on the prior fulfilment of basic needs and in 1962 Herbert Marcuse made a related point when he argued that it was possible for revolution to spring not only from poverty but also from affluence. During the hedonistic psychedelic years, having freed themselves from any substantial concerns with basic needs like food and survival, members of the youth culture began increasingly to pursue 'meaning' in life and to explore spiritual paths vastly different from those associated with mainstream western values. It was these young people—collectively referred to by historian Theodore Roszak as the 'counter-culture'—who followed the lead of figures like Alan Watts and Timothy Leary in the pursuit of mystical revelations, and I myself was among them. It was a time of high idealism and also a time when many young people believed collectively that they could work miracles in the transformation of those around them. As Julian Beck wrote in his poem 'Paradise Now':

> we want
> to zap them
> with holiness
> we want
> to levitate them
> with joy
> we want
> to open them
> with love vessels[34]

In one of the most symbolic occurrences of the psychedelic period, in October 1967, Abbie Hoffman, Jerry Rubin and a large group of counter-culture devotees organised the National Mobilization demonstration at the Pentagon in Washington DC. An underground publication, *The East Village Other*, called for the presence at this event of 'mystics, saints, artists, holymen, astrologers, witches, sorcerers, warlocks, druids, hippies, priests, shamen, ministers, rabbis, troubadours, prophets, minstrels, bards (and) roadmen' in a magical ceremony that would attempt to levitate the Pentagon. This was a period of quasi-surreal political activity in which a group of hippies formed the Youth International Party and the so-called 'yippies' were formed, as a 'cross-fertilisation of the hippie and New Left philosophies'.[35] And even though the magical levitation did not of course occur, this very public magical ceremony would nevertheless come to symbolise in the popular mythology of the day the encounter between the cosmological forces of love and magic on the one hand, and the symbolic military might of the Pentagon on the other—a clear distinction between the country's rulers, with their symbols of external political strength, and the youth-culture with its internal vitality and magic.

The era of the psychedelic counter-culture is now widely regarded as a time of hedonistic indulgence which didn't really amount to much, and there were many who held this view all along. In the words of the somewhat cynical anthropologist Marvin Harris: 'The counter-culture is doomed so long as everyone is doing his own thing. Head trips and meditation, a million chanting messiahs and love-ins will not appreciably affect material conditions . . . It feels good while it changes nothing.'³⁶ And yet there were consequences and outcomes of a more diffuse nature, which were perhaps less obvious but which would affect later generations—including devotees of the New Spirituality in the 1990s.

There are numerous instances of individuals who had mystical experiences on psychedelic drugs in the first instance, and who later began to pursue meditative and spiritual practices as a result. A significant number of key figures in the transpersonal movement—including Stanislav Grof, Joan Halifax, Jean Houston, John Lilly, Baba Ram Dass, Ralph Metzner, Michael Harner and Andrew Weil—have also undertaken both personal and scientific investigation of psychedelic states of consciousness at various times in their careers. LSD is now seen as an amplifier of natural and innate processes in the brain rather than as a chemical agent capable of producing 'artificial' states of consciousness. It also remains one of the most potent psychedelics known to humanity and as such deserves the respect which the exuberant youth culture of the 1960s and 1970s for the most part failed to provide. As Alan Watts remarked in *The Joyous Cosmology*, with reference to psychedelics in general,

> . . . these drugs . . . provide the raw materials of wisdom, and are useful to the extent that the individual can integrate what they reveal into the whole pattern of his behaviour and the whole system of his knowledge . . . the hours of heightened perception are wasted unless occupied with sustained reflection or meditation upon whatever themes may be suggested.³⁷

Many have looked back on this period as a time of personal transformation. Professor Allan Cohen, who studied psychology under Timothy Leary at Harvard, saw the aftermath of the counter-culture period as a time of 'tremendous reawakening of the spirit' and John Lilly has spoken recently of Leary's 'insight and courageous facing of transiting to beyond the biophysical realities'.³⁸

Others, though, have warned of the limitations of self-centredness, a trait often associated with the so-called post-war 'baby boomer generation'. As Jerry Rubin put it, 'One of the problems, and dangers, of the consciousness movement is that it is thoroughly individualistic. People are very much into the concept of "me first", and then they imbue that "me first" with religious and psychological justifications . . .' Rubin also cautioned against the new spiritual authority figures embraced by members of the youth culture:

> These gurus, swamis, *high people*, talk about universals, talk about bringing everything together and reaching a higher consciousness. But if you really watch the process, and not the content, they often have a very ego-centred, individualistic approach . . . I think that, wherever we are going, there are many different ways to get there and I think it is unfortunate that so many advocates of these disciples regard their own way as 'the answer'.[39]

Rubin was also critical of certain religious groups, especially the guru-oriented ones, because in his view they tended to diminish personal self-worth. However he strongly supported those aspects which assisted self-empowerment:

> If you take the consciousness movement as a whole, it *is* putting forward a healthy definition of the human being as such. It is also a compendium of very valuable techniques—yoga techniques, meditation techniques, communication techniques, self-awareness techniques that can help people reach higher power within themselves.
>
> The contemporary consciousness movement also has a political function. One of the things we learnt in the sixties is that political change is just political change, it's not psychological change. Many people who were politically active in the sixties were just as screwed up as the people they were attacking . . . Now people look at themselves in a much deeper way than we did in the sixties. And that is politics itself. Politics is *living*. So by taking seriously the techniques offered in the growth movement, you can change yourself and eventually that in itself becomes political change.[40]

Although Rubin was referring here to the aftermath of the 1960s and 1970s, these themes are also central to the New Spirituality of the 1990s. In many ways the spontaneous and often haphazard visionary approach which characterised the American counter-culture has re-emerged in our own era, tempered with the wisdom of hindsight and a broader understanding of the meditative and holistic tools available. One can argue, I think, that the approach to transpersonal states of consciousness is now more respectful, but the belief remains that we hold our spiritual destinies in our own hands. The choice for transcendence is essentially ours to make.

# 2
# Mystical Experience and Religious Belief

*In the province of the mind, what is believed to be true is true or becomes true, within certain limits to be found experientially and experimentally. These limits are further beliefs to be transcended. In the province of the mind, there are no limits.*

—Dr John Lilly

For most people, religious belief is enmeshed in cultural tradition, and large parts of what they believe are inherited in the form of pre-existing teachings, practices and doctrines. However, although religious traditions and values are these days entrenched within a matrix of institutions—within churches, temples, synagogues, monastic orders, missionary organisations, health and educational centres, and more recently within media and marketing organisations—it is worth considering that religions have a much more intangible, and non-institutional, beginning.

All great historical religions, and even many of the minor ones, have their origins in the visionary, or mystical, experience. Religions, by their very nature, are intended as pathways towards some sense of transcendence. They provide an intimation of a much bigger picture of the universe and our place as human beings within the cosmos. They point to a Greater Mystery, and they endeavour, on behalf of their devotees, to provide a deeper and broader framework of spiritual understanding than that provided by the prevailing secular and materialistic models of reality.

Whether we think of this Greater Mystery as a god, a spirit or an energy, or regard it in an abstract way as the very basis of the manifested universe—as an innate dimension of life which provides the ground and sustenance of our being—essentially we are dealing with concepts that transcend our intellectual understanding. This invariably leads religious exponents to employ the language of myth, symbol and metaphor as an expression of what lies beyond. Indeed, all religious and mystical systems make use of such metaphors to convey what they perceive to be a 'higher truth'.

With our limited perceptions as human beings—our spectrum of awareness necessarily limited by the complex filtering processes that maintain social reality and thereby keep us 'sane' and 'rational'—most of us can hardly hope to grasp the total magnitude of the Greater Mystery which underlies the religious experience. But it is also clear that at different times in history the sheer potency of this transcendent spiritual domain has inspired prophets and seers, and the founders of our major traditional religions. The numinous energy of mystical consciousness has also inspired sacred art and music and given rise to profound and sensitive poetry and many other forms of creative endeavour.

But there is another side to spiritual enlightenment, and that has to do with the nature of 'authority'. At times, personal experience of the Greater Mystery brings with it its own sense of certainty: the feeling that a sublime depth of being has been revealed, that a more profound perspective on life has been attained, and perhaps even that 'God' has spoken to us in a unique and individual way. However, it is important to remember that any spiritual encounter of this sort is, in itself, an altered state of consciousness—or what Maslow would call a 'peak experience'. By their very nature, evoking as they do feelings of ineffability, awe and intangibility, it becomes extremely difficult to communicate the essential profundity of mystical experiences like these, and to explain fully what has occurred. And yet it is important that we endeavour to explore this intangible territory—for if we desist we may instead find ourselves open to the manipulations and distortions of belief itself.

In the case of institutionalised religions—especially in the West, where there is more emphasis on faith and doctrine, and much less on individual religious experience—we often find the revelations of the founder-visionary perpetuated in specific ways by devotees who appear to have no personal perspective on the mystical origins of their own religious traditions. So often the damage and division associated with religious factions results from a fundamental misunderstanding of the core visionary experience itself, and a type of literalism begins to assert itself which is then used by some religious followers to defend the 'unique' nature of the founder's revelation. Profound insights and perceptions experienced by the founder-visionary become 'miraculous events' and a cause, perhaps, of bitter doctrinal wrangling.

While by definition exclusivist thinking is alien to most devotees of the New Spirituality—their eclectic belief systems emerging from various and multiple blendings of both Eastern and Western religious traditions—for those who follow institutional religious beliefs there are more specific consequences, and even possibilities for serious dissent. In extreme cases exponents of some religious traditions may feel that God has revealed a particular teaching only to them and not to others; that the teaching is an exclusive revelation, never to be repeated or modified at future times in history, and even that the followers of other teachings or doctrines will be damned for all eternity for failing to heed such a unique revelation. Religious attitudes of this kind imply that 'truth' can be exclusively contained, that other spiritual or religious revelations are necessarily inferior, less enlightened, heretical, and possibly even 'evil'.

In such ways, and within a variety of cultural settings, belief systems spawn and build, producing edifices of doctrine and dogma. Of course, as the edifice grows larger and becomes ever more rigid, it engenders new types of conformity. The message to the followers from those in power may then become even more assertive: do not stray from these confines; here is the orthodox teaching—complete and unequivocal. Such an attitude provides us with the very basis for fanatical extremism and in some cases for religious wars or political attacks against those of another persuasion. The rise of fundamentalist Islam in several countries, including Egypt and Algeria, and the emergence of militant factions within conservative Judaism in Israel are examples in our own time, while the persecutions inflicted upon 'heretics' during the medieval Crusades and the Inquisition remain a major blight on Christian history.

It seems to me that conflicts and problems like these arise some time after the initial visionary experiences have taken place, at a time when the religious founder has been elevated or 'mythologised' to a position of spiritual authority. And such problems, when they do arise, are usually brought on by the extremist views of the followers rather than by the visionary who received the revelations in the first instance. Almost without exception, conflict is caused by those with lesser vision—by those compelled by the exclusivist nature of their own belief system to protect their own specific cause, and who feel potentially threatened by those making competing claims elsewhere.

## FOUNDER-VISIONARIES

At this point, then, it might be useful to consider the spiritual careers and visionary experiences of three historical founders of religions, all of whom, in varying degrees, have had their core revelations institutionalised and their teachings variously interpreted by dissenting groups and factions. However by looking at the experiences of the founder-visionaries themselves we are able to gain an insight into the processes of mystical revelation. The core nature of mystical experience is in itself a major concern of devotees of the New Spirituality and, as we have already seen, as a broad-based movement the latter may in turn be seen as a shift away from institutionalised religions towards more individually based experiential frameworks of belief and spiritual practice. However it is also fascinating, from the viewpoint of the spiritual humanism which I believe characterises this movement, to see how and in what circumstances religions begin. Who better than to provide us with examples of spiritual transformation than Gautama Buddha, Jesus and Muhammad?

### Siddhartha Gautama Buddha (563BC–483BC)

The term 'Buddha', meaning 'enlightened one', was a name later given to the Indian prince Siddhartha Gautama, who was born in Lumbini Garden in the Himalayan foothills.

The accounts of Gautama's birth are unavoidably shrouded in mythic language. It is said that many aeons before, an ascetic called Sumedha had taken the vows of a Bodhisattva (a Buddha-to-be) and while in the Tushita Heaven determined that he would be reborn into the Shakya clan. His parents would be King Shuddhodhana, a ruler of this clan, and his wife Mayadevi.

According to legend, Mayadevi received Gautama into her body in the form of a white elephant—a symbol of pefect wisdom and royal power—and when he was born, the trees in Lumbini

Garden burst into beautiful blooms. Later a horoscope was drawn up which identified Gautama as a 'universal monarch' and an *arhat*—'one worthy to be honoured'.

Gautama grew up in an environment of great privilege and luxury. Cared for by 32 nurses and provided with three palaces—each intended for different seasons of the year—he enjoyed a world filled with dancing, singing, beautiful music and fragrant flowers. He married his cousin, Yashodhara, when he was sixteen, and she subsequently gave birth to their son, Rahula.

However, Gautama's life of elegant seclusion was not destined to endure. He urged his father to allow him to see the world at large—not realising that it contained evil and suffering. And so, with Channa his charioteer, he rode through the streets of the city on what would become a transformative journey. He saw a wrinkled, toothless old man whose body was so weak with age that he was bent over, supporting himself with a stick; he saw a diseased man, stricken with fever and pain; he saw a corpse wrapped in cloth and being carried by family and friends to the funeral pyre; and finally he saw a monk, serenely begging with a bowl in his hand. Gautama now felt he had to find the means whereby he could maintain such inner calm and composure in the face of the evils of human existence—old age, sickness and death.

Gautama began his spiritual quest with what is now known as 'The Great Renunciation'. On the very night that his son was born, and with the help of his servants, Gautama secretly left his courtyard, rode off on his horse Kanthaka and journeyed until daybreak. He removed his princely garments, donned the clothes of a huntsman and cut off his hair with a sword. From now on he would not be a prince but a seeker of enlightenment.

In due course he studied under Alara Kalama, practised yoga and engaged in severe dietary abstentions for a period of six years. But the physical toll eventually became intolerable:

> Like dried canes now became my arms and legs, withered through this extremely scanty diet; like the foot of a camel became my buttock; like a string of beads became my spinal column with the vertebrae protruding.
>
> Just as the roof beams of an old house sharply protrude, so protruded my ribs; just as in a deep well the little water-stars far beneath are scarcely seen, so now in my eye-balls the sunken pupils were hardly seen; just as a gourd freshly cut becomes empty and

withered in the hot sun, so now became the skin of my head empty and withered.[1]

Gautama remained completely immobile during his ascetic period. He sought no shade from the sun, wind or rain. However it eventually became apparent to him that both his body and mind were deteriorating and he decided to break his fast to build up his strength. And yet, in ceasing austerities he did not revert to a life of sensuality, but decided to follow a 'middle path', allowing himself to beg for a little food now and then as he wandered around.

One day, at a place called Gaya, he decided he would sit down under a bodhi tree and would not rise again until he had found enlightenment. It is recorded that Gautama, who was then 35 years of age, sat beneath the bodhi tree for 49 days before becoming a Buddha.

During the 49 days, according to legend, Gautama was severely taunted by Mara, the Tempter. Mara is said to have offered Gautama dominion over 'the four great continents and their 2000 attending isles' but he responded by saying: 'I have no wish for sovereignty. I am about to make the 10 000 worlds thunder with my becoming a Buddha'.

Mara assembled a huge army and when he attacked Gautama all the gods in the 10 000 worlds fled, leaving him alone. Mara now launched against him a whirlwind, a huge rainstorm, showers of rocks, weapons, hot ashes and mud—but to no avail. Mara then taunted him, saying that there was no-one to bear witness for him. Gautama, sitting in a lotus position with his left hand resting palm up on his right leg, now reached down with his right hand to touch the ground, thereby 'calling the earth to witness'.

According to legend, the earth is said to have thundered: 'I bear you witness' with 100, 1000, 100 000 roars, and then Mara withdrew, frustrated in his attempts to lure Gautama from his task.

Meanwhile the moon rose and Gautama passed into a state of deep meditation. He reviewed his previous incarnations, rose to higher levels of consciousness where he was able to understand the nature of his human self, and finally attained a state of pure enlightenment, or Buddhahood.

After attaining enlightenment in this way, it is said that the Buddha remained in a meditative position for a further 49 days, contemplating the truths that had been revealed to him. Mara approached him again, tempting him to enter Nirvana, but Gautama decided instead to continue his earthly existence, and share his spiritual knowledge with others.

He now travelled to Sarnath, north of Benares, and was joined by five ascetics who had left his company earlier, when he had broken his pattern of austerities. At Deer Park he gave a sermon which contained the four noble truths and the eight-fold path. These teachings, in essence, were as follows:

- Life is suffering (*dukkha*).
- The cause of this suffering is desire (*tanha*).
- Suffering can be eliminated when desire is extinguished.
- Desire can be eliminated by pursuing the eightfold path which comprises:
  Right understanding
  Right aspiration
  Right speech
  Right conduct
  Right vocation
  Right effort
  Right mindfulness
  Right concentration.

From this time onwards, Gautama Buddha believed that his main task was to bring the teaching (*Dhamma*) to the world, and he sought to do this for a further 45 years, gaining many converts and also ordaining his son Rahula. At his death he is said to have passed through a number of mystical realms, finally entering *Parinibbana*, or total bliss.

## Jesus (circa 4BC–33AD)

According to the biblical account of Matthew, Jesus was born in a stable at Bethlehem. His mother Mary was betrothed to a carpenter named Joseph but before they came together she discovered she was pregnant. Joseph felt he should separate from Mary to avoid any embarrassment but he then had a dream in which an angel told him:

> Joseph, son of David, do not fear to take Mary as your wife, for that which is conceived in her is of the Holy Spirit; she will bear a son, and you shall call his name Jesus, for he will save his people from their sins.[2]

Mary and Joseph travelled to Bethlehem to comply with a decree from Caesar Augustus that there was to be a census, and all Jews were to return to their place of tribal origin. Joseph and Mary arrived in Bethlehem and it was clear that she was about to give birth to Jesus. No rooms were available in the inn, so the couple spent the night in the stable. It was here that Jesus was born.

As with Gautama Buddha, Jesus' birth was nevertheless the occasion for dramatic portents. It is said that a star in the East indicated that the King of the Jews had been born, and three wise men from the East fell down and worshipped the child, offering him gifts of gold, frankincense and myrrh.

Much has been made of Jesus' humble birth and it has always been implied that his father Joseph was a 'simple carpenter'. However, according to a recent report by Father Ugo Vanni, a lecturer in New Testament studies at the Gregorian University affiliated with the Vatican, Jesus came from a middle-class family and would have been considered a cultured citizen of Galilee, enjoying a high standing in his community. Father Vanni maintains, on the basis of twenty years' research, that Jesus was 'not a simple carpenter, but more like a successful builder, a professional artisan like his earthly father, Joseph'. The biblical word *tekton*, commonly translated as 'carpenter', in fact implied a high level of professional training and craftsmanship—'something more like a surveyor'.[3] Nevertheless, like Gautama Buddha before him, Jesus embraced ascetic spiritual values and principles of simplicity, and frequently associated with the poor, despised and outcast in society.

We know very little about the early years of Jesus' life. In all likelihood he would have celebrated his *bar mitzvah* at the age of thirteen and would have studied the Hebrew scriptures, probably receiving instruction at the local synagogue.

The turning point in his spiritual career came, however, at the age of 30, when he went to the River Jordan to be baptised by John. John the Baptist was himself a somewhat eccentric figure—he preached repentance in the wilderness of Judaea and subsisted on a diet of locusts and wild honey. Many came to him to confess their wrongdoings and to be baptised. John proclaimed that his baptisms were of water, symbolising repentance, but warned that a more formidable figure was coming: 'He who is coming after me is mightier than I, whose sandals I am not worthy to carry; he will baptise you with the Holy Spirit and with fire'.

Soon after this, Jesus presented himself to John to be baptised. According to Mark's account, 'When he came up out of the water, immediately he saw the heavens opened and the Spirit descending upon him like a dove; and a voice came from heaven: "Thou art my beloved son; with thee I am well pleased."'⁴ Inspired by this divine illumination—the Bible says he was 'driven by the Spirit'—Jesus wandered in the wilderness of Judaea, fasting for 40 days. It was here that he was tempted by Satan in a similar way to Gautama's encounter with Mara.

Satan confronted Jesus with three temptations. First he challenged him, in his newly revealed role as the Son of God, to change stones into loaves of bread. Jesus resisted this act of magic. Then Satan took Jesus to the parapet of the Temple in the holy city of Jerusalem and challenged him to throw himself down, arguing that if he were really the Son of God he would be protected by the angels. Jesus rejected this act of potential vainglory by declaring: 'You shall not tempt the Lord your God'. Then, in the final temptation, Satan went with Jesus to a high mountain and showed him the different kingdoms of the world. Satan offered to give him these domains if he would in turn worship him as Lord—again, a comparable temptation to that of Mara. Jesus once again denied Satan, affirming: 'You shall worship the Lord your God, and only Him shall you serve'.

Jesus subsequently began to teach the love of God and one's fellow man, calling for everyone to repent of their sins in the assurance that God would be merciful to the righteous. Mark records Jesus' first commandment: 'Hear, O Israel! the Lord our God, the Lord is one, and you shall love the Lord your God with all your heart, and with all your soul, and with all your mind, and with all your strength!' His second commandment was: 'You shall love your neighbour as yourself. There is no other commandment greater than these.'⁵

Jesus also counselled his disciples to pray to God in the manner described in Matthew's gospel ('Our Father, who art in Heaven . . .') and according to John's gospel believed that baptism was essential for spiritual salvation: 'Unless one is born of water and the Spirit, one cannot enter the Kingdom of God'.

It can be argued that it was the confusion between spiritual and physical realities that led to Jesus' death. Jesus clearly regarded his relationship with God the Father as extremely personal—a characteristic which distinguishes his visionary experiences from Eastern accounts of mystical illumination, which tend to be less anthropocentric.

In several biblical accounts Jesus speaks of his role in terms that would seem extraordinarily egotistical were one to interpret them other than as statements made from a mystical perspective: 'I am the living bread that came down from Heaven'; 'Whoever eats of this bread will live forever'; 'I am the light of the world; whoever follows me will not walk in darkness but will have the light of life'; 'You are from below, I am from above; you are of this world; I am not of this world'; 'I am the way and the truth and the life; no-one comes to the Father but by me'.

In fact, it was because statements of this sort were taken literally, and because he affirmed his special role as the Messiah, that Jesus was condemned for blasphemy, brought to trial and crucified by the Roman governor, Pilate. Jesus was affirming his special relationship with God—that, in his being, the Spirit was made flesh. When Jesus was taken before 'all the chief priests and the elders and the scribes' he was asked:

> 'Are you the messiah, the son of the Blessed?' Jesus said: 'I am, and you will see the Son of Man sitting at the right side of Power and coming with the clouds of Heaven.' And the high priest tore his coat and said: 'Why should we need further witnesses? You have heard this blasphemy. What is your decision?' And they all condemned him as deserving death.[6]

Jesus clearly believed he was the Anointed One—the Messiah anticipated by the Jewish prophets. As Janet and Thomas O'Dea have noted, Jesus told his disciples that he was the Messiah, and thus identified himself with the deepest yearnings and aspirations of the Jewish people:

> Jesus entered a Jewish context where God was seen as Lord of history, about to intervene to bring about its redemption and apotheosis. The Jews were the people of the covenant. There was a hope that God would intervene, would send his anointed one, would redeem Israel and begin a new age of the world for all men. Thus it was that Christianity was founded by a prophetic Jewish figure who took his stand within the Jewish religious tradition and in the consciousness of his messianic mission announced its imminent fulfilment.[7]

Jesus was condemned to die on the cross and his last words are recorded in Psalm 22: *Eli, Eli lama sabachthani?*: 'My God, my

God, why have you forsaken me?' However, despite this sense of spiritual isolation at the end of his life, for Christian believers it was the affirmation of Jesus' spiritual message after his resurrection which made his role in history unique. According to the Gospel of Mark, following Jesus' resurrection and his miraculous appearance to the Apostles, Jesus gave a very clear, almost stark, statement of his religious purpose: 'Go into all the world and preach the gospel to all creatures. Whoever believes and is baptised will be saved . . .'

## Muhammad (circa 570AD–632AD)

Muhammad was born in Mecca, the son of prominent members of the Quaraysh clan. His father, Abdullah, died a few days before he was born and his mother, Aminah, when he was only six years old. He was looked after by his grandfather, Abd al Muttalib, until he was eight and then, after his grandfather's death, by a paternal uncle, Abu Talib, who was the leader of the clan.

Muhammad grew up as a caravan trader on the camel routes. He is believed to have travelled with Abu Talib to Syria and also to have encountered other religious groups, including Jews and Christians. By the age of 25 he had been placed in charge of transporting the merchandise of a wealthy widow named Khadijah. She was fifteen years older than him and finally proposed that they be married. Muhummad accepted the offer and by all acounts their marriage was very happy. They had six children, the best known being Fatimah, and Muhammad took no other wives until Khadijah died in 619AD (after which he is believed to have had eleven other wives).

Khadijah's considerable wealth allowed Muhammad a certain amount of freedom and independence, and he liked to stay in the hills near Mecca. Sometimes he would visit a cave on Mount Hira, where he would engage in fasting, meditation and contemplation. It was during an all-night vigil towards the end of the month of Ramadan when he was 40 years old that he experienced the first of several revelations—a vision of a majestic being later identified as the archangel Gabriel. Gabriel demanded that Muhammad:

> Recite in the name of thy Lord who created!
> He createth man from a clot of blood.
> Recite; and thy Lord is the Most Bountiful,

He who hath taught by the pen,
taught men what he knew not.[8]

The next morning, as he was leaving the cave, he again heard the archangel's voice, this time proclaiming: 'Muhammad, you are Allah's messenger . . .' The archangel stood before him, bathed in brilliant light, and Muhammd tried to turn his face away from the visionary being. However, at all turns Gabriel confronted him—and then suddenly vanished. Muhammad now hurried home to tell Khadijah that either he was possessed by a spirit or truly called to the role of a prophet. Khadijah reassured him, believing that he had experienced an authentic revelation. She also told her Christian cousin, Warakah Ebn Nowfal, about Muhammad's visions and he advised her that her husband had apparently encountered the same angel who had appeared to Moses.

Muhammad had several further revelations, which he believed came directly from God. During these experiences he would go into a cold sweat, and some commentators have suggested, probably incorrectly, that he may have suffered from epileptic fits. Be that as it may, Muhammad's revelations were sometimes written down and at other times memorised by his followers. Eventually they were collected and put into written form in 650AD. This collection of writings, the Qur'an, or Koran—the sacred book of Islam—has remained unchanged to the present day.

Muhammad had grown up in a world abounding in idolatry. Mecca was dominated by the Sabian religion, whose devotees venerated the fixed stars and planets, and who also worshipped a plurality of gods and spirits transposed into their culture from Graeco–Roman counterparts. The Temple of Mecca was consecrated to Zohal, or Saturn, and there were also Sabian counterparts of Jupiter, Mercury and Sirius the Dog Star. The Arabs around Mecca also worshipped a number of idols including the lion-shaped Yaghuth, and Hobal, introduced from Syria, who was believed to bring rain when required. Muhammad disliked idolatry instinctively, and after his revelations from Gabriel became determined to wipe it out altogether.

His principal cause as God's Prophet subsequently became to proclaim the worship of the One God—Al Ilah, or Allah. In due course Muhammad divided Islam (which means 'submission') into *Iman* (faith) and *Din* (practices, prayer, alms, fasting and the pilgrimage to Mecca). His teachings included belief in God, his angels, his prophets (Muhammad considered himself to be the last of 28 prophets sent by God, his predecessors including Adam, Abraham, Jesus, and John the Baptist), the resurrection and Day of Judgement, and God's control of good and evil.

Muhammad gained few converts at first—Khadijah was one, and so too were his cousin Ali, his adopted son Zyad, and a merchant named Abu-Bakr. Soon, however, the Quaraysh clan into which he had been born came to regard Muhammad as a threat to their privileged position in Meccan society and he and his followers were persecuted and assaulted. At one point Muhammad's own life was in danger but his uncle, Abu Talib, was able to protect him. However, he urged Muhammad to abandon his new religious perspective.

When Abu Talib died in 619AD, Muhammad was once again vulnerable. However a delegation of twelve men who regarded themselves as Muslims visited him from Medina (Yathrib) in 621AD, and the following year a larger group from this city invited him to join them. Muhammad agreed but, just before departing, he had to contend with an assassination plot. He was able to reach Medina, which lay some 300 kilometres north, in 622AD. His flight is now known as the *Hegira* or *Hijrah*, meaning 'to sever kinship ties'.

Subsequently, Muhammad helped to plan raids on caravans coming from Mecca and mounted a number of substantial military manoeuvres against the Meccan infantry and cavalry. In due course he negotiated treaties with the Meccans to remove the threat of raids from Medina and was able to procure the surrender of Mecca without bloodshed. Muhammad entered Mecca in 629AD, married the sister-in-law of his uncle and, after putting down a further Meccan uprising under Abu Sufyan, re-entered the city as both a political leader and the Prophet of God—a potent combination. At this time all remaining idols in the Ka'ba, the sacred centre of Mecca, were destroyed and Muhammad was able to proclaim the worship of Allah from both a spiritual and a political point of view.

## THE TRANSFORMATION EXPERIENCE

Obviously different social and political factors determine the continuation of a major religious faith, but when we consider the core transformative events in the lives of these three religious founders, distinct factors emerge. And these seem to be crucial components in the attainment of mystical experience.

All three had a clear sense of purpose, a desire to look beyond the more familiar domain of everyday existence and to open themselves to the universe on a broader level of understanding. Thus Gautama left the security of home and family to expand his horizons of experience. His resolve culminated, after many years, in 49 days of meditation spent beneath the bodhi tree in order to penetrate the veils of illusory appearances and to understand the mysteries of human existence. Jesus accompanied John the Baptist in the Judaean wilderness and experienced the symbolic transformation of baptism, which became for him a rite of passage into the cosmos—the realm of spirit. And Muhammad sojourned in the hills near Mecca—a setting removed from domestic, trade and political issues and the anathema of idolatry, where he could fast and meditate, attuning his mind to more spiritual concerns. It was in this setting—a remote cave on Mount Hira—and not amidst the clamour of the traders' caravans, that he received his revelations from Gabriel.

If we extrapolate these experiences in a contemporary way, we might say that Gautama, Jesus and Muhammad were each, in their own way, dispensing with their domestic or social 'programming' as a prelude to the core transformative experience of mystical revelation. Both Gautama and Jesus had dramatic encounters with the Tempter—events which personify the universal battle with the forces of the ego, vanity and pride. The latter are all manifestations of 'individual' rather than 'cosmic' consciousness.

All three, too, had withdrawn to an environmental setting that enabled them to focus on the inner, spiritual aspects of the universe rather than remain caught up with the logistics of the external world. And each received his revelation while in an altered state of consciousness—characterised in Gautama Buddha's case by profound philosophical insights into the nature of reality and in the case of Jesus and Muhammad, by archetypal encounters with the Spirit (the voice and dove coming from God, and Gabriel serving as a 'messenger' from Allah).

To this extent the transformative experiences themselves appear not to have been accidental but occurred in the type of setting and context one might expect. The spiritual 'authority' of each of these religious leaders thus lies in the magnitude and profundity of the spiritual and perceptual breakthroughs gained in each case. At the same time, I believe we need to 'de-mystify' the process of mystical illumination in order to place it in an appropriate perspective. While the Buddha and Jesus have both been mythologised (Gautama as a white elephant; Jesus born of a virgin and resurrected from the dead), such metaphors are really an attempt to convey that the worlds of sacred and human reality have co-existed at special times in history. This process need not be taken too literally, however. From the perspective of the New Spirituality, the real reason why humanity should revere Jesus, Muhammad and the Buddha is because they each had a special spiritual capacity to perceive the world in a more profound and insightful way than most other human beings before or since. It is not so much that Jesus, for example, was the unique Son of God but that, for a unique time, God, or Spirit, dwelt in him: he was open to God and became 'one with God the Father' in a privileged state of grace. Similarly, Gautama was able, during his meditations, to see beyond the veils of illusion and to enter the domain of pure enlightenment. In like manner, after his mystical revelations, Muhammad felt that he had become a messenger or 'vehicle' for expressing the Oneness of Allah.

We see in such transformations a fusion of human and spiritual qualities on a profound level of awareness. However it remains a truism among adherents of the New Spirituality that potentially all human beings have the same capacity for such spiritual realisation—that potentially everyone may become 'god-like' in terms of their innate quest for transcendence and unity with the Cosmos. The tragedy, if one can call it that, is that most of us live lives which filter such realisations from our consciousness.

I believe we can explore the factors relating to the visionary breakthrough quite dispassionately. Most adherents of the New Spirituality, I feel sure, would not support the view that the Universal God-Energy (call it what you will) has selected various individuals or groups in history and favoured them exclusively over other groups. Similarly, there would be little emphasis placed on ranking states of enlightenment or speculating on whether the spiritual teachings of Jesus, for example, were 'superior' or 'inferior' to those of Muhammad or Gautama Buddha. Indeed, we are not obliged to look at the visionary process through the constraints of any particular belief system.

Institutionalised belief systems, by their very nature, develop only after the visionary breakthrough of the founder has occurred, and as mentioned earlier these beliefs are often consolidated into religious doctrines by those who have not actually participated in the visionary process themselves. Religious beliefs are essentially a secondary phenomenon: they gather momentum as the initial mystical impulse is transmuted by the prevailing cultural, political, linguistic, ethical and philosophical preferences of the particular society in which they occur.

From the perspective of the New Spirituality it is more important to consider the process which underlies and leads to the visionary experience in the first place—for if we can begin to understand that, it becomes potentially attainable for all of us. For Dr John Lilly, a writer whose views have greatly influenced the New Spirituality, it is important that we stay completely open to all visionary and mystical possibilities and discard the limitations of entrenched perspectives. In his important book, *Simulations of God*, Lilly offers these thoughts on the limitations, and potentialities, of belief systems:

> Dogma arises when one asserts the exclusiveness and 'truth' of a specific belief system. Mystical experiences can be used to support dogma . . . to extend into proofs of belief systems. All we are calling to attention here is that if one forms the basic belief that these phenomena originate from a God Out There, from the results of one's use of rituals directed to a God Out There and from a prayer to a God Out There, then one is not exploring all the possibilities.[9]

According to Lilly,

> To remain open-ended one's God must be huge—in order to include one's ignorance, the unknown, the ineffable. Instead of God as the Belief, the Simulation, the Model, one adheres to God as Mystery, God as the Unknown. The explorer of the inner spaces cannot afford the baggage of fixed beliefs. The baggage is too heavy, too limited and too limiting to allow further exploration.[10]

Clearly, it is not a matter of following someone else's vision so much as discovering that infinite visionary source which dwells deep within oneself—and which also unites us with all other beings. This is not to say that one cannot learn profound lessons from the spiritual teachers who have preceded us, but simply that in the final analysis we owe it to ourselves to discover our own sacred depths—unencumbered, and in our own way. When we engage in this deep and reflective self-exploration our beliefs can then be enriched by our own experience, and do not derive—as is the case with inherited religious doctrine—primarily from the experiences of others. If our realisations are sufficiently profound, tending towards states of transcendence and away from the entrapments of the ego, they will necessarily lead us towards feelings of connectedness with others and with the planet as a whole.

## COMMON DENOMINATORS

Interestingly, certain factors arise time and time again when we consider the nature of the visionary breakthrough. We usually find that some, though not necessarily all, of the following elements are present in the mystical experience:

- A focus on inner attentiveness
- Withdrawal from social 'programming'/sensory isolation
- Lifestyle modifications resulting in biochemical changes to the body (such as fasting, and changes to one's rhythm of breathing)
- The use of symbols or ritual as a catalyst to attaining transcendental experiences
- A genuine sense of personal 'openness' and humility.

### Inner Attentiveness

If we look beyond cultural differences, we find that all mystical traditions emphasise that we should pay less attention to our external self, or persona, and place more emphasis on our inner self, which is the pathway to our infinite and universal spiritual essence.

In modern western society most of us find that we are obliged to engage in activities which enhance our perception of distinctiveness. To attain success in the cut and thrust of contemporary life we are obliged to project our personal image and to respond to external perceptions of who we are or should be. The focus is invariably on ego-fulfilment, on individual careers, on pride in possessions—and with this, for many of us, comes a strong sense of competitiveness and 'getting ahead'. We have to show that we are more efficient, more capable, more adept at business, more successful and assertive than others—for these are the admired qualities in our culture. However, if this is the case, our lives are surely ego-dominated. By contrast, the experiential mystical perspective advocated by adherents of the New Spirituality movement urges us to look within, to pay attention instead to the realities beyond the world of ego—to touch the deep source of our inner nature which not only provides us with our core sense of meaning and being but also links us to all other living creatures and to the universe as a whole.

Meditation, Tai Chi, and the various methods of visualisation utilised in yoga are all 'inner attentiveness' techniques embraced by adherents of the New Spirituality and will be discussed in subsequent chapters of this book.

### Social Deprogramming/Sensory Isolation

If we accept the view that in everyday living we develop various routines and 'filters' for systematising our daily activities, it follows that for any radically different mode of awareness to break through into consciousness, a certain amount of 'deprogramming'—or at least a substantial shift in one's personal orientation—would have to occur first.

We find this time and again in mystical and spiritual history. As noted earlier, Gautama Buddha, who had grown up in a privileged world of luxury and who had a particularly protected lifestyle, had his transformative vision only after leaving his protective context and encountering death, old age and suffering—first-hand. Jesus had his profound spiritual insights at the River Jordan, while roaming the wilderness of Judaea or while reflecting silently in the Garden of Gethsemane. Muhammad withdrew from Mecca to the caves on Mount Hira, where he engaged in fasting, prayer and meditation. However, revelatory or transformative mystical experiences are not confined to the founders of major religions. Seeking direct mystical enlightenment remains one of the central elements of the New Spirituality.

Obviously many mystical and deeply reflective experiences occur naturally—perhaps as we wander in the wilderness, inspired by beautiful forests, mountains or rivers, or simply as we are uplifted by the transcendent stillness and peace of open space. However in modern society most of us live in cities and the attainment of inner peace and tranquillity is much harder to obtain. One of several solutions to this problem has come with the development of the sensory isolation chamber, popularly known as the 'float tank', which is part of the current holistic health scene. On an individual level these tanks do much the same thing as the cave did for Muhammad: they remove all awareness of the routine external world and allow the person floating in total darkness to focus within.

The original tanks—which utilised seawater—were pioneered by Dr John Lilly in the 1950s while he was working for the National Institute of Mental Health in the United States. Lilly believed that because the experience gave an impression akin to floating gravity-free in space, it would lead to 'inner security and a new integration . . . on a deep and basic level'. Lilly's design was modified by Glenn Perry to replace the seawater with Epsom salts, which had no effect on the skin or hair. In the new tanks—sometimes known as Samadhi tanks—the participant floats for around 45 minutes in salinated water heated to ambient skin temperature (35.2°C). During the float, in a process akin to meditation, one is able to surrender one's stresses and tensions and retreat from the sensory pressures of the outside world. Floating in total darkness in this way is thought to also stimulate right-hemisphere brain function, enhancing one's capacity for creativity and intuition. Lilly has documented his own visionary float-tank experiences in his books *Center of the Cyclone* and *The Deep Self*.

## Biochemical Changes in the Body

In the mystical traditions it has not been uncommon to engage in practices which alter the body's biochemistry. Some of these practices are primarily purificatory, while others may help facilitate altered states of consciousness.

Fasting is widely believed to act as a precursor to mystical revelations. Japanese Buddhists fast as part of their asceticism and as Dr Imamura Motoo has noted: 'Religious ascetics, who led their lives abstaining from food, came to the conclusion that fasting improved not only their spiritual state but also their physical condition, and through fasting many diseases could be cured.'[11]

Fasting is a way of detoxifying the body and shedding excess body weight but it also helps practitioners to focus their spiritual resolve. Moses is said to have fasted for 40 days and 40 nights before receiving the Ten Commandments in a state of visionary consciousness on Mount Sinai, as did Elijah before reaching the

Mount of God. Later, Jesus continued this practice in the wilderness, and in the fourth century the 40-day period was officially adopted by the Christian Church as a time of preparation for Easter. Fasting was also practised in the Greek mystery cults as a prelude to receiving divine revelations in dreams.[12]

Techniques of breath control are similarly associated with altered states of consciousness, and feature in both Indian *Pranayama* (breath yoga) and in contemporary holistic modalities like rebirthing and Holotropic Breath Therapy. The latter uses a connected-breath cycle to produce a state of hyperventilation which can often appear rather dramatic, with spasms in the hands and feet. While hyperventilation is regarded in some medical circles as a pathological condition, Dr Stanislav Grof, who developed Holotropic Breath Therapy, believes this type of breathing can be useful in overcoming emotional blockages. This modality is discussed further in Chapter 5.

Physiologically, hyperventilation reduces the amount of oxygen transmitted to the cortex of the brain, producing a natural 'high'. It is therefore not surprising that techniques of hyperventilation and yogic breath retention have been used to attain mystical states of consciousness.

### Rituals and Symbols

As mentioned earier, the visionary experience often comes about by withdrawing from the familiar external environment—which has its own patterning or automated behaviour patterns and expectations—to another domain where the inner self can be revealed. This can be an area of sensory isolation—a cave, a mountain-top or a desert—or, closer to home, in a float tank or in a private 'sacred space' at home that has been put aside as a meditation chamber. Sometimes sacred symbols can be used to adorn the interior of this sacred space, and also to trigger transcendent or archetypal awareness.

Using this approach, one comes to a sanctified place—a temple, a church, a special place in Nature—for specific purposes associated with one's spiritual practice. This domain is sacred: it is distinct from the outside or secular world. Just as churches are erected as 'houses of God' for religious ceremonies, many within the New Spirituality movement—especially devotees of Eastern meditation and Western neo-pagan practices—have their own private 'temples'. Here, within the sacred precincts of the meditation room, or within the ritual circle that symbolises unity and wholeness, a space is put aside where spiritual transformation may occur. And in the same way that many Christian churches feature sacred images—representations of Jesus and the Virgin Mary and exquisite stained glass allowing the Spirit to break through into the everyday world, so too meditators and neo-pagan devotees alike may surround themselves with motifs and symbols associated with the mystical task at hand—be it a private prayer to Krishna or an invocation to a mother-goddess like Isis or Demeter. The concept underlying such symbolic practices is to shift one's focus of awareness away from the mundane to the cosmic, away from the everyday to the archetypal.

## Humility

It has to be said that vain human striving for 'the greater mystical reality which lies beyond' can bring its own range of problems. If the quest is solely for personal fulfilment, rather than a humble desire for greater self-knowledge in the service of others, then there may well be the flaw of ego in the outcome. Across a wide range of alternative spiritual practices—from Eastern mystics to devotees of Western neo-paganism—many with a position of spiritual authority have been prone to excesses of the ego. In the world of ceremonial occultism it has been common for group leaders to develop ritually enlarged egos, regarding themselves as initiated illuminati and subsequently engaging in power-play with their followers or neophytes. Several of the more flamboyant contemporary Eastern gurus, meanwhile, have been known to use their 'spiritual' charisma to enchant and dominate compliant followers, abusing their position for sexual or monetary gain.

At the same time, it is of little communal benefit if, in pursuing a spiritual path, so much time is spent within an *ashram* or spiritual retreat that one's inner attentiveness renders one unable to operate in a meaningful way in the outside world later on. From the perspective of the New Spirituality the task is ideally a blending of mystical and physical—assimilating the profound mysteries of the spiritual world within the context of familiar reality, in this way bringing greater vision to our everyday lives.

Humility is an appropriate state of mind for this endeavour, whatever spiritual traditions or practices one might follow, and regardless of our degree of apparent social or business 'success' in the secular world. Humility means recognising the limitations of our perspective, while opening ourselves to the vast possibilities that exist along the spectrum of consciousness. Arrogance and pride are states of mind which produce a type of boundary where one perceives oneself to be superior to others. Humility, on the other hand, can be regarded as a state of openness. All mystical traditions agree that it is in the inner world where the real insights lie, and where our dreams and visions first take form. According to the perspective of the New Spirituality it is up to us whether we let those visionary insights shape and guide our lives in the physical world.

# 3
# Ideas from the East

*When the ten thousand things are viewed in their oneness, we return to the origin and remain where we have always been*
—Zen Master Sengstan

*Beyond words, in the silencing of thought, we are already there*
—Alan Watts

One of the major distinctions between the major Eastern and Western religions is that Eastern perspectives tend to be cyclic and Western frameworks linear, in dealing with their essential concept of Creation. Eastern mystical traditions emphasise cycles of birth and rebirth over vast aeons of time, whereas Judaism, Christianity and Islam embrace a linear model of time extending from the Creation through to the Last Judgement. The noted scholar of comparative religion, Mircea Eliade, has referred to this as the distinction between *cosmos* and *history*: one framework embracing continuous cycles of time, the other dealing with finite beginnings and endings. One can make a clear contrast, for example, between the Indian concept of cyclic *yugas*—each of them vast eras of time preceded and followed by a 'dawn' and 'twilight' and reaching across eternity, and the Hebrew tradition which limited the world to seven millennia.[1] Similarly, in Christianity the world of Creation ceases as such with the second coming of the Saviour—for here, as Eliade observes, Christianity 'translates the periodic regeneration of the world into the regeneration of the human individual'.[2]

## REBIRTH AND SPIRITUAL LIBERATION

Eastern thought, by way of contrast with the Judaeo-Christian tradition, embraces the concept of cyclic rebirth, of a multiplicity of incarnations, and the idea that individual existence is ultimately illusory—individual existence being simply a small part of a timeless, transcendent whole. Gautama Buddha's vision of Creation was that all forms and beings have emerged from the universal Void (*sunya* or *sunyata*)—a Void which by definition transcends form.

According to Buddhist tradition, when Gautama began to teach his doctrine of the Void most people could not embrace such a concept in its entirety for it seemed remote from the world of everyday appearances. In due course, Buddhism divided into two schools—the Vibhaijjauadins (subsequently known as devotees of southern or Hinayana Buddhism—sometimes also known as Theraveda) and the Sarvastivadins (devotees of northern or Mahayana Buddhism). The teaching of *sunyata* was embraced more completely by the Mahayana Buddhists while Hinayana Buddhism became a more pragmatic, external form of Buddhism. In effect, Buddhism now had an esoteric tradition (Mahayana) and an exoteric, or more mainstream tradition (Hinayana). Gautama Buddha realised that most human beings need a more tangible explanation for their existence than the Void and so, as the distinguished Indologist Heinrich Zimmer recounts,

> . . . he committed the deeper interpretation of reality to an audience of Nagas (serpents) who were to hold it in trust until mankind should be made ready to understand. Then to his human disciples he offered, as a kind of preliminary training and approach to the paradoxical truth, the comparatively rational and realistic doctrine of the so-called Hinayana division of Buddhism. Not until some seven centuries had passed was the great sage Nagarjuna, 'Arjuna of the Nagas', initiated by the serpent kings into the truth that all is Void (*Sunya*). And so it was he who brought to man, the full-fledged Buddhist teachings of the Mahayana.[3]

To this day the southern Hinayana Buddhists who live in such countries as Thailand, Sri Lanka and Burma do not follow the doctrine of the Void to the same extent as their Buddhist counterparts in the north. Mahayana Buddhists also place more emphasis on Bodhisattvas, beings who have achieved supreme insight into reality and who can assist mankind through their wisdom. In the north there is an elaborate cosmology of divine emanations and a greater emphasis on yoga meditation as the pragmatic means to experience the Great Realisation, whereas in the south yoga is more a theoretical study than a practice.[4] Northern Buddhism expounds an esoteric, or mystical, interpretation of the Trinity, *Tri-Kaya* (the first three emanations of the Universal Essence), whereas in the south there is more of a fundamentalist adherence to the text of the Pali Canon.[5] In summary, Mahayana Buddhists do not reject what the Hinayana advocates profess; they simply claim that it is incomplete and capable of a more profound interpretation.

Not surprisingly, it is the Mahayana tradition in Buddhism, and specifically its expression in the *Bardo Thodol* or *Tibetan Book of the Dead*, that has had the strongest appeal to devotees of the New Spirituality in the West. Tibetan Mahayana Buddhism presents a very extensive cosmological framework related to the cycle of living and dying, and for many has provided a more complete picture of our essential relationship with the universe than is found in Western theologies. Aldous Huxley, a practising Buddhist, prized the *Bardo Thodol* and alluded to it in his famous book *The Doors of Perception*. The *Bardo Thodol* was also chosen by Timothy Leary, Ralph Metzner and Richard Alpert (later known as Baba Ram Dass) as a framework for exploratory psychedelic consciousness expansion.[6]

The *Bardo Thodol* is addressed primarily to the living, for they are the ones who must necessarily face the inevitability of death, but it was also read to the dying and addressed to the spirits of the recently departed. The book recounts what one may expect in the hereafter and describes a sequence of post-mortem visions—successive *Bardo* phases of consciousness—which arise in between separate incarnations. From the Mahayana Buddhist viewpoint, each person must face the essentially illusory but nevertheless at times frighteningly real, sensory impressions which are presented in the after-death state. The challenge is then to transcend these illusory states and attain the Great Liberation which frees the individual from the need for rebirth.

In the *Bardo Thodol* the climax comes first, for the text begins with references to the loftiest experience of all: the first

*Bardo* of the Clear Light of Illumination, experienced as the beholder loses his own ego in favour of the Void. This is a condition of transcendent equilibrium and knowledge, a state of well-being and Unity with All. It is also a state of sublime liberation from the constrictions of the sensory world.

According to the *Bardo Thodol*, if this state of being cannot be maintained it yields to the Secondary Clear Light. In this mystical level of consciousness the beholder is illuminated in an ecstasy that Timothy Leary has referred to as *wave energy flow*: '. . . the individual becomes aware that he is part of and surrounded by a charged field of energy, which seems almost electrical'. If one is able to ride with the flow it is possible to sustain this level of consciousness. However should the individual attempt to control it, this in itself indicates an act of ego, reflective of *duality*—that is to say, a sense of oneself *distinct* from one's surroundings. The flow of energy associated with the experience of Unity consciousness now gradually ebbs away and the individual begins to fall into lower levels of mind referred to in the *Bardo Thodol* as the *Chonyid Bardo*, or karmic hallucinatory stages.

In this *Bardo*, strange sounds, weird sights and disturbed visions may occur. These can awe, frighten and terrify unless one is prepared. The appropriate response from a Buddhist perspective is to remain composed and neutral as these mental events array themselves within one's field of consciousness, for in the second *Bardo*, 'any and every shape—human, divine, diabolical, heroic, evil, animal, thing—which the human brain conjured up or the past life recalls, can present itself to consciousness; shapes and forms and sounds whirling by endlessly . . .'[7]. And yet it is one's own brain that is producing these visions, for in essence they do not exist. According to the Mahayana viewpoint nothing exists in these *Bardo* states unless one's own consciousness gives them life.

It is in the second *Bardo* that Tibetan Buddhists believe they will encounter the Seven Peaceful Deities and the Seven Visions of the Wrathful Deities, incorporating 58 embodiments of the human personality couched within traditional, culturally delineated forms and shapes. These, together with a number of lower forces and potencies, constitute the Tibetan religious pantheon. As W. Y. Evans-Wentz has written:

> . . . the chief deities themselves are the embodiments of universal divine forces, with which the deceased is inseparably related, for through him, as being the microcosm and the macrocosm, penetrate

all impulses and forces, good and bad alike. Samanta-Bhadra, the All-Good, thus personifies Reality, the Primordial Clear Light of the Unborn, Unshaped *Dharma-Kaya*. Vairochana is the Originator of all phenomena, the Cause of all Causes. As the Universal Father, Vairochana manifests or spreads forth as seed, or semen, all things; his *shakti*, the Mother of Great Space, is the Universal Womb into which the seed falls and evolves as the world-systems. Vajra-Sattva symbolizes Immutability. Ratna-Sambhava is the Beautifier, the Source of all Beauty in the Universe. Amitabha is Infinite Compassion and Love Divine, the *Christos*. Amogha-Siddhi is the personification of Almighty Power or Omnipotence. And the minor deities, heroes, *dakinis* (or 'fairies'), goddesses, lords of death, *rakshasas*, demons, spirits, and all others, correspond to definite human thoughts, passions and impulses, high and low, human and sub-human and super-human, in *karmic* form, as they take shape from the seeds of thought forming in the percipient's thought-content.[8]

The third phase, or *Sidpa Bardo*, is the period of 're-entry'—the descent from the heights of mystical and archetypal consciousness to the more familiar world of everyday 'reality'. In Tibetan society a person able to bring full knowledge of Unity-consciousness to his or her temporal existence would be considered an avatar or saint. However within Mahayana Buddhism, various levels of inspirational attainment are recognised, ranging from greater-than-normal human perception down to the lowest forms of animal consciousness manifest, or re-awakened in humanity.

As we have seen, the levels of mind which the beholder finds himself engaging in are directly related to his ability to flow with his perceptual field. It is important, however, that he should not be 'captured' or seduced by its imagery. Mahayana Buddhists also believe that during the phase of 're-entry' the will should be focused as much as possible on integrated spiritual values rather than symbols of the ego. Otherwise one may become enmeshed in judgement visions related to karmic projections from one's own personality, debased sexual fantasies, or other manifestations of neurosis.

In essence the core teaching of the *Bardo Thodol* is the attainment of the Great Liberation that frees the individual from the cycle of endless rebirths. This state is achieved by ego-loss, or the death of the ego. It may be achieved in the first *Bardo* of the Clear Light, or by transcending the archetypal images of deities in the second *Bardo*. Below these levels the ego gains more and more strength and seeks 'rebirth' in the world of the senses where it is able to assert itself once more as dominant. Most of us are doomed to return to 'normality' and are locked into seemingly endless cycles of rebirth. However, training for these transcendent levels of consciousness allows for greater familiarity with the most sacred realms of the mind. From the Buddhist viewpoint the choice for Liberation will have to be taken sooner or later.

## KARMA

Implicit here is a belief that ultimately we are all masters of our own destiny. The Hindu/Buddhist concept of *karma* which underscores the *Tibetan Book of the Dead* emphasises that there are consequences arising from good or bad actions. According to a number of Hindu texts 'A man of good deeds becomes good, a man of evil deeds becomes evil', and this concept has filtered through into the New Spirituality as the truism that 'we create our own reality'. However there is a moral imperative which rises above selfish motivation. Ideally one should earn good karma (or 'fate') through an attitude of detachment rather than by focusing on personal gain, 'Karma', writes Edward Rice,

> is the effect of any action upon the doer, whether in a past, present, or future life . . . most Indian sects believe that karma works as a kind of automatic moral safeguard ensuring that the righteous move toward liberation from the cycle of birth and rebirth, while the evil-doers are more and more bound to it, to their own detriment. In classical terms the series of lives is known as *samsara*, or stream current; it is also compared with a vast ocean 'fraught with dangers and whirlpools'. Man is caught in the stream (says the Katha-Upanishad) and 'Like wheat man ripens [and dies] and like grain he is born again'.[9]

In Mahayana Buddhism karma is a universal law from which there is no escape. Each individual has brought into this life the karma of past lives and through his or her present existence continues to accumulate even more. It is up to the individual to break out of the patterns which threaten to enfold him and this can only be done through an act of will. As Rice comments, 'In the end, nothing but relentless striving—not prayer, sacrifice, offerings, austerities, and penances—will free the individual from the chains of karma'.[10]

## REINCARNATION

Obviously the concept of karma is closely associated with the idea of reincarnation. The belief that each of us may already have lived many lives on this Earth, with many more yet to unfold, is widely accepted in the East—by Hindus, Buddhists, Jains, Sikhs and Taoists alike. Many Hindus believe also in the possibility of regression—that in certain circumstances one may be reborn as an animal: this variant is sometimes known as transmigration or metempsychosis. However, Buddhists incline to the view that once a soul has achieved human status the path of spiritual development continues in a predominantly upward spiral, and it is unlikely that one will revert to an animal form.

It is widely believed in the East that consciousness determines form, a quite different perspective from that adopted by many contemporary neuroscientists in the West, who assume that human consciousness is a by-product of biochemical processes in the brain. In the following section of *The Mahabharata* it is clear that *soul* is the 'first principle':

> Hear how a man . . . enters the womb. Within the womb of a woman he obtains as the result of action a body good or bad . . . [The Soul] is the seed of all beings; by that all creatures exist. That soul, entering all the limbs of the foetus, part by part, and dwelling in the seat of the life-wind (i.e. the heart), supports them with the mind. Then the foetus, becoming possessed of consciousness, moves about its limbs. As liquefied iron being poured out assumes the form of the image, such you must know is the entrance of the soul into the foetus. As fire entering a ball of iron heats it, such too, you must understand, is the manifestation of the soul in the foetus. And as a blazing lamp shines in a house, even so does consciousness light up bodies. And whatever action he performs, whether good or bad, everything done in a former body must necessarily be enjoyed or suffered . . .[11]

Similarly, Sankharacharya, the Hindu founder of the Advaita School of Vedanta, notes in his renowned work *The Crest Jewel of Wisdom* that 'for living beings . . . liberation is not to be attained without holiness perfected through a hundred myriad lives'.[12] And Gautama himself taught that the spiritually enlightened had the capacity to recall many former lives, as mentioned in the *Samannaphala Sutta*:

[Buddha speaks:] With his heart thus serene, made pure, translucent, cultured, devoid of evil, supple, ready to act, firm and imperturbable, he [the saint] directs and bends down his mind to the knowledge of the memory of his previous temporary states. He recalls to his mind . . . one birth, or two or three . . . or a thousand or a hundred thousand births, through many an aeon of dissolution, many an aeon of both dissolution and evolution.[13]

And the belief in spiritual rebirth has a strong resonance today as well. In his memoirs, *My Land and My People*, the Dalai Lama mentions that it was his belief in karma and reincarnation that sustained him during the Chinese invasion of Tibet. For him such perspectives could only lead to compassion in the face of tragedy:

Belief in rebirth should engender a universal love [because] all living beings and creatures, in the course of their numberless lives and our own, have been our beloved parents, children, brothers, sisters, friends. And the virtues our creed encourages are those which arise from this universal love—tolerance, forbearance, charity, kindness, compassion . . . If belief in afterlife is accepted, religious practice becomes a necessity, which nothing else can supplant, in the preparation for one's future incarnation . . . By whatever name religion may be known, its understanding and practice are the essence of a peaceful mind and therefore of a peaceful world. If there is no peace in one's mind, there can be no peace in one's approach to others, and thus no peaceful relations between individuals or between nations . . .[14]

Responsiblity for one's own actions, coupled with the sense of inner fulfilment and self-empowerment that this brings, is a powerful undercurrent within the New Spirituality, and in my view goes some way to explaining why self-determining spiritual philosophies like Tibetan Buddhism have such strong appeal in the 1990s. Most individuals drawn to the frameworks embodied in the New Spirituality are open to the idea of karma and past lives and see themselves involved in a spiritual growth process which may encompass many millennia and a succession of lifetimes. The planet is often referred to as a school for human experience, and we are all here to learn its lessons—at our own appropriate pace. While Western institutional religions tend to focus instead on a decision for personal salvation *taken in this lifetime*, the Eastern concept of self-liberation over a number of lifetimes has a certain appeal and for many makes more sense.

## MEDITATION

For numerous devotees of the New Spirituality the path of meditation is a first step on the path towards spiritual realisation. Meditation is not exclusively Eastern—it is also found within Christianity and Islam—but it is an integral aspect of both Hinduism and Buddhism and is more generally associated with Eastern spiritual traditions than with Western religious practice. Meditation has become increasingly popular in the West, partly as a result of the widespread interest in the teachings of the Maharishi Mahesh Yogi and the Transcendental Meditation (TM) movement, and also through the influence of other modalities like Siddha Yoga.

It has been suggested by the researcher R. K. Wallace, who studied Transcendental Meditation, that meditation itself may actually be an identifiable state of human consciousness similar to, but distinct from, sleeping, dreaming and waking. Essentially meditation produces heightened powers of awareness and deep tranquillity, and also has positive benefits for health. Those who practise meditation systematically and regularly believe it leads to a greater sense of 'centredness', heightened powers of creativity and decision making, increased efficiency at work, and a lesser incidence of negative emotions and mental tension. Adherents of the New Spirituality who link their spiritual practice with concepts of holistic health also maintain that many ailments which are stress-related can be eliminated or reduced by meditation. These include migraine and tension headaches, high blood pressure, and menstrual cramps.

Despite an increasing number of devotees a misconception continues to persist that meditation is a type of passive introversion—a peaceful but ineffectual form of self-centredness. However meditation is actually a form of mind control, and it is more appropriate to regard it as a means of broadening one's sense of being. As Baba Ram Dass once said, 'meditation frees your awareness' and opens new horizons of perception. And, according to Dr Christopher Magarey—a physician as well as a devotee of Siddha Yoga—the holistic approach to inner health means entering a state of deep, inner stillness:

> This is why meditation is the key to health. When we begin to focus our attention towards the stillness and strength which is our own inner Self and we begin to realise who we really are, then we

can watch our minds. We can watch the play of our thoughts and we can see them creating our experience of the world. Then we can begin to take control of our minds so that instead of creating stress and illness we can begin to create happiness and health.[15]

Because it is highly effective in reducing stress, meditation has also been used by some health practitioners to alleviate psychosomatic factors contributing to potentially life-threatening conditions like heart disease and cancer. According to the Melbourne-based psychiatrist Dr Ainslie Meares, who for many years treated cancer patients with a Buddhist meditation technique based on stilling the mind, the anxious or distressed person—a person who is not coping adequately with the stresses of life—places increased pressure on his or her hormonal balance and through the nervous and endocrine systems produces larger amounts of cortisone than usual. Unfortunately, cortisone inhibits the body's immune system and therefore renders the body more vulnerable to disease. While all of us are probably manufacturing aberrant cancer cells in our bodies, normally the immune system can overcome these problems. The person who develops cancer is one whose immune system has weakened, allowing the cancer cells to take hold and multiply. Because meditation seeks to lessen tension it also lessens anxiety and thereby reduces the cortisone level of the body. This in turn helps restore the balance in favour of the immune system and allows the physical organism the possibility of returning to its normal state of health.

There are basically two approaches to meditation. The first focuses on powers of concentration, the second emphasises detached awareness.

### Concentration

This approach requires that the attention be focused on a meditative symbol, a sound or chant, or a body process like breathing. Sometimes Sanskrit *mantras*, or sacred utterances, like *Om Namah Shivaya* ('I honour my own inner state') are employed—this particular one is an appeal to God the Destroyer of all illusion and ignorance which forms a barrier to perfect Union. In other forms of 'concentration' meditation the teacher may give the pupil a more personal mantra on which to meditate, once or twice a day. The idea is to turn the processes of thought inwardly until the mind transcends thought itself.

## Detached Awareness

The focus here is on what is happening *now*. The task is not so much to elevate consciousness to a 'higher state' but to become increasingly aware of the present moment. From that position one gains an awareness of the flux of life and the ebb and flow of human experience.

The *Visuddimagga*—the Path to Purification—by the fifth century monk Buddhaghosa describes the meditative approach from the Buddhist point of view, and in some respects encompasses both elements referred to above. One of the major disciplines of the Buddhist meditator is to eliminate distractions, with the aim of attaining a 'unification of mind'. As the practitioner learns to meditate for an extended period, such factors as agitation, scepticism and doubt begin to disappear and a feeling of one-pointedness (bliss) begins to dominate. The meditator becomes absorbed in thought—a process known as *jhana*—and moves deeper and deeper, finally acquiring an awareness of infinite space. Many Buddhists, however, regard the pursuit of various *jhana* levels as secondary to the Path of Mindfulness which leads, finally, to *nirvana*. The meditator learns to break out of stereotypes of thought and perceives every moment of familiar everyday 'reality' as if it were a new event. The ego becomes comparatively less important and the manifested universe is seen to be in a state of total and ever-changing flux. This leads to the sense of detachment from the world of experience, a gradual abandonment of all desires, and finally to the dissolution of the ego itself.

Another well known approach to meditation—a complete system within itself, and one which has exerted enormous influence on the New Spirituality in the West—is the ancient Hindu tradition of Kundalini yoga. This tradition of enhancing spiritual awareness involves focusing on the *chakras*—symbolic spiritual energy centres within the body.

## KUNDALINI YOGA

Kundalini yoga is a form of *Tantra*, a Hindu philosophy of life which regards the universe as the divine playground of the goddess Shakti (representing the creative principle) and the male deity Shiva (often known as the destroyer, but also associated with love and tenderness). Between them these two gods give rise to, and sustain, the manifested world. According to practitioners of Kundalini yoga the latent *Shakti* energy can be systematically awakened and raised through the different chakras of the body. As a method of expanding consciousness, Kundalini yoga encompasses many specific techniques, among them the use of mantras, visualisation, the development of the five senses and breath control. It may also involve deities from Indian mythology (each ascribed to different chakras), symbolic animals (each characteristic of different aspects of mystical consciousness) and meditation on the five Hindu elements, or *tattvas*: Earth (*Muladhara*), Water (*Svadisthana*), Fire (*Manipura*), Air (*Anahata*) and Spirit (*Visuddha*).

Kundalini yoga presents the essential aim of yoga perhaps more clearly than any of the other related spiritual paths. The very word 'Yoga' itself comes from the Sanskrit *yuj*, meaning 'to yoke', and the aim of yoga is union—with the Higher Self, the Godhead, Brahman. In Kundalini yoga this union is expressed as the merging of the two polar opposites, Shakti and Shiva, and as Swami Muktananda observed, 'once the Kundalini is awakened, then you become the very nature of bliss'.[16] While the Higher Self (Atman) is represented as male, all created forms, all manifestations of life energy, intelligence, will, thoughts and feelings are considered to be female—and aspects of Shakti. As the Great Goddess, she encompasses the three aspects of creation known as the *gunas*—sattva (purity), *rajas* (activity) and *tamas* (inertia)—as well as the five elements from which the universe is formed and as Swami Sivananda Sarasvati lucidly expresses it,

> She is the primal force of life that underlies all existence. She vitalises the body through her energy. She is the energy in the Sun, the fragrance in the flowers, the beauty in the landscape . . . the whole world is her body. Mountains are her bones. Rivers are her veins. Ocean is her bladder. Sun and Moon are her eyes. Wind is her breath. *Agni* [Fire] is her mouth.[17]

Beyond the realm of manifestation is the transcendental domain of Lord Shiva. The essential task in Kundalini yoga is to arouse the energy of the Goddess so she may be once again united with him in the supreme bliss of *Samadhi*. Considered the highest state of consciousness in yoga, *Samadhi* is referred to in the *Bhagavad Gita* as 'seeing the self in all things and all things in the self'.

Kundalini yoga clearly identifies within all human beings a potentially cosmic process. The gods are within—the purpose is to bring them to life, to unleash their energy.

## ENERGY CHANNELS AND THE CHAKRAS

There are numerous energy channels in the body. According to some yogic sources there are as many as 350 000, but the principal one in Kundalini yoga is the one path which the *Shakti* energy should take in passing through the chakras to the crown of the head. This is *Sushumna*, the *nadi* (or energy channel) that corresponds to the central nervous system of the body. Around it are coiled two other major channels: *Pingala*—which is masculine and associated with the heat of the Sun, and *Ida*—which is feminine and represented by the cool, reflected light of the Moon. Ida and Pingala meet in the lowest of the chakra energy centres in the body, known as Muladhara, and again in the sixth centre known as Ajna. The essential purpose in arousing the Kundalini from the base chakra is to lift the Shakti-energy from the 'gross' levels of physical existence to the pure and transcendent level represented by *Sahasrara*—the highest chakra in the body. In so doing, the practitioner's awareness of the universe and its sacred energies gains new meaning, for Shakti 'leads the individual from chakra to chakra, from plane to plane, and unites him with Lord Shiva'.

So Kundalini yoga is essentially about energy, and that is reflected in the use of mantras (energy as sound) and in the visualisation of specific colours (energy as light). It is also demonstrated by the dance of Shiva and Shakti as they united one with the other, dissolving old forms and forever creating the universe anew (energy as movement). The chakras are themselves sources of subtle energy depicted as 'wheels' (the literal meaning of the word) or as 'lotuses' (*padma*). In some Kundalini tracts it is said that the petals of the lotus droop downwards until the Shakti energy is aroused to bring them to life, and the Sushumna channel then becomes a conduit for powerful spiritual energies as each chakra is progressively transcended. The process involves flowing from one chakra to the next by visualising each tattva in turn, dissolving it in the associated mantra vibration, and then merging it with the next tattva in sequence. The five tattva elements—Earth, Water, Fire, Air and Spirit—which in turn are associated with the first five chakras, are in due course integrated as the meditator moves ever higher in raising the Shakti energy. Then, in an act of transcendence, Shakti is united with her consort Shiva in the sixth sphere, Ajna. The seventh chakra, Sahasrara, is said to lie beyond the realm of human experience and to this extent is somewhat like the Void in Buddhism and the Limitless Light in the Kabbalah—beyond manifested form or human consciousness altogether.

Some Western interpreters of Kundalini yoga have identified the chakras with specific nerve plexuses, ganglia and glands in the body. However yoga authority Haridas Chaudhuri notes in his article 'Yoga Psychology' that this is misleading and contrary to Tantric teaching.[18] Chaudhuri describes the chakras as 'consciousness potentials' which only assume meaning as the Kundalini is aroused. The chakras themselves are said to lie within the *Brahmanadi*—the innermost channel within the Sushumna. And while there is a correlation between the chakras and various parts of the body, the chakras do not equate with them. The 'locations' are nevertheless necessary for visualisation purposes, and may be summarised as follows:

*First chakra*: Muladhara—at the base of the spine, near the coccyx (associated with the pelvic plexus, testes and ovaries)
*Second chakra*: Svadisthana—two inches below the navel in the sacral region (associated with the hypogastric plexus and adrenal glands)
*Third chakra*: Manipura—three inches above the navel in the lumbar region (associated with the solar plexus, pancreas and liver)
*Fourth chakra*: Anahata—near the heart (associated with the cardiac plexus and thymus gland)
*Fifth chakra*: Visuddha—near the Adam's Apple in the throat (associated with the pharyngeal plexus and thyroid gland)
*Sixth chakra*: Ajna—between the eyebrows (associated with the nasociliary plexus and pituitary gland)
*Seventh chakra*: Sahasrara—on the crown of the head (associated with the cerebrum and pineal gland)

As with any metaphysical system, it is important not to take the symbolism and metaphorical imagery too literally. Kundalini yoga, after all, describes transformations of consciousness and is very much a process of exploring one's inner spiritual reality rather than representing a tangible, quantifiable endeavour. We find on examining the literature that there is also a certain amount of disparity, both with regard to the structure of the lotus chakras and the colour symbolism of the tattvas, and even in perceptions of the experience itself. For example, Mahav Pandit ascribes a ten-petalled lotus to the heart chakra, Anahata, while Heinrich Zimmer and Swami Sivananda Radha describe it as twelve-petalled. Some writers represent the tattva for Akasha (Spirit) as a black egg, others as a white circle, while the tattva for Svadisthana is given by some as a silver crescent and by others as a white one.

In terms of experiencing the arousal of Kundalini itself—something which Tantric scholar and swami Agehananda Bharati describes as a basically 'imaginary' rather than a 'physical' process[19]—there is also a certain amount of variance. According to Mircea Eliade, author of the classic work *Yoga: Immortality and Freedom*, the authentic arousal of the Kundalini through all the chakras of the body is not only difficult but 'according to the tantric scholars themselves . . . rarely successful'[20]—usually because the breath cannot be restricted long enough to allow the Shakti-energy to rise the full length of the Sushumna. However, according to Eliade, when it does occur the authentic release of the Kundalini invariably generates intense heat and the lower part of the body becomes correspondingly inert and cold.

This is confirmed by Gopi Krishna, a yogi from Jammu in northern India, who aroused his Kundalini unexpectedly and experienced searing heat within his body—to such a dramatic extent that he feared he would die. Indeed, Gopi Krishna's unleashing of the Kundalini energy proved to be unbalanced and required further visualisation to negate the heat. Suspecting that he had raised the energy not through the Sushumna, but through the hot, solar channel Pingala, he subsequently visualised the arousal of Kundalini through the cool, lunar channel Ida, and was able to counteract the 'devouring fire within'. Krishna's account highlights the value of visualisation and lends credence to Bharati's view that the arousal of Kundalini is, in essence, imaginal rather than biophysical:

> With my mind reeling and senses deadened with pain, but with all the will-power left at my command, I brought my attention to bear on the left side of the seat of Kundalini, and tried to

force an imaginary cold current upward through the middle of the spinal cord. In that extraordinary extended, agonised, and exhausted state of consciousness, I distinctly felt the location of the nerve and strained hard mentally to divert its flow into the central channel. Then, as if waiting for the destined moment, a miracle happened.

There was a sound like a nerve thread snapping and instantaneously a silvery streak passed zig-zag through the spinal cord, exactly like the sinuous movement of a white serpent in rapid flight, pouring an effulgent, cascading shower of brilliant vital energy into my brain, filling my head with a blissful lustre in place of the flame that had been tormenting me for the last three hours. Completely taken by surprise at this sudden transformation of the fiery current, darting across the entire network of my nerves only a moment before, and overjoyed at the cessation of the pain, I remained absolutely quiet and motionless for some time, tasting the bliss of relief with a mind flooded with emotion, unable to believe that I was really free of the horror. Tortured and exhausted almost to the point of collapse by the agony I had suffered during the terrible interval, I immediately fell asleep, bathed in light, and for the first time after weeks of anguish felt the sweet embrace of restful sleep.[21]

While accounts like Gopi Krishna's confirm the subjective nature of the Kundalini experience, this is not to deny its experiential 'reality' for, as in many techniques of meditation and visualisation, the power of the creative imagination and its importance in maintaining a state of spiritual balance can hardly be overstated.

In the East, the arousal of the Kundalini is generally attended by a guru. As evidenced by the case of Gopi Krishna, intense psychic energies may be unleashed in the Sushumna, and if these energies flow into the wrong channel or prove too powerful, the experience can be both disturbing and painful. For this reason it is often emphasised that meditators using the Kundalini yoga system of visualisation should proceed with care and work at a level that feels comfortable.

Having said that, it appears also to be the case that the balanced arousal of the Kundalini can be a profound and awesome experience, in which life literally takes on a new quality and meaning. Mystical teachers often emphasise that if one is proceeding on a spiritual path of this sort that one should approach one's meditation with humility and pure intent. The essential task is to surrender the limitations of the ego to the potentially infinite vision of the Higher Self.

## THE ROLE OF THE GURU

Obviously, as we have just seen, a meditator like Gopi Krishna—straying unawares into the high-energy realms of the aroused Kundalini—could well have benefited from the guidance of a guru, or spiritual teacher. This leads us inevitably to the role of the guru itself, and also to the issue of how one should choose one's spiritual leader.

Most individuals in contemporary Western society are not involved in meditation practices at the same level of depth as Gopi Krishna, so the issue arises of whether one needs a guru at all. Are gurus simply alternative spiritual authority figures to whom one turns in the flight from institutional religion? Are gurus an excuse for us not to make our own decisions? Are gurus actually disempowering those whom they profess to lead?

In an era of extraordinary spiritual diversity, it would seem that there are now gurus everywhere we turn: not only in the ashrams and meditation centres but also on the television networks, on the academic lecture circuits, and at the body, mind and spirit festivals. Gurus may even be seen from time to time gracing the social lives of pop singers, actors and social celebrities. Given this spiritual array, how does one choose? Obviously it is a deeply personal decision, and one which perhaps must be taken intuitively. It is also something of a truism that, as with politicians, we may finish up with the guru we deserve!

The authentic role of the guru is to lead the *chela*—the guru's pupil or follower—towards self-knowledge and mystical transcendence. In theory, the guru represents the sacred divinity within each of us, and is a catalyst for self-enlightenment. The real quest is the flowering of more complete spiritual awareness within the individual.

Some gurus give their chelas individual mantras upon which to meditate, and there is usually an unfolding programme of lessons and spiritual exercises appropriate to the level of the pupil. At times the interaction between the guru and chela may become quite complex and may involve a process whereby the guru challenges the concepts and self-image of the chela in order to reduce the pupil's ego, in this way allowing a new spiritual awareness to dawn.

In some traditions the chela is required to submit totally to the spiritual leader, the underlying principle here being that the guru embodies the divine consciousness required for self-realisation. Devotees of Siddha Yoga believe that simply being in the presence of one whose Kundalini is already aroused may act as a stimulus to spiritual growth in itself. As Dr Magarey writes: 'A holy person, a Siddha, awakens that awareness spontaneously and initiates the process of inner transformation quite naturally and effortlessly.'[22]

However, others observing the contemporary spiritual scene are not so sure. Indeed, in some circles a distinct cynicism has attended the upsurge of gurus coming to the West to assuage our widespread spiritual thirst. There would also appear to be a clear potential for spiritual exploitation and deception. After all, many gurus charge excessive fees for their spiritual guidance, some adopt a lifestyle of luxury and material abundance while professing to transcend it, while others have been known to exploit their devotees sexually in the name of spiritual liberation. Gurus, then, come in all shapes and sizes and with varying degrees of credibility.

Certainly there are gurus on the current scene who do not operate from a position of dominance or power and who teach that essentially we have within our innate potential the path for our own spiritual liberation. There are also populist gurus who are somewhat less discerning and who adopt Western marketing methods to attract their audience. And then there are other individuals—not really gurus at all—who present themselves as mystical leaders while in fact adhering to a quite different agenda.

A recurring theme among a number of gurus who currently grace the contemporary scene is that their teaching in some way precludes that of other, competing teachers. Perhaps the teaching is said to be 'more enlightened' or 'more ancient' than other teachings. Or the doctrine derives from a revelation that only this particular guru has earned. Invariably, there is also a distinct sense of hierarchy: there are those who *know* (the guru and those who have been 'initiated') and there are those who *don't know* (the other, newer followers or those who have not yet joined the cause). Often, too, there is a comparatively rigid belief system which flows from the guru's knowledge. Any competing teaching would be deemed as impure or an adulteration. Sometimes, the guru is elevated to a position of godliness by virtue of his or her claimed achievements.

A biography of the Indian spiritual leader, artist and musician, Sri Chinmoy, relates that in one particular calendar year:

. . . Sri Chinmoy painted over 120 000 works of art depicting higher realms of meditation. His poetry and music became just as voluminous. On November 1st . . . Sri Chinmoy demonstrated the creative dynamism of meditation by writing 843 poems in a 24-hour period. Fifteen days later he painted 16 031 works of art in another 24-hour period. Three days later Sri Chinmoy celebrated a year in which he had completed 120 000 paintings. Since arriving in America he has composed over 5000 songs and musical compositions, earning the praise of such notable composers as Leonard Bernstein and Zubin Mehta.[23]

Presumably this extraordinary data about Sri Chinmoy, released in a press kit to the media, was intended to establish him as a role model for his prospective followers. As Sri Chinmoy himself explained,

Our goal is always to go beyond, beyond, beyond. There are no limits to our capacity because we have the infinite divine within us. Each painting, each poem, each thing that I undertake is nothing but an expression of my inner cry for more light, more truth, more delight.[24]

However, while one could hardly fail to admire the sheer volume of his output, the effect of such statistics upon his followers would surely have been to disempower them, rather than uplift them. After all, who else but Sri Chinmoy could maintain such an exalted pace of creative manifestation?

There was also a call for devotees to come to his musical concerts, no doubt to admire him but also to gain privileged insights from his music. As a publicity notice for one of his concerts revealed: '*Unlike other musicians*, Sri Chinmoy's music is not composed for entertainment but as a guide to higher states of awareness' (my italics). The author of this publicity notice clearly believed that Sri Chinmoy was the only musician capable of providing this special path to higher consciousness . . .

Prior to the demise of his ashram in Oregon, Bhagwan Shree Rajneesh also exercised a remarkable charismatic power over his followers. Each day *sannyasins*, or devotees, would file in procession to watch as the Bhagwan drove past in his gleaming Rolls Royce, flanked by security guards armed with Uzi semi-automatic guns. And yet, double-think was clearly in evidence at Rajneeshpuram. Bhagwan's principal assistant, Ma Anand Sheela, later to be jailed for conspiracy, food poisoning and attempted murder at the ashram, described during a cable network interview what Bhagwan was doing: 'What he is teaching is to be individual, to become free, free of all limitations, free of all conditioning, and just become an integrated individual, a free being.'[25]

In fact Bhagwan gave each of his followers 'spiritual names', insisted on their wearing pendants bearing his photographic image, and allowed his devotees to wear clothing only of specific colours. His organisation also charged substantial fees for experiential spiritual growth workshops. Such are the paradoxes of spiritual leadership.

Admittedly the charismatic Bhagwan Shree Rajneesh and his ashram in Oregon represent an extreme case, but it is one which persists in the memory. It is not so long since Bhagwan departed the scene, and one must ask the question, as with any guru: Are these teachings purely for my spiritual growth and enlightenment? How enlightened is the teacher? Are any other agendas operating? What is the cost?

As transpersonal commentator Ken Wilber has wryly observed, there are many people looking for new spiritual alternatives who have opened their hearts at the expense of bypassing their brains.[26] In the end it is up to each of us to decide for ourselves which path we are on and which spiritual teacher we should follow—if indeed we choose to follow one at all.


## ORIENTAL HEALING ARTS

With the enormous growth of interest in Eastern philosophies over the last decade, it is not only the gurus and their meditation techniques whose influence has been felt in the West. Many oriental healing therapies have also attracted widespread attention, and these too have become amalgamated within the New Spirituality. They tend to emphasise the interrelatedness of body, mind and spirit and equate health and well-being with harmony and balance. Among the best known and most widely practised oriental modalities are acupuncture, shiatsu, macrobiotics and Tai Chi.


### Acupuncture

Traditional Chinese medicine dates from as early as 3000BC and is based on a philosophical approach which is fundamentally different from that found in Western medicine. While in the West the principal focus is on defective organs or biological systems considered in isolation, the Chinese believe that disease results from an imbalance of life-energy in the organism and they therefore take the whole body into consideration when treating a patient.

Chinese medicine is based on the philosophy of Taoism which urges a respect for the laws of Nature and for the polarities that affect all things in the universe. Two forces, Yang and Yin, govern Nature and, in turn, human health. Yang is masculine, positive and warm, and is associated with the sky and sun. Yin is feminine, passive and cold and is associated with the earth and the moon. While this may seem a rather chauvinistic division, traditionally it was not intended in that light. Rather, it was designed to show symbolically the dynamic and ever-changing flux of opposite forces at play in the processes governing life itself. According to the *Nei Ching*, or *Yellow Emperor's Classic of Internal Medicine*—a work which dates from the second century BC— 'Those who disobey the laws of heaven and earth have a life-time of calamities, while those who follow the laws remain free from dangerous illnesses'.

The ancient Chinese sages discovered that the skin could be stimulated at different points by fine needles or finger-pressure to alleviate pain and increase the flow of energy to the inner organs. The Chinese evolved the concept of a network of meridians linking the inner organs to the body surface. Chinese medicine has twelve basic meridians, coupled in pairs: male and female. These meridians incorporate most of the acupuncture points used in medical practice and are linked to Yin and Yang organs as follows:

| Yin | Yang |
|---|---|
| Lung | Large intestine |
| Spleen | Stomach |
| Heart | Small intestine |
| Kidney | Bladder |
| Liver | Gall bladder |
| 'Circulation–Sex'* | 'Tri-Heater'** |
| (* linked to the endocrine system) | (** linked to the organs of respiration and reproduction) |

There are also two other major meridians, known as the *Yang Governing Vessel*, which follows the mid-line course of the spine over the head to the face, and the *Yin Conception Vessel*, which starts between the anus and the genitals and passes up the mid-line of the body to the lower lip. In addition, there are interconnecting canals between the meridians known as *Lo*, or *Luo*, and these can be used by the acupuncturist to regulate the flow of energy up or down.

According to the practitioners of Chinese medicine, *Chi* ('breath' or 'life force') must flow unimpeded through the body if it is to remain healthy. If the flow is blocked, the person will become unhealthy and that imbalance will manifest as disease in a specific organ. The acupuncturist therefore uses his needles to stimulate points along the meridians, bringing the flow of energy in the body back into balance.

The acupuncturist begins the treatment by analysing the patient's skin colour, hair texture and rate of breath, and then reads the pulses at different points along the radial artery. Too much warmth indicates an excess of Yang, while coldness indicates excess Yin. Needles are then inserted along key meridian pathways to rectify the energy imbalance. The needles, which nowadays are made of stainless steel, are kept in position for around 30 minutes and then removed.

In China, acupuncture is used to treat a wide variety of complaints. These include neuralgia, migraine, lumbago, tooth-ache, spasm, rheumatoid arthritis, gout, muscular diseases, asthma, hypertension, cardiac arrhythmia, corneal ulcers, deafness and angina pectoris. Acupuncture is used in some health clinics and hospitals to induce a state of anaesthesia for surgery, and also has a useful application in some cases of paralysis because stimulation applied to an actively functioning part of the body can produce an energy response—via the meridian—in the paralysed part.

## How Does Acupuncture Work?

There seems to be a high correlation between acupuncture points and visceral, cutaneous and nervous reflexes in the body. Of the 300 acupuncture points used in active practice, half lie along nerve pathways and the other half are within half a centimetre of a nerve. According to Chinese acupuncturist Dr Pui Sinn, 'the results of clinical practices and scientific experiments have proved that acupuncture anaesthesia depends upon the normal functions of the nervous system'.[27] The Heart Meridian, for example, runs along the internal cutaneous and ulnar nerves, and the Bladder Meridian along the sciatic nerve. The anaesthetising or pain-killing effect seems to take place because the needle or finger-pressure stimulates the brain to release naturally occurring pain-killers. These are known as endorphins and resemble opiates in chemical structure. Acupuncture—despite its continuing 'alternative' status in some Western medical circles—therefore confirms the orthodox scientific model that sensations are received in the cerebral cortex through stimulation of sense organs which transmit messages, via nerves, to the brain. Where acupuncture differs from Western medicine is in its emphasis on the vital flow of energy through the body, connecting all organs by means of the network of meridians. Although the philosophy of Taoism, on which acupuncture is based, may seem mystical rather than scientific, there are clearly overlapping medical applications where both East and West can learn from each other.

## Shiatsu

Shiatsu is a modern Japanese application of Chinese medicine, and remains a popular 'alternative' modality in holistic health communities. The word 'shiatsu' derives from the Japanese *shi*, meaning 'finger' and *atsu*, meaning 'pressure'. As a health modality shiatsu has many characteristics in common with acupuncture although finger, elbow and heel pressure rather than needles are used. In shiatsu the acu-points are called *tsubo* and there 365 on the body. The concept of the vital energy flow—called *Ki* by the Japanese—is identical to that found in acupuncture, and there is a similar emphasis on the link between balance and health. Shiatsu treatments employ a variety of techniques to stimulate the pressure points. These include *Anma* massage, finger and elbow pressure of varying intensities (light, soft, firm) and the squeezing, rubbing and kneading of the skin. Pressure can be applied with the thumbs, the knuckles, the fingers, and the heel of the hand. Sometimes the hand is closed into a fist, at other times the hand is cupped. Practitioners also apply pressure with the feet by walking along the patient's back and digging in with the toes and heel.

Many alternative health practitioners prefer shiatsu to acupuncture because individual patients eventually can apply the techniques themselves, rather than continue to visit a specialist.

### Macrobiotics

Macrobiotics, a term meaning 'great life', focuses on the principles of a healthy, balanced diet and was formulated by the Japanese philosopher George Ohsawa. Drawing on the Taoist polarities of Yin and Yang, it recommends that each meal should be complete in itself and should contain a harmonised blend of nutrients. Foods should be consumed in their appopriate seasons and should preferably be grown in the district where one lives, rather than imported. Ohsawa classified foods as predominantly Yin or Yang according to the following criteria:

| Yin | Yang |
|---|---|
| Grown in a hot climate | Grown in cold climate |
| Generally acidic | Generally alkaline |
| Grown high above the ground | Grown below the ground |
| Fruits, leaves | Roots, seeds |
| Sweet and hot foods | Salty and bitter foods |
| Foods that are purple, blue or green in colour | Foods that are red, yellow or orange in colour |
| Foods that contain more water and perish quickly | Foods that are dry and store well |

Many foods have both characteristics and the macrobiotic cook should consider the dominant qualities in preparing the meal. But the essence of macrobiotics is that a balanced diet helps promote health and well-being.

Cereal crops comprise around 50–60 per cent of the macrobiotic diet and, where possible, the whole grain is consumed. Recommended cereals include wheat, barley, oats, brown rice, maize and rye. Fresh vegetables, soya beans, lentils and edible seaweeds, as well as miso and tofu, are also popular components of the macrobiotic diet. Processed foods and dairy products are generally avoided, as are meat and sugar. Fruits and nuts are an optional, rather than essential, part of the diet.

Overall, the macrobiotic approach puts into practice the principle that 'we are what we eat'. By recognising the natural, complementary balance of Yin and Yang, one is able to learn to live in harmony with the environment and gain nourishment from appropriate and natural foods.

## Tai Chi Ch'uan

Tai Chi, as it is usually known, is motion, unity, dance—a surrendering to the natural flow of energy in the Universe. The Chinese expression *Tai Chi* itself translates as 'supreme ultimate' and has some of the same connotations as Yin/Yang. Ch'uan means a 'fist' or 'boxing' and demonstrates the links between the oriental martial arts like Kung Fu and Karate, and the more contemplative practice of Tai Chi. The latter replaces aggression and hostility with sensitivity and the capacity to yield to an overidding calm.

Tai Chi is a means of exploring the processes of mind and body through creative movement and reflects the view expressed in the I Ching—the revered Taoist divinatory text—that Nature is always in motion. A person learning the basic movements of Tai Chi—which soon become very much an individual expression—begins to experience inner transformations and a renewed sense of energy vitalising the body.

Tai Chi is said to have originated with the meditation of the Taoist monk Chang San-feng. As he looked out of a window he watched a magpie trying to attack a snake. The snake teased the bird and remained always just out of reach, writhing and curling in a spiral motion. Similar movements are now an integral part of Tai Chi.

Several symbols recur in Tai Chi: the image of water, to represent the flow of energy and the yielding adaptability of its form within a container; the symbol of earth as a 'centring link' between person and planet, and the use of circular forms of expression to show unity, containment and polarity change.

In Tai Chi all movements complement each other. According to Chang San-feng, 'the inner strength is rooted in the feet, developed in the thighs, controlled by the waist and expressed through the fingers'. All movements begin with stillness and manifest a sense of revitalisation while producing a profound feeling of serenity and well-being.

There are various forms of Tai Chi—*Yang* and *Wu* for example—but they tend to overlap. Traditionally Tai Chi techniques were passed from master to pupil but today in the West many practitioners conduct Tai Chi workshops on the art of creative self-expression and the more formal aspects are disappearing.

One of the best known international exponents of Tai Chi is <u>Al Chung Liang Huang</u>, who has taught Tai Chi in many countries and has been closely associated with the personal growth movement focused at Esalen. Al Huang is associated with a free-form style of Tai Chi that has become extremely popular. One of his basic expressions relates to the Five Elements of Taoism: fire, water, wood, metal and earth.

Following a period of meditative stillness we begin by stepping forward on the right foot. This is an energy step and fire is visualised shooting from the palms. Then the energy is pulled back into the body and the weight transferred to the left foot: water (at this time water may be visualised cascading over you like a life-giving shower). Turning to the left we let the palms rotate and curve back towards the right. The arms are moved in a sweeping, circular motion to symbolise wood. The body continues to turn to the right with both feet fixed: metal. Then the left leg is brought around and we return to the centre: earth. All energy is focused in the body.

Tai Chi is a form of self-actualisation and in keeping with other holistic philosophies emphasises the interrelatedness of mind, body and spirit and the importance of the natural and unimposed flow of energy. Tai Chi is also a process of self-discovery and, like yoga, demonstrates the link between body movement and posture, and contemplative states of being. It has been said that Tai Chi seeks 'serenity in activity' and this captures the essential paradox. We live in both the inner and outer worlds—the inner domain of thought and reflection, the outer world of force and action. Tai Chi provides a means of blending these worlds together with the aim of expressing unity and fulfilment.

# 4
# Ideas from the West

*You never enjoy the world aright*
*Till the sea itself flows in your veins*
*Till you are clothed with the stars*
—Thomas Traherne

The New Spirituality has unquestionably drawn substantially on Eastern mysticism but much of its esoteric orientation derives from the West. It seems to me that if one is looking for specific antecedents within Western cultural history—for the seeds which have shaped the New Spirituality of the present decade—then one must look back in the first instance to the Gnostic sects which existed in the first, second and third centuries of our historical era.

## GNOSTIC AND MEDIEVAL PRECURSORS OF THE NEW SPIRITUALITY

The Gnostics embodied a principle which also characterises the 1990s distinction between having faith in a specific religious tradition and deriving one's spiritual perspective from broad-based personal experiences—perhaps gained through meditation or some other personal growth modality. For the Gnostics, the key element in gaining greater personal awareness was the concept of *gnosis*, or spiritual knowledge. The Gnostics believed that it was possible to look within oneself, to make contact with one's innate divinity—a divinity intrinsic to all human beings—and that in this way one could come to know about the 'higher worlds' and the spiritual origins of the universe. This is clearly a very different attitude to the more orthodox Christian perspective, which emphasises redemption and spiritual salvation as an exclusive gift from God. The Gnostic attitude, mirrored in the New Spirituality of the 1990s, affirms that the initiative for spiritual growth lies essentially with humanity—rather than with some remote, albeit at times intrusive, God.

If we take the view that the Judaeo-Christian tradition has dominated the rise of Western culture and civilisation, then it is also fair to say that the New Spirituality is the most recent spawning in a series of subordinate belief systems which have trickled along as part of a spiritual undercurrent through the centuries. Not that these belief systems have necessarily seen themselves as anti-Christian, simply as not wholly Christian. Whether that necessarily makes them anathema is a matter of individual choice. But since the time of the Gnostics there have existed at different periods in Western history clusters of mystical adherents who, taken cumulatively, represent a minority tradition committed to a substantially different perspective from mainstream spiritual beliefs.

It is possible to regard this minority tradition—whose most recent expression can be found in the New Spirituality of the 1990s—as beginning with those Gnostic sects whose tenets were firmly discarded as heresy by the early Christian Councils of Nicea and Constantinople, and then continuing with the Neoplatonists and Hermeticists who kept alive the concept of a universe consisting of different spiritual, hierarchical levels that these days we would call 'levels of consciousness'. These levels of spiritual reality could be tapped through prayer, magical invocations and certain rites of initiation but, again, the spiritual initiative lay with the individuals themselves if they wished to have access to these levels of mystical awareness and 'knowledge'.

As we will consider later in more detail, the Western esoteric tradition gained a special impetus through the groups of Jewish Kabbalists who adhered to a minority belief system grounded within the Judaic spiritual tradition. The central work in the Kabbalah is the *Zohar*, or *Book of Splendour*, ascribed to Moses de Leon and completed *circa* 1286AD. It provides a mystical framework which clarifies the symbolic relationship between the domain of the Godhead (the trinity), the world of Creation, and the archetypal man, Adam Kadmon. However, as the eminent authority on Kabbalism, the late Gershom Scholem, pointed out, Kabbalism was really a form of Gnosis. It was an oral tradition that sought to provide an esoteric or mystical interpretation of the Judaic Torah (law or doctrine) and Talmud (commentaries), and it embraced a symbolic interpretation of the Creation process which, as with the Gnostics and Neoplatonists, assumed different 'spheres', emanations, or levels of consciousness between the Godhead—or supreme Reality in the universe—and humanity. These symbolic spheres have modern-day correlates in contemporary meditational practice and are the Western esoteric counterparts of the chakras.

In the Kabbalah there are ten levels of consciousness which are known as *sephiroth*, or spheres, upon the Tree of Life. The Tree of Life, in turn, symbolically encompasses all levels of 'reality', or manifestation, between the infinite levels of the transcendent Godhead—*Ain Soph Aur*, the Limitless Light—and the physical world of familiar perception. According to the Kabbalah, of the ten spheres of consciousness on the Tree, the first three represent a spiritual 'trinity', and the remaining seven the Days of Creation. They also provide a type of sacred map— these days one might call it a 'meditative framework'—for humanity to recover its lost divinity.

The ten spheres of the Tree of Life are as follows:

*Kether*: This is the first manifestation of Creation, manifesting as the first point of radiance from the Infinity of non-existence (the Limitless Light) which extends beyond the Tree of Life. The sphere of *Kether* is neither male nor female.

*Chokmah* and *Binah*: As the great impulses of force and form, these emanations are symbolised by the Great Father (*Chokmah*), who provides the spark or sperm of creative manifestation, and the Great Mother (*Binah*) who is the womb of the World.

The seven 'Days of Creation' now follow lower down on the Tree, and are presided over by a Great Father archetype who acts as guardian of the world (the Judaic image of 'God the Father'—the tribal Yahweh):

In *Chesed* and *Geburah*, the Great Father shows his two faces— Mercy and Severity respectively—revealing the universe as a domain associated with the ongoing process of life, destruction and renewal.

*Tiphareth* is the consciousness level of the God-man—the divine Son who mythologically encompasses the Sun and the process of spiritual rebirth. Mythically this is also the domain of the Messiah, who in the Judaic tradition leads his people back to the realm of God the Father.

*Netzach* is one of three subsequent emanations which reflect in mythological terms lesser aspects of the Great Mother and in turn are linked mythologically to the Moon. *Netzach* represents emotional love and equates with the love of the divine Son for the world.

*Hod*, the eighth sephirah, like *Tiphareth*, is a 'lower' masculine potency and bears a strong relation to *Chokmah*.

The other levels of consciousness upon the Tree of Life are the ninth and tenth sephiroth, *Yesod* and *Malkuth*, which are feminine in focus and represent the sexual instincts and the fertile earth itself.

In the Kabbalah, these ten sephiroth are sometimes shown superimposed upon the body of Adam Kadmon—the archetypal man, who in Judaic thought represents humanity as a whole. In the esoteric tradition one of the approaches to working one's way back, as it were, to the Godhead, would be to meditate in turn on each of the ten sephiroth, retracing the path of Creation from *Malkuth* through to *Kether*—the source of all being. While orthodox Jews had a comparatively tribal view of religion—with Jehovah (or Yahweh) ever ready to intrude into historical affairs—the Kabbalists had a more transcendental emphasis. The supreme reality in the Kabbalah is not Jehovah, but *Ain Soph Aur*—the Limitless Light—an idea which has more in common with the Mahayana Buddhist notion of *sunyata* (the 'Void') and with concepts of energy in quantum physics than with the model of an often bellicose and at times merciful Father-God situated somewhere in the heavens above suffering humanity.

Other belief systems which rose up in the Middle Ages were also antecedents of the New Spirituality. Medieval alchemy presented a series of metaphors relating to the purification of metals. Underlying the philosophy of alchemy, at least for the more mystical alchemists, was the idea of portraying the transformation of humanity from its 'leaden', impure state to a 'golden', pure condition where the Philosopher's Stone or the Pearl of Great Wisdom—symbolic of spiritual knowledge or Gnosis—might also be attained. Figures like Paracelsus, Basil Valentine and Thomas Vaughan certainly understood alchemy on this level: it was much more than a rudimentary pre-chemistry aimed at discovering an elixir for prolonging life.

Allied to this, too, are the medieval traditions of Free-masonry and the Tarot, which also provide symbolic models of the universe. In the case of Freemasonry, which flourished among the guilds of stonemasons, the concept arose of God as the Divine Architect of the universe—an idea which many Christians and non-Christians alike would not find uncongenial. However, there is nothing especially 'exclusivist' in the Masonic god—Masons are only required to believe in a supreme being, not necessarily the Christian God. So Masonry lends itself, at least theoretically, to an almost pantheistic world-view in which the universe is meaningfully constructed by transcendent forces.

The Tarot is perhaps more relevant to understanding the origins of the New Spirituality, however, because it continues as one of the metaphorical systems in the contemporary 'alternative' subculture, whereas Masonry as a social institution no longer retains its 'esoteric' label. The Tarot, on the other hand, is much more than a simple divinatory tool, for it describes a number of archetypal images, personified in turn by the 22 cards of the Major Arcana. These take the form of various male archetypes, including the Magician, the Emperor and the High Priest, and certain female counterparts like the High Priestess, the Empress, Justice and the Moon. There are also symbolically 'neutral' cards—that is to say, neither male nor female symbolically—like the World, Death and the Wheel of Fortune. Beneath the seemingly decorative imagery of this set of cards—the 56 Minor Arcana correspond to modern playing cards, with four suits—is a structure which again is central to the thinking that underlies the New Spirituality.

In the Tarot the cards of the Major Arcana—the 'mythic' cards—represent paths to transcendent reality, a type of spiritual journey through the maze of the mind and soul: in the Western esoteric tradition they have been incorporated onto the Kabbalistic Tree of Life as a type of framework of Western mythic consciousness. However, from a historical and symbolic perspective the Tarot is in no way Judaeo-Christian. In some Tarot packs there are Egyptian motifs—the Wheel of Fortune, for example, is sometimes shown with the Graeco-Egyptian jackal-headed god Hermanubis, and the High Priestess is invariably shown seated between Egyptian-style temple pillars. However, figures like the Magician, while medieval in terms of their imagery, are nevertheless essentially Gnostic in tone. In most Tarot packs the Magician is shown directing spiritual energy from a higher source—the Infinite World of Light—down to the manifested world of form, represented in turn by the symbols of Earth, Water, Fire and Air. The Magician thus represents a level in the spiritual hierarchy—an archetype, as Jung would say, in the inner universe of the Collective Unconscious.

## WEST MEETS EAST

It is by no means coincidental that the esoteric traditions described above all came to form part of the occult revival that occurred in England and Europe in the late nineteenth century, and which has had a direct bearing on the present-day New Spirituality. The end of the last century saw the emergence of several 'new' religious sects, such as Mormonism, Christian Science and Theosophy, but significantly it also saw the first real interest in comparative religion. Influential scholars such as the German philologist Max Muller began to translate works like the *Rig-Veda Sanhita* (Sacred Hymns of the Brahmans) and Theosophy, in particular, advocated the idea that there was a wisdom tradition, encompassing both East and West, which represented a type of universal esoteric knowledge. This knowledge was held in its most complete form by 'initiates', and could be communicated only to those most worthy to receive it. Madame Helena Blavatsky, co-founder of the Theosophical Society in 1875, believed that she received her teachings from Tibetan spiritual 'Masters'—Mahatmas—and that she had privileged access to them. There is nothing new about such claims, of course, and one finds distinct echoes of this phenomenon both among the various New Age 'channellers' who have proliferated in California, and also among a number of Eastern gurus whose teachings and devotional practices are now part of the New Spirituality.

The key point here, however, is that Theosophy—in helping to bring Eastern mysticism to Western shores—had much to do with promulgating the idea of a universal wisdom tradition that could be accessed through different religious systems and metaphors of transcendence. From the Theosophical viewpoint, God was perceived as an all-pervasive, universal constant—the Ground of All Being—and there were many routes up the mountainous path to spiritual enlightenment: they all led to the same place. This is a rather different proposition, however, from the Christian belief that God sent his only-begotten son into the world to save the whole of humanity. The Christian perspective does not share Theosophy's eclecticism, for Jesus is the Messiah and is not regarded as simply another 'master' alongside, say, Gautama Buddha, Muhammad or Madame Blavatsky's inner-plane teachers. Theosophy epitomised, and continues to advocate, the comparative approach, and acknowledges that one may find wisdom and 'salvation' in many different places concurrently.

## THE GNOSTIC MAGIC OF THE GOLDEN DAWN

During the last decades of the nineteenth century, at a time when Theosophy was establishing itself, first in New York and later in London, a number of other individuals were also seeking to amalgamate Western esoteric beliefs into a composite and practical approach to mystical consciousness. This process eventually culminated in the establishment of the Hermetic Order of the Golden Dawn in London in 1888. The Order of the Golden Dawn—essentially a magical secret society—is significant because it represents the most important historical source of contemporary occult information. It exerted a profound influence on the 1960s 'Aquarian' subculture and has also permeated the New Spirituality in indirect ways, even though many devotees may not actually have heard of it, nor explored its origins.

The Golden Dawn brought together all of the esoteric strands referred to earlier, and added some of its own. Its principal founder, Samuel Liddell MacGregor Mathers, took as his framework of spiritual knowledge the Kabbalistic Tree of Life which, as we have noted, represented ten levels of consciousness between the Godhead and the manifested world of everyday reality. He then prepared a number of ceremonial rituals that were intended to focus the awareness of his fellow occultists on each of these levels of consciousness in turn, from the lowest to the highest. Some of the Golden Dawn rituals had rather grand names like the Grade of Philosophus and the Consecration Ceremony of the Vault of the Adepti, and the ritual practitioners each took specific ceremonial roles. The central idea was to identify with the symbolic qualities of the god-energies summoned in ritual: to become like them and to share their essence. This is a central aim of 'High Magic'—the notion that the most

profound levels of spiritual inspiration can be activated by invocation and ritually focused acts of imagination.

The Golden Dawn included the Tarot within its 'special
knowledge' lectures and also provided its followers with symbolic
explanations of alchemy, Freemasonry, the Hindu *tattvas*, the
Enochian 'keys' of the Elizabethan astrologer Dr John Dee and
a solid grounding in medieval magical symbolism. More important, perhaps—especially as we are considering the Golden Dawn
as a precursor of the New Spirituality—was the fact that several
of its members practised forms of guided visualisation and trance-
work which have their present-day counterparts in 'creative
visualisation' and 'guided imagery' workshops. Some of the most
interesting Golden Dawn accounts of 'travelling in the spirit
vision' date from as early as 1893 and thus pre-date both Freud
and Jung and the contemporary interest in the imagery of the
unconscious mind.

One should not overlook the fact, either, that the Golden
Dawn had within its ranks some extremely talented individuals.
MacGregor Mathers was particularly adept at composing poetic
rituals designed to inspire the imagination, and Arthur Edward
Waite was responsible for formulating, with Pamela Colman
Smith, the so-called Rider Tarot pack, which remains one of the
most popular New Age Tarot decks, even today. Other leading
figures in the Golden Dawn included the renowned Nobel prize-
winning poet William Butler Yeats, the distinguished Welsh
novelist Arthur Machen, and the notorious but nonetheless
influential occultist Aleister Crowley.

Arguably the most important female member of the Golden
Dawn was Violet Firth, better known as Dion Fortune. Firth joined
the Order in 1919 and was interested in Jung's theories of archetypes and the Collective Unconscious. She worked as a lay
psychologist and also wrote a number of mystical novels. In 1922
she helped establish an occult group known as the Fraternity of the
Inner Light, which developed the idea of *visionary* magic—the
concept being that by using guided visualisations based on the Tarot
images and other archetypes, one could explore the heights of
mythic consciousness. This approach continues today through an
international group called the Servants of the Light whose leader,
Dolores Ashcroft-Nowicki, is a prominent and internationally published occult writer and magical devotee.

Once can say, then, that the contemporary revival of interest
in the occult or 'hidden' esoteric traditions has had a great deal

to do with the writings and techniques developed either within the Golden Dawn itself, or by its individual followers. Aleister Crowley's magical writings, in particular, were revived as part of the international hippie culture and his face appears in the colourful montage which makes up the cover of the Beatles' famous *Sergeant Pepper's* album. Arthur Edward Waite's writings on the Kabbalah, the Holy Grail, ceremonial magic and the Tarot were also republished in the 1960s and became central to the occult strands of the counter-culture. Their influence within the New Spirituality continues to this day.

## WICCA, NEOPAGANISM AND GODDESS WORSHIP

One of the most interesting elements in the New Spirituality is the ongoing interest in what is now often referred to as Sacred Psychology and the archetypal Feminine principle. A direction of this sort in contemporary society is hardly surprising. As the international feminist movement helped rectify an imbalance in the socio-political sphere during the 1960s and 1970s it was only a matter of time before such expressions flowed through into different forms of feminine spirituality.

Acknowledgement of the Feminine takes many different forms. It may be expressed through the sacred metaphor of Gaia—embodiment of the living planet and the increasing global awareness—or it may derive from the feminist perception that a largely male-dominated society should learn to acquire the 'feminine' gifts of nurturing and intuition. It is mirrored, too, in the contemporary revival of interest in the esoteric Wiccan and neopagan traditions that honour the Universal Goddess through different ritual, ceremonial and meditative expressions.

Modern witchcraft is often referred to as Wicca, from the Old English words *wicca* (masculine) and *wicce* (feminine) meaning 'a practitioner of witchcraft'. The word *wiccan*, meaning 'witches', occurs in the Laws of King Alfred (*circa* 890AD) and the verb *wiccian*—'to bewitch'—was also used in this context. Some witches believe the words connote a wise person, and Wicca is sometimes known as the 'Craft of the Wise'.

Witchcraft in essence is a Nature-based religion with the Great Goddess as its principal deity. She can take many forms: the Great Mother or Mother Nature or, more specifically, Artemis, Astarte, Athene, Demeter, Diana, Aphrodite, Hathor,

Isis or Persephone—among many others. The High Priestess of the coven incarnates the spirit of the Goddess in a ceremonial context when the High Priest 'draws down the Moon' into her body. In witchcraft, the High Priestess is the receptacle of wisdom and intuition and is symbolised by the cup, whereas her consort is represented by a short sword or dagger. Many witchcraft rituals feature the act of uniting dagger and cup to symbolise sexual union, and there is also a comparable relationship in Celtic mythology between the sacred oak tree and Mother Earth. Accordingly, the High priest, or consort, is sometimes known as the Oak King—a reference to the Oak of the Celts—and at other times as Cernunnos, 'The Horned One'. In witchcraft the Horned God personifies fertility, and in ancient Greece the Great God Pan—the goat-footed god—was a symbol of Nature and the universal life-force. There is no connection between the Horned God of witchcraft and the Christian horned Devil although this has been a common misconception since the witchcraft persecutions of the Middle Ages.

Wiccan covens vary in size although traditionally the members number thirteen—six men, six women and the High Priestess. When the group exceeds this number, some members leave to form a new coven. Wiccans take special magical names which they use in a ritual context and they meet for their ceremonies at specific times of the year. These meetings, or *sabbats*, are related to the cycles of Nature and the traditional times for harvesting crops.

The four major sabbats are:

Candlemas (2 February) known by the Celts as *Imbolc*
May Eve (30 April), or *Beltane*
Lammas (1 August), or *Lughnassadh*
Halloween (31 October), or *Samhain*.

In addition, there are four minor sabbats—the two solstices at midsummer and midwinter, and the two equinoxes in spring and autumn.

In pre-Christian times, *Imbolc* was traditionally identified with the first signs of spring; *Beltane* was a fertility celebration when the sacred oak was burned, mistletoe was cut, and sacrifices were made to the gods; *Lughnassadh*, which was related to autumn and the harvesting of crops, celebrated both the gathering-in of produce and the continuing fertility of the earth; and *Samhain* represented the transition from autumn to winter and was associated with bonfires to keep away the chilly winter winds. *Samhain* was also a time when the spirits of the dead could return to earth to be once again with their loved ones.

Contemporary witches still meet in their covens to celebrate these Celtic rites although, in the southern hemisphere, most Wiccan practitioners adjust the sabbats to equate with the appropriate season. Sabbats are a time for fellowship, ceremonial and initiation, and after the rituals have been performed there is feasting, drinking and merriment.

Wiccan ceremonies take place in a magic circle which can either be inscribed on the floor of a special room set aside as the 'temple', or marked on the earth at a designated meeting place—for example, in a grove of trees or on the top of a sacred hill. The earth is swept with a ritual broomstick for purification and the four elements are ascribed to the four directions: Earth in the north, Air in the east, Fire in the south and Water in the west. The altar is traditionally placed in the north. Beings known as the 'Lords of the Watchtowers' are believed to govern the four quarters and are ritually invoked for blessings and protection.

Within the circle and present on the altar are the Wiccan's *Book of Shadows* (a personal book of rituals and invocations), a bowl of water, a dish of salt, candles, a symbolic scourge (representing will and determination), a bell, a cord to bind candidates in initiation, and consecrated symbols of the elements: a pentacle or disc (Earth/feminine); a cup (Water/feminine); a censer (Fire/masculine) and a wand (Air/masculine). The High Priestess has her own *athame*, or ritual dagger, and the sword of the High Priest rests on the ground before the altar.

Contemporary Wicca recognises three initiations. The first confers witch-status upon the neophyte, the second promotes a first-degree witch to the position of High Priestess or High Priest, and the third celebrates the bonding of the High Priestess and High Priest in the Great Rite: either real or symbolic sexual union.[1]

There is also an emphasis in Wicca on the three-fold aspect of the Great Goddess in her role as Maid (youth, enchantment), Mother (maturity, fulfilment), and Crone (old age, wisdom). This symbolic personification of the phases of womenhood are represented, for example, by the Celtic triad Brigid—Dana—Morrigan, the Greek goddess in her three aspects Persephone—Demeter—Hecate, or by the three Furies, Alecto (goddess of beginnings)—Tisiphone (goddess of continuation)—Megaera (goddess of death and rebirth), and these three-fold aspects are particularly emphasised by feminist Wicca groups in their development of 'women's mysteries'. As American neopagan Z. Budapest writes in her *Holy Book of Women's Mysteries* (Part Two): 'Images of the Mother Goddess, female principle of the universe and source of all life, abound . . . [for she is] the goddess of ten thousand names'.

On a practical level Wiccan ceremonies can involve spells of enchantment, invocations for healing, and initiations which lead a coven member from one grade of advancement to the next. Witches also conduct their own type of weddings known as 'handfastings'—binding Wiccans for a specified time ranging from a year and day to 'eternity'—and also 'wiccanings', the pagan counterpart of christenings. Coven members tend to become close friends and the group functions rather like a family, with the High Priestess and High Priest taking a caring, parental role over other members of the coven.

It should perhaps be mentioned that in Wicca, as in other contemporary forms of esoteric practice, magic is usually classified as 'black' or 'white' and this has very much to do with intent. Black magic is pursued in order to cause harm to another person—through injury, illness or misfortune—and it also aims to enhance the personal power of the magician in bringing about this result. White magic, on the other hand, seeks a beneficial outcome and is often associated with rites of healing, with eliminating evil or disease, and with the expansion of consciousness. It is the latter which has the most appeal within the New Spirituality movement. As Wisconsin-based Wiccan Selena Fox says: 'We're working with the energies of the earth, and we're very much tuned into a love consciousness. We're seeking to do those kinds of things that religions around the world have as their essence, which is working with healing, working with love and working to achieve an inner balance.'[2]

Contemporary Wicca has a direct connection with the Golden Dawn tradition via Gerald Gardner and Arnold Crowther, both of them practitioners of modern witchcraft. Gardner and Crowther visited Aleister Crowley in Hastings, a year before his death in 1947, and discussed various fusions of witchcraft and magic. Gardner's brand of witchcraft, which honours sexual freedom and working 'sky-clad', or naked, in ritual, is now a mainstream element in contemporary American neopaganism.

Margot Adler, granddaughter of the famous psychologist Alfred Adler and the acclaimed author of *Drawing Down the Moon*—a detailed study of American neopaganism—is an initiated Gardnerian Wiccan and currently works as a reporter for National Public Radio in New York. Adler says that she first fell in love with the Greek gods and goddesses when she was twelve years old. A leading spokesperson for the neopagan movement in the United States, she feels strongly that the esoteric mystical traditions provide the opportunity for direct spiritual experience.

In an interview published in *East West*,[3] she told journalist Victoria Williams that practising Wicca involved 'seeing the earth as sacred, seeing human beings and everything else as part of that creation, seeing divinity as immanent and not transcendent, and seeing people as basically good'. She told me much the same thing when I interviewed her in New York for a television documentary:

> I think that one of the reasons that so many people in the United States have come to paganism is that they see in it a way of resacralising the world, of making it animated, of making it vivid again, of having a relationship to it that allows for harmony and wholeness. Perhaps this can help create a world that is more harmonious with Nature and can end the despoliation of the planet.[4]

However she also emphasised that one of the areas where Wicca differed from more organised religions was in its conviction that the divine principle could be found, potentially, within every living person—a formal structure or belief system was not required: 'The fundamental thing about the magical and pagan religions is that ultimately they say that within yourself you are the god, you are the goddess—you can actualise within yourself and create whatever you need on this earth and beyond.'

Another key figure in the Wiccan movement is Miriam Simos, otherwise known as Starhawk, a San Francisco-based writer, counsellor and political activist. Author of *The Spiral Dance* and *Dreaming the Dark*, Starhawk studied feminism at UCLA. She regards her magical craft as the ability to transform consciousness at will and believes the female practitioner has a special and privileged role. As a representative of the Goddess, the female Wiccan is, metaphorically, a giver of life:

The images of the Goddess as birth-giver, weaver, earth and growing plant, wind and ocean, flame, web, moon and milk, all speak to me of connectedness, sustenance, healing, creating.

If you think of magic as an art, art implies imagery and vision. The basic principle of magic is that you work with visualisation, making pictures in your mind through which you direct energy. Ritual is simply a patterned movement of energy that opens channels to the marvellous living force we are all part of. Magical systems are highly elaborate metaphors, and through them we can identify ourselves and connect with larger forces. If magic is the art of causing change in accordance with will, then political acts—acts that speak truth to power, that push for change—are acts of magic. My model of power says that the world itself is sacred and the Goddess is simply our name for the living organism of which we're all a part.[5]

While magical and neopagan perspectives have clearly become a major element in the New Spirituality of the 1990s—especially through their role in honouring female spirituality, other branches of the so-called 'occult arts' have retained a mixed status. Divination, for example, remains a popular metaphysical pastime although usually as an adjunct to more far-reaching spiritual philosophies.

Many would argue that systems of divination are not in themselves spiritual perspectives. By their very nature they are employed to 'predict' the future and thereby provide reassurance, but in themselves they are rarely transformative or self-empowering and do not offer a path to self-realisation or spiritual transcendence. One could also argue that most forms of divination are simply superstitious and not at all efficient as predictive systems. Did any astrologer in the world accurately, and with any sense of detail, predict the recent tragic death of Princess Diana, popular and internationally famous though she was?

Astrology, nevertheless, somehow remains a special case. It evokes a sense of cosmos, it positions humanity within a matrix of archetypal forces and at times its symbolic assertions on personality traits may seem uncannily accurate. Indeed, in an era that values free will and self-realisation, astrology becomes a lot more interesting if we begin to think of it as a metaphorical and symbolic system rather than as an approach to divining the future.

## ASTROLOGY, HEREDITY AND SPIRITUAL POTENTIAL

From the time of their very first perception of the universe around them, humans have been overawed by the vastness of space and by the wonders of the Sun and Moon, the planets and the stars. Even today, when humanity's scientific skill has penetrated the depths of space, the wonders of the universe remain mysterious and powerful. In their personalising of the universe, some have attributed to the stars and planets relationships with, and influences over, their own lives.

Traditionally, astrology is the study of the relationships between the heavens and the Earth and between humans and the planets. It is one of the oldest documented studies, having played an important role in every highly developed civilisation of the past, from those of Egypt and Babylonia to India, China and South America. Astrological study of the heavens led eventually to the emergence of the scientific discipline of astronomy, while the rules, methods and principles of astrology have been refined over thousands of years.

Astrology proceeds on the basis that the planets exert influences on the Earth that affect individuals, as well as groups. Individuals are especially affected by the cosmic situation in existence at the time of their birth, and the qualities inherent in the individual can, to a large degree, be determined by that situation. In the light of scientific knowledge regarding the influences of cosmic radiation upon the Earth, the theories of astrology are perhaps not so fantastic, although it can be argued that the most important time as far as the individual is concerned is the moment of conception rather than the moment of birth.

Astrology attributes different influences to different planets and conjunctions of planets. A 'map' of the heavens at the moment of birth is drawn up to determine the planetary influences upon an individual; this is known as a horoscope and its accuracy depends very much on a specific knowledge of the location and the exact time of the individual's birth. In general terms, individuals can be placed under the influence of any of the twelve signs of the zodiac, according to the date of their birth, but the more subtle influences of the planets and their conjunctions mean that these basic zodiacal types are subject to wide variation. The popular newspaper-column type of astrology presents only a rather crude parody of the discipline, for contemporary scientific and psychological approaches to astrology involve mathematical precision and detailed analysis of astronomical data unique to each individual case.

There are two main types of astrology. The first is mundane astrology, which concerns itself with large-scale phenomena, such as wars, natural disasters and political and social trends. This is based upon the premise that cosmic influences affect large groups of people—and even the physical structure of the Earth. Horoscopes can be drawn up for nations, societies or even races, but most astrologers acknowledge that these are necessarily far less accurate than those drawn up for individuals.

The second type, horary astrology, is based upon the premise that a chart can be drawn up not only for an individual born at a specific moment in a specific place, but indeed for anything to be 'born', or inaugurated, at that place at that time. Hence horoscopes can be used to determine the advisability or otherwise of undertaking certain activities at particular times.

The basic premise upon which astrology is founded is that the universe is not a fragmented collection of individual pieces, but a unified, organic whole in which every part is dependent upon, and in some way connected to, every other part. The universe is seen to be coherent, meaningful and ordered; it has pattern and rhythm and is, to a large extent, cyclic. Humans first gained a sense of order and rhythm from their close relationship with the cycles of Nature and their observance of the movement of the planets and the stars. Gradually they came to the conclusion that these patterns could be interpreted and understood and, therefore, anticipated.

Astrology works on the assumption that the Earth is the centre of both the solar system and the universe—and, for all practical purposes, this is a valid assumption in that the universe does revolve around it, as far as humanity is concerned. Astrology pictures the Earth as being at the centre of a series of concentric circles: the paths of the planets and the signs of the zodiac. The zodiac is a hypothetical sphere around the Earth, divided into twelve sections—the popularly known 'signs' of the zodiac. Each of the signs is classified as being either positive or negative, and has one of the basic elements of traditional occultism (earth, air, fire and water) attributed to it. The Sun appears to move around this zodiac, passing through the various signs. The sign against which it appears to rise on the day of an individual's birth dictates the sign under which the person is said

91

to be born. Thus a person born on 4 November will be a Scorpio, because the Sun appears to rise in the sign of Scorpio at that time. And the Sun, representing the powerful, energetic and creative principle, is seen as the most important factor in the horoscope.

But the Earth also revolves on its own axis, and so there is a 'rising sign' too (that is, the sign against the eastern horizon at the moment of birth), and this is said to be the second most important factor in the horoscope. The actual point of sunrise is called the 'ascendant', and this determines a further classification of twelve houses, equal to the twelve constellations. For example, a person born with Scorpio as his or her Sun sign, with the ascendant in Scorpio, would be very different in personality from someone born at a similar time but with a different ascendant; in the former case, all the characteristics of Scorpio would tend to be emphasised and reinforced.

After these basic influences, astrology considers the influence of the Moon (the second most important 'planet') and the other planets. Not only the positions of the planets at the time of birth, but also their relationships to each other, must be taken into account to establish a whole 'plan' of the universe at that moment. Different planets in different positions, as well as various combinations of planets, will result in different influences and differing degrees of influence. A fair degree of mathematical skill and accuracy is necessary for such subtle and complex interpretations, and to draw a horoscope properly involves considerable knowledge and ability. The very complexity of such analyses also means that popular accounts of the zodiacal types can never be more than very generalised statements about a whole category of people, all of whom probably display more differences than similarities. All Scorpios, for example, are not necessarily alike, and there are important and subtle influences which only a detailed analysis will reveal.

Nevertheless, there is a significant body of modern scientific evidence that supports at least some of the basic assumptions of astrology. Much of this evidence has to do with psychological aspects of astrology and its relevance to the study of human personality.

One of the most often quoted sources of astrological data is that of Michel Gauquelin, who began in 1951 to gather the birth-times of successful French people who had pursued a number of different professions. He soon came to the view that the distribution of planetary positions in his study diverged sharply from the norm and the results could not simply be written off as chance. Gauquelin's initial survey of 6000 individuals showed a very strong tendency for champion athletes to be born when the planet Mars had just risen over the horizon—data eventually acknowledged even by sceptical scientific researchers like George Abell of UCLA, Paul Kurtz of the State University of New York and Marvin Zelen of Harvard. Gauquelin also found that Jupiter was linked with success in politics, cinema, theatre and journalism; Saturn with success in science, the Moon with creative writing, and Mars with military pursuits, top executive positions and the role of physician. Gauquelin's replications in 1982 of 1400 eminent Americans and additional French individuals also produced positive results. However Gauquelin also began to think of the personality attributes and character traits associated with certain planetary types. On this basis he was able to broaden his span considerably and some of his associations are provided below:[6]

*Jupiter:* ambitious, authoritarian, harsh, lively, conceited, independent, proud, talkative, witty, wordly
*Saturn:* cold, conscientious, discreet, introvert, meticulous, reserved, sombre, timid, uncommunicative
*Mars:* active, belligerent, brave, combative, dynamic, energetic, spontaneous, strong-willed, tough, valiant
*Venus:* agreeable, attractive, benevolent, charming, considerate, courteous, gracious, polite, seductive
*Moon:* amiable, disorganised, easy-going, friendly, helpful, imaginative, impressionable, impulsive, spontaneous

While Gauquelin concedes that planetary influences are difficult to explain, he believes that some clues may lie in research on hereditary predispositions of temperament. For Gauquelin, the astrological 'effects' of the different planets would be easier to explain if they were somehow symbolically linked to heredity.

According to Gauquelin, children must come into the world under the same 'planetary' conditions as their parents and the birth of a child is somehow linked to a 'cosmic indication' through a process that may be hormonal. A recent study established that the planetary effect in heredity was twice as marked in children born on a day of strong solar activity than children born on days with less solar activity. However Gauquelin has also found that if doctors interfere and induce a caesarian birth, evidence of the planetary influence in heredity disappears.

Gauquelin's research is certainly suggestive, and his correlations of astrological planets and personality traits confirm broad impressions which many people find intuitively to be broadly correct.

Meanwhile, the Swiss astrologers Bruno and Louise Huber have recently affirmed that the future of astrology itself lies in aligning it philosophically with the pursuit of individual freedom and spirituality. The Hubers believe that astrology offers an essentially expansive view of the universe and one which requires a holistic picture of Nature, life and creation. For the Hubers, any inclination towards using astrology for prediction implies an essentially fatalistic approach and an innate vulnerability—the very opposite effect from what is called for in the quest for individual freedom and personal responsibility. And while the Hubers acknowledge the extensive interest in the astrology of personality, and its capacity for symbolically demonstrating the strengths and weaknesses of any given individual, they see its potential unfolding in much more diverse and profound ways. Astrologers are already aligning their skills and techniques with other personal growth modalities like psychosynthesis, Jungian psychology, transactional analysis and Bioenergetics and, according to the Hubers, the principal thrust of astrology in the future will be spiritual:

> Of the highest significance for astrologers is the possibility of spiritual development: a state in which a person is striving towards an ever-increasing realization of his one-ness with the Soul and with the Greater Cosmic Whole. Astrology deals here with the qualities of the Soul and its influence on the personality, and thus becomes a spiritual science, leading to a new experience of religion. For many people astrology can be of help in finding out about the inner goal of incarnation, in acquiring knowledge about the tests, difficulties and special tasks on the spiritual path. This expansion of consciousness brings astrology into a much wider orbit. It deals with our earthly span of life as a segment of a greater evolutionary cycle.[7]

The late Dane Rudhyar, who was not only a notable astrologer but also a distinguished musician and philosopher, similarly considered astrology to be a type of 'spiritual psychology' and he saw in the human soul a 'complex network of psychological-mental processes which must be harmonized, chorded [and] made

organic, if man is to become master of himself and of life . . .'.
In his influential essay 'Whence, Why and Whither' Rudyar
writes:

> Astrology shows us how to work out soul-harmony, how to build
> the inner soul-organism into which the Breath of Spirit will descend
> when it has become 'viable' after a definite period of interior
> spiritual gestation. It shows us, by extension and analogy, how the
> collective life of a group, a nation, and ultimately humanity, can
> be made organic, harmonious and efficient . . . Astrology reveals
> the law of the universal process. It deals with life itself, with its
> most fundamental and general operations. Its value is not that we
> should know what events are in store for us, but rather that 'we',
> as individual selves, should accept the task of becoming 'immortal
> souls', by harmonizing the many forces, inner and outer, which every
> year, every month presents to us . . .[8]

For Rudyar, as for the Hubers, the key to astrology may be
found not in its role as a method of divination but in its value
in symbolising the dynamics of the unconscious mind and the
spiritual potentials latent in all human beings. It is in this area
that astrology appears to have most of its credibility, for it is
here that it may be able to provide insights into the nature of
human personality and the possibilities for spiritual growth.

## 'NEW AGE' MYSTICISM

However, if the debate on the value of astrology must still be
considered open, there are also elements within the New Spirituality movement which appear very superficial, and there are
signs everywhere of what Chogyam Trungpa has called 'spiritual
materialism'. Many of these elements have been subsumed under
the heading of the 'New Age'—which I do not equate with the
New Spirituality *per se*, but which unquestionably reside at the
commercial end of the metaphysical spectrum. If one can believe
the popular media image, a New Ager is a person who believes
in channelling spiritual 'masters' and developing telepathic
bonds with dolphins, eats organically grown fruits and cereals
while listening to the chime of wind-bells, is obsessed with the
healing power of crystals, casts a daily horoscope or regularly
consults the *I Ching*, talks to trees, and has a personal philosophy
that is so optimistic that it makes naivety into an art form. It
has not helped that in a consumerist society where anything in

demand can be marketed, that assuaging spiritual thirst has itself become a commodity.

And so we find in our midst a vast array of personal and metaphysical 'transformation' courses—many of them marketed for excessively high fees. Some might come with the tag, for example, that money is simply 'a unit of power and energy' and that 'prosperity consciousness' is potentially available to all of us if we can but 'take the responsibility' to recognise our own self-worth. Approaches of this sort have certainly worked for 'human potential communicator' Anthony Robbins, author of motivational bestsellers like *Awaken the Giant Within* and *Notes from a Friend*. Robbins, who charges $795 per person for people to attend his seminars on overcoming fear, reputedly earns $150 000 a day and owns an entire island in Fiji. And while he is among the most successful international self-promoters in the consciousness-raising business, there are many others who aspire to follow in his footsteps.

I have in my possession a recent copy (Fall 1997) of an American magazine called *Interface*, which lists an extraordinary number of personal transformation seminars and workshops—all of them available at a price. Some of the random offerings on tap: 'The Necessity of Meeting God in the Darkness'; 'Embracing the Shadow and Reclaiming our Wholeness'; 'Freedom from Emotional Eating'; 'The Seven Stages of Money Maturity'; 'Evolving Culture through the Chakras'; 'The Tao of Now' . . . and so the list continues. No doubt some of these may be meaningful and worthy, but one cannot help forming an impression that in popular American culture—a culture which ultimately permeates everywhere else—spirituality and transformation can be purchased in weekend workshops like goods from a supermarket.

On a certain level, what has been called the New Age appears glossy, yuppie, materialistic and potentially elitist. First there is the price of participation but then there is also the possibility that those who graduate to these new levels of self-realisation might come to feel themselves a class apart—as a distinct category of more 'evolved' human beings, or 'spiritual illuminati'. Then there are the executives for whom expanding consciousness really means improving the bottom line in profit-making in business and who are therefore drawn to the New Age for its promise of material abundance and an end to 'poverty consciousness'. And there are those whose sense of self-confidence is perhaps so fragile that they grasp at all manner of oracles—from divination and predictive astrology through to the fortune telling aspects of the *I Ching* and the Tarot (as distinct from their archetypal applications).

The New Age is also a movement with its own superstars—from American actress Shirley MacLaine through to the mega-guru Deepak Chopra. During one of her New Age lecture tours, while emphasising the divine potential latent in all human beings, Shirley MacLaine would tell her audiences: 'I am God'. When a woman in New York rose from her seat to object, MacLaine is said to have replied: 'If you don't see me as God, that's because you don't see yourself as God'.[9] Although such statements seem incredibly brazen at first glance, it is likely that Shirley MacLaine was intending to convey the sense that every human being is animated by the spark of the universal God-head—a basic principle in the wisdom tradition of both the East and West. And as one writer put it, 'She believes that each person is the centre of creation and that power, wisdom and the strength to overcome resides in every individual'.[10]

This, of course, is hardly different from the message which emerged from Esalen in the 1960s—a type of humanism laced with spiritual potential. However, where the New Age's credibility seems to have crumbled is in its bland mix of self-help, 'channelled' inspiration, confused mythologies and show-biz therapies. There is now a multi-million dollar international market in experiential workshops, lectures, crystals, relationships counselling and 'rebirthing', presented in a way which often tends to trivialise the more important findings of humanistic and transpersonal psychology. Thus we find the motivational psychology of Abraham Maslow and Alfred Adler replaced on a more popular level by organisations like Est and its later counterpart Forum. And there are numerous workshops on loving relationships, discovering the inner child, dialoguing with the inner voice, recovering the inner song, or reawakening the inner pulse—all of them variants on Carl Jung or the encounter group therapies of the 1960s.

The spiritual healer Deepak Chopra, meanwhile, is in a class of his own. Acclaimed as 'Hollywood's surgeon for the soul', Chopra has a certain credibility because he trained as a conventional doctor. Born and educated in India, he eventually discarded Western medicine for Indian Ayurvedic medicine, because he was less concerned with curing disease than promoting holistic health.

However, where Chopra shines is in his capacity to promote his message—and his products. In little over a decade he has transformed himself into being what one commentator has called 'the rock star of the new spirituality'. His fifteen books—among them *The Seven Spiritual Laws of Success*—have sold more than six million copies, he has written a film script with former Eurythmics guitarist Dave Stewart and pop lyricist Michael Jackson, he earns millions of dollars each year from the sale of his tapes and alternative health products, and he receives a rapturous reception at each of his many seminars around the world.

Singer Olivia Newton-John has claimed that the charismatic health guru helped her overcome her breast cancer, and Chopra also has a close personal following among many of the Hollywood glitterati, including Elizabeth Taylor, Winona Ryder and Demi Moore, as well as television hostess Oprah Winfrey and Beatle George Harrison. He is also possibly the first New Age spiritual guru to claim wealth is God-given. 'I have no qualms about being a millionaire and I want everyone else to know that they can do it too', he has said. 'People who have achieved an enormous amount of success are inherently very spiritual.'

## Self-Transformation

Deepak Chopra's charismatic impact notwithstanding, it remains a truism in the New Age—and within the New Spirituality generally—that one should transform oneself before endeavouring to transform others. While at times, and perhaps with justification, this might appear to be an extremely self-centred attitude, the broader intent—at least, in theory—is to move beyond exploring the facets of one's own individuality to developing an integrative state of awareness in one's relationship with others, and then within one's environment and the planet as a whole. However it is clear that the process of individual integration needs to occur on a number of levels—physical, mental, emotional and spiritual. A diverse range of alternative 'mind, body and spirit' modalities—some more authentic than others—has sprung up to cater for this need. And underlying all of these modalities is a common theme of self-transformation and the credo that if we all were to transform ourselves and raise our culture to 'the next phase of human evolution' then the world would surely be a much better place to live in.

However, while bodywork therapies like massage, chiropractic, the Alexander Technique and yoga are now reasonably mainstream and uncontroversial, and while Transcendental Meditation and the various relaxation and visualisation techniques have demonstrated their worth to many, it is in the New Age approaches to the Spirit that one finds the most questionable concepts and practices.

### Channelling from the Spirit World Beyond

One of the most controversial practices of this sort is channelling—an activity associated with New Age personalities like Kevin Ryerson, Shirley MacLaine, J. Z. Knight and the late Jane Roberts (the last two of these being channellers of Ramtha and Seth respectively). Channelling is really a new name for spiritualism or mediumism. Here the psychic is believed to act as a channel for communications from the spirit-world. Channellers claim to obtain information which can in turn be offered to their clients or workshop participants as advice for managing their day-to-day affairs. Kevin Ryerson, for example, is currently offering a 'Directions Workshop' at $85 per head on 'Social and Spiritual Directions for the Millennium'. In his workshops, according to Ryerson's promotional advertising, 'a trance channelling with Spirit will address current social and spiritual trends and how they will influence us in the future. Spirit will also address how we, as spiritual beings, influence both our personal communities as well as the Global Community'.[11]

Sometimes channelled entities purport to provide spiritual messages of great spiritual significance. In November 1987, J. Z. Knight channelled these thoughts from Ramtha:

> God is both male and female and yet neither. That which lives in the woman is as powerful and divine as that which lives in the man . . . God is the essence, it permeates your entirety. Within you lies the ability for profound knowingness. Like the Mother Earth, a wisdom, a courage, a dignity to evolve . . .

While such pronouncements seem now like banal platitudes—hardly life-shattering or controversial—Ramtha also spoke of a huge wave which would soon engulf Sydney. Ten years later, in the city chosen to host the Olympic Games in the year 2000, this has not eventuated. And yet several people in J. Z. Knight's audience were so perturbed by Ramtha's pronouncements that they decided, there and then, to move to the relative safety of the Blue Mountains, or even further away. J. Z. Knight also advised members of her audience to hoard their gold supplies and mentioned too that governments would soon act to reduce citizens' financial free will—further statements that caused unwarranted alarm.

From a psychological perspective, vulnerability to such messages would seem to reflect a sense of individual disempowerment and low self-esteem. And such a position is not assisted by the belief that any advice emanating from the spirit world must necessarily be superior to everyday commonsense. Regrettably, there are many individuals within New Age circles who fail to heed what the New Age is actually telling them: that they can come to valid personal conclusions by drawing on their own resources and the intuitive voice within.

### Healing with Crystals

Another New Age practice that has attracted widespread media ridicule and which has come to personify the more credulous aspects of the New Age is the idea of healing with crystals. In an article in the alternative publication *Southern Crossings*, Lynette Mayblom described how:

> crystals have wonderful uses in the area of personal healing but they can also be used on a greater scale for world healing. Crystals can be used to focus love and light on important buildings and places, to construct triangles of light in the planet's etheric body, to assist the growth of plants, and to protect and purify your home.

Mayblom went on to relate how crystals could also be used in spiritual meditation:

> Triangles of light can be set up between three people by meditating daily at the same time with crystals. These people can visualise light flowing from their third eyes to the other two, creating a triangle of light and visualising the encompassed area filled with light. Distance is of no consequence . . .[12]

Crystals are by no means a cheap commodity and it needs to be emphasised that only the more affluent New Agers can hope to afford crystals of any size. New Age enthusiast Bianca Pace told journalist Mark Chipperfield that she marketed quartz crystals for between $600 and $4000 each, and that her crystals had 'the power to cure diseases and transmit human and cosmic thoughts'. Crystals, she maintained, 'are part of the energy grid of the planet'.[13]

Some New Agers continue to attend regular therapy sessions where their chakras are 'balanced' or 'aligned' by the healing power of crystals. For Mark Chipperfield, who was admittedly somewhat sceptical, crystal healing had no tangible effect at all and any potential benefit was somewhat undermined by the accusing tone of the therapist he visited. 'It's a wonder you're still walking around,' she told him. 'For a start, your third eye is turning completely inwards and your chakras are almost not working at all.'

In fairness to the less gimmicky aspects of the personal growth movement, however, it must be emphasised that there are also other approaches, philosophies and techniques that have much greater claims to recognition and acceptance, and several of these have already been mentioned. One can gauge their respective merits not in terms of the 'quick cosmic fix' provided by channelled advice and crystal healing, but through their capacity to assist the process of personal transformation. It is really only those approaches representing the pathways to trans-personal consciousness that have any claim to defining the New Spirituality of the 1990s. Some of these approaches, and their advocates, are considered in the following chapter.

# 5
# Spirit, Myth and Cosmos: The Transpersonal Movement After Maslow

*Furthermore, we have not even to risk the adventure alone; for the heroes of all time have gone before us; the labyrinth is thoroughly known; we have only to follow the thread of the hero-path. And where we had thought to find an abomination, we shall find a god; where we had thought to slay another, we shall slay ourselves; where we had thought to travel outward, we shall come to the centre of our own existence; where we had thought to be alone, we shall be with all the world.*
—Joseph Campbell

As Abraham Maslow and Anthony Sutich anticipated, Esalen Institute would play an important role in the transpersonal movement, and would provide a context for encouraging systematic research into human consciousness in general. This was made even more likely when Dr Stanislav Grof was appointed scholar-in-residence at Esalen in 1974. However Grof's role in consciousness research also highlights a somewhat controversial aspect of the New Spirituality—that many of the breakthroughs and developments in consciousness which have impacted upon the New Spirituality in the 1980s and 1990s owe a debt to earlier exploration with psychedelic drugs. It was Grof—a world authority on LSD—who first indicated that this potent psychedelic is basically an amplifier of innate biochemical and physiological processes in the brain, and that much of what we know now about transpersonal states of consciousness might have taken a lot longer to discover had psychedelics not been available. As I mentioned in Chapter 1, many of the key figures of the New

Spirituality were involved with psychedelic research in the early 1970s although most have now gone on to pursue non-psychedelic approaches to mystical consciousness. Stanislav Grof is a case in point. He and his wife Christina are now primarily associated with their work in the field of Holotropic Breath Therapy—which we will look at shortly—but Grof's early models of human consciousness, and his reasons for rejecting the Freudian model of the mind derive completely from his medical research on LSD.

## THE GROF MODEL OF CONSCIOUSNESS

Born in Prague in 1931, Grof emigrated to the United States in 1967, becoming head of Psychiatric Research at the Maryland Psychiatric Research Center and Assistant Professor of Psychiatry at Johns Hopkins University School of Medicine. Grof's research programme in the late 1960s and the early 1970s focused on the medical use of LSD in easing the pain of terminally ill cancer patients. His framework of transpersonal states of awareness, formulated initially on the basis of his LSD research and complemented later by his experiences with holotropic breathwork, remains one of the major models of consciousness to have emerged from the personal growth movement. In fact, it is one of three major models—this chapter will also discuss the other two, those of John Lilly (produced in conjunction with Oscar Ichazo) and Ken Wilber.

According to Grof there are basically four levels in the psychedelic encounter with the mind. The first of these, experienced at the most superficial level, involves sensory and aesthetic phenomena—for example, visionary episodes characterised by vibrant colours, geometric patterns, and experiences of beautiful natural vistas and exquisite architectural forms. At this level there is also an increased awareness of sounds—humming, chimes and so on.

The next level Grof refers to as the 'biographical' level and its content includes important memories, emotional problems, repressed material and unresolved conflicts from one's present life. Basically this is the realm of the individual unconscious, associated with areas of the personality accessible in usual states of awareness—the unconscious mind as conceived by Freud. Grof coined the term 'COEX System' to describe a 'specific constellation of memories consisting of condensed experiences (and related fantasies) from different life periods of the individual' and he recognised early on that these COEX patterns in individual patients could be triggered into conscious awareness using LSD in a therapeutically controlled environment.[1]

However, Grof felt obliged, on the basis of the data he was uncovering, to move beyond Freud's model of the mind, because he came to believe that restricting his framework of the unconscious to one based only on 'biographical' or ego-based elements was no longer tenable. When I interviewed Grof at Esalen in the mid-1980s he explained this to me:

> I was brought up and educated as a Freudian analyst, and so when we started doing the LSD work I expected that we would be mostly working with biographical material. I was looking for a tool that would somehow bring out the unconscious material much faster, so that it would deepen and intensify psychoanalysis. To my surprise people would not stay in the biographical domain which, according to western psychology, is considered to be the only domain available—memories from childhood and the individual unconscious. Without any programming, and actually against my will, my subjects started moving into realms that hadn't been charted in psychoanalysis at all. The first encounter was powerful . . . death and birth. People started having sequences of dying and feeling reborn, frequently with details of their biological birth. But this experience of death then reversed and became like a gateway to the transcendental, the archetypal—the transpersonal as we call it now. All this material emerged as a great surprise for me.[2]

Grof's third level of consciousness encompasses levels 'characterised by a degree of experiential intensity that transcends anything that is usually conceived to be the limit for the individual human being'. This might involve a 'deep, overwhelming confrontation with the existential realities of death and dying, pain and suffering, birth and agony' but could also open the individual to profound religious and spiritual experiences.[3]

Grof calls these third-level realms of perception—which relate closely to the process of birth and the intra-uterine experience—*Basic Perinatal Matrices* (BPM), and he identifies four of them (BPM 1–4). Grof believes that each of these four matrices in turn can be linked to different types of religious or spiritual experience:

*BPM 1* is associated with the intra-uterine bond of the foetus to the mother, a type of 'symbiotic unity' reflected in the mystical experience as feelings of cosmic unity, tranquillity, bliss and transcendence of time and space—they are often what Grof calls 'good womb' experiences. Grof correlates BPM 1 with Maslow's 'peak experiences' and has described them as 'an important gateway to a variety of transpersonal experiences'.[4]

BPM 2 is related to the first clinical stage of biological delivery, a process characterised by muscular uterine contractions while the cervix is closed. This is experienced as a feeling of 'no exit', of cosmic engulfment, or being trapped in a torturous domain. Understandably, it is often a terrifying time for the subject, who feels overwhelmed by increasing levels of anxiety, unseen sources of danger and sometimes a strong sense of lurking evil. Grof correlates this level with Hell states and the 'expulsion from Paradise'.[5] Examples of this type of experience include Prometheus chained to a rock and tortured by an eagle who feeds on his liver, Christ's visions in the Garden of Gethsemane, and the Dark Night of the Soul as described by St John of the Cross.

BPM 3 is associated in the birth process with the second stage of delivery, when the cervix is dilated. Here, although the uterine contractions are still continuing, the open cervix offers the prospects of survival, albeit through a process of struggling along the birth canal. Grof associates this, in the LSD experience, with death–rebirth struggles, and says that at this time the individual can still have frightening encounters with repulsive materials— the experience of eating faeces, drinking blood and urine, and so on. However there is also the sense of impending release—the distinct impression that transcendence is possible. Grof believes that this level sometimes produces visions associated with bloody sacrifice—mythic images of Moloch, Astarte, Kai, or Aztec/Mayan ceremonies—but he also associates BPM 3 with the 'the transcending aspects of the crucifixion and of Christ's suffering, as well as the positive aspects of the Last Judgement'.[6]

The final matrix, BPM 4, is associated with the spiritual experience of death and rebirth and, according to Grof, is linked in the birth process with the actual birth of the individual. LSD subjects entering this phase report visions of vivid white or golden light, the universe is perceived as indescribably beautiful and radiant, and those experiencing it feel cleansed and purged, as if they have entered a state of spiritual redemption or salvation. Grof associates this state mythically with the rebirth of

Osiris—brought back to life by Isis, after being murdered and dismembered by Set—and also with the resurrected Christ, who is crucified on the cross but triumphs over death.[7]

However, Grof does not believe that the correlations between the birth process and the levels of consciousness accessed through LSD are coincidental. Sometimes individuals appear to relive their actual birth experiences and even seem to tap into the thought processes experienced by their mothers at the time. He also believes that his LSD research confirms the presence of Jungian archetypes in the collective unconscious—that it is no longer appropriate to consider such a concept as simply theoretical:

> LSD subjects frequently report that in their transpersonal sessions they have had a vivid and authentic sense of confrontation or identification with archetypes representing generalised biological, psychological or social types and roles; these can reflect various levels of abstraction and different degrees of generalisation. The Old Wise Man, Good Samaritan, Conqueror, Martyr, Fugitive, Outcast, Tyrant, Fool or Hermit are examples of the more specialised archetypal images. The most general archetypes always have strong elements of numinosity, as exemplified by the Great Mother, Terrible Mother, Father, Child-King, Great Hermaphrodite, Animus and Anima, or Cosmic Man. Frequently transpersonal experiences of this kind have concrete cultural characteristics and take the forms of specific deities, demons, demi-gods and heroes . . . Quite common also are experiences with spirits of deceased human beings and suprahuman spiritual entities . . .[8]

Significant and powerful though they are, Grof does not however regard perinatal and archetypal experiences as the most profound or transcendent levels of human awareness. In his view, it is possible to extend still further on the spectrum of consciousness—from the four perinatal levels to an experience of the complete transcendence of human individuality. Here, he writes, 'we begin to free ourselves from the preconception that consciousness is something created within the human brain. Transpersonal consciousness is infinite, rather than finite, stretching beyond the limits of time and space'.[9] For Grof, and this perhaps confirms the views both of the Mahayana Buddhists and a wide range of indigenous peoples across the world, consciousness would seem to be an innate characteristic of the natural universe:

> Mind and consciousness might not be exclusive privileges of the human species but [may] permeate all of Nature, existing in the most elemental to the most complex forms. Struggle as we might, we seem

unable to free ourselves from preconceptions imposed on us by our culture and by what we believe to be common sense. However, if we are to maintain these illusions it becomes necessary to ignore a vast body of observations and information coming from modern consciousness research and from a variety of other scientific disciplines. From all these sources comes evidence strongly suggesting that the universe and the human psyche have no boundaries or limits. Each of us is connected with, and is an expression of, all of existence.[10]

## Grof's Holotropic Breath Therapy

When research into the medical and therapeutic potentials of LSD became politically untenable in the mid-1970s, Grof was forced to explore other techniques of achieving transpersonal states. Gradually he began shifting his emphasis towards what he now calls Holotropic Breath Therapy, an approach that resembles the more widely known technique of 'rebirthing'. The latter was developed by Leonard Orr in California during the early 1970s, and both rebirthing and Holotropic Breath Therapy derive substantially from *Pranayama*—the Indian Yoga of breath—which employs a connected breathing rhythm to produce an altered state of consciousness. In both therapies the subject lies horizontally in a comfortable position with a facilitator, or helper, sitting nearby to assist in any experiential crisis. The session begins as the subject engages in rhythmic in-and-out breathing, with no pauses in between. As Orr has written: 'You merge with your breath, flowing, glowing, soaring, relaxing profoundly, your mind melting into your spirit, surging, awakening your inner being and the quiet sounds of your soul . . .'

In Holotropic Breath Therapy, however, the technique is somewhat more intense and the results more sudden and dramatic. The breathing is accompanied by recorded music which is chosen to reflect different phases of the cathartic process. As Grof explains:

> The music is the vehicle itself, so at the beginning we start with some very activating, powerful music. Then, maybe an hour into the session, we move into a kind of culminating, 'breakthrough' type of music—for example using the sounds of bells or similar, very powerful, transcendental sounds.'[11]

His musical selections are very varied, including African tribal rhythms, Sufi chants, Indian *ragas*, Japanese flutes and various forms of ambient music.

Paradoxically, the type of hyperventilation breathing employed in the holotropic approach actually reduces the amount of oxygen transmitted to the cortex of the brain, producing a natural 'high'. The technique simulates the experience of mystics who live in high altitudes where the air is more rarefied and is therefore ideal, as Grof himself says casually, for those who can't make the trip to the Himalayas! However, more importantly, Grof has found that holotropic breathing, like LSD psychotherapy, can resolve profound emotional problems associated with the birth process, and can also take subjects into the furthest transpersonal realms. A significant finding of his more recent work is that Grof's original model of consciousness remains basically unchanged: the same transpersonal levels of awareness can be accessed either through psychedelics like LSD or through non-drug-induced, altered-state modalities like holotropic breathwork. The human mind and the universe are as they are. There are different ways of arriving.

## JOHN LILLY AND THE SPIRITUAL POTENTIAL OF SENSORY ISOLATION

Another contemporary pioneer of psychedelic consciousness, whose work on belief systems has already been referred to, is Dr John Lilly. Lilly was born in 1915, graduated from the California Institute of Technology, and received his doctorate in medicine from the University of Pennsylvania in 1942. He then worked extensively in various research fields of science including biophysics, neurophysiology, electronics and neuroanatomy. However he first attracted international attention for his work with dolphins, which spanned a period of 25 years: Lilly's research was perhaps the first systematic attempt by human beings to communicate with another intelligent species and led to the publication of two books, *Man and Dolphin* and *The Mind of the Dolphin*, before his acute awareness of the sensitivity and intelligence of dolphins caused him to have ethical objections to further clinical research on these creatures. He adopted the position that it is preferable for a scientist to be his own guinea-pig rather than inflicting himself on his subjects.

Lilly thus began to switch his emphasis to the study of human consciousness, using his own experiences as a focal point. A few years after gaining his doctorate he decided to test the idea that a person remains awake because he is bombarded with sensory stimuli. It was while working for the National Institute of Mental Health in Bethesda, Maryland, that he developed the first prototype of the float-tank. His idea was to produce an environment of solitude, isolation and confinement where sensory input was minimised as far as was humanly possible, and see what happened. Wearing a special latex rubber mask fitted with a breathing apparatus, Lilly floated naked in quiet solitude and darkness, in seawater heated to a constant 93° Fahrenheit, the temperature at which one is neither hot nor cold. In the darkness Lilly felt as if he were floating in a gravity-free dimension. He discovered that the brain compensates for the reduction of sensory stimulation by producing a marked degree of heightened *inner* awareness. 'I went through dream-like states, trance-like states, mystical states', he wrote later. 'In all of those states I was totally intact.' He remained simultaneously aware of his floating body and the nature of the experiment.[12]

This inquiry into sensory deprivation was Lilly's first scientific contact with mystical reality. It seemed to him that, under these conditions, the brain—or 'biocomputer'—released a particular 'programme' of sensory experiences. The programme would be directly related to one's concepts and beliefs, that is to say, one would only perceive things within the grasp of the imagination. A person with narrow conceptual confines would find himself in a barren, constricting 'space' when his mind-contents were revealed to him.

Lilly found that, potentially, sensory deprivation states offered tremendous freedom. External reality had been shut out and he could programme a mental journey to any place which his imagination could conceive—his choice of programme could take him to various specific 'spaces', or to states of consciousness representing various levels of transcendence.

During the early 1960s Lilly also took LSD for the first time, and he found that he was capable of entering mystical dimensions by this means. He had been raised as a devout Roman Catholic in his youth and he knew full well that, at death, the pure soul winged its way to God. Now, years later, while listening to Beethoven's *Ninth Symphony* under the influence of hallucinogens, Lilly found himself experiencing a similar flight of the soul. He saw angelic beings and an aged patriarchal God seated on a throne—the programmed religious learning from his youth had been reactivated by the LSD! 'Later', wrote Lilly, 'I was to realise that the limits of one's belief set the limits of the experience'.

Sometimes on his inner journeys Lilly contacted entities he called his 'two guides'. However, he resists describing these beings beyond indicating that they represented a particular type of direction and knowledge applicable only to his own wanderings on the inner planes. On occasion they appeared to epitomise his higher self talking down to the more constricted personality, showing the way towards a state of more integrated being. At other times they took the form of 'karmic' conscience, reminding Lilly that he had commitments to his friends and family and so he could not be an 'inner-plane drop-out' without dire consequences.

As he continued to explore the various states of inner space, Lilly also began to seek what he called a 'safe place', a point of reference: the dark and silent void of the water tank—'absolute zero point'—a place 'out of the body, out of the universe as we know it'. Before him were endless planes of possibility barred only by the limits of the imagination.

On one occasion Lilly found himself in a space that he called 'the cosmic computer'. It seemed to him that he was a very small and insignificant part of *someone else's* macro-computer, in much the same way that Jorge Luis Borges writes of an individual 'dreamed' into reality by the power of another person's imagination. Lilly sensed tremendous waves of energy, of the same intensity as those described in the Tibetan *Bardo* of the Secondary Clear Light. However, there was no sense of well-being or order. Instead he found himself in total terror, engulfed by a whirlpool of swirling, meaningless energy—a loveless cosmic dance with 'no human value'.

Afterwards Lilly thought over his conceptions of the origin of the physical universe, which had been formulated during his scientific training. There had been no room here for mystical trance elements or doctrines of 'love' and 'meaning'. His negative *Bardo* visions showed that a new 'programme' was necessary. He had failed to acknowledge the energies of the Godhead working through him.

Later Lilly had discussions with Alan Watts about Eastern mysticism. At Esalen he talked over the merits of Gestalt Therapy with Fritz Perls and Ida Rolf, and here too he met Baba Ram Dass, who had returned from India.

Ram Dass introduced him to the *sutras* of Patanjali—a classic text on yoga—and a major consequence of this was that Lilly came to realise that if he wished to find Union with the Infinity of the Void he would have to stand back both from the programmer and the programme. He would have to see his results and his frameworks in a new light, for the two-fold division of seer and seen could no longer apply in a state of Unity Consciousness. He would later write: 'Beyond transcendence is an infinite variety of unknowns . . . Beyond these unknowns, now unknown, is *full complete Truth*'.

For Lilly this meant that even when we hold to a set of beliefs they must always remain open-ended, for they cannot hope to encompass the Transcendent Unknown and contain it within finite expressions and concepts.

Lilly subsequently had a close involvement for a time with Oscar Ichazo, a mystical teacher who headed a mystery school in Arica, a town on the Pacific coast of Chile. With Ichazo he discussed the concept of 'negative spaces' and the 'burning of karma'. A high degree of concentration was called for: in this approach negative qualities would be mentally 'seized' and ruthlessly exhumed in transcendentally negative spaces where they would fail to exert further influence on one's state of being. Never again would they register on one's personal map of inner consciousness.

Oscar Ichazo's system was based substantially on the teachings of George Gurdjieff, a mystical teacher of Greek and Armenian parentage. Gurdjieff had a personal growth centre in Paris in the 1940s and in many ways was a precursor of guru-therapist figures like Fritz Perls, who would become icons of the counter-culture generation. Gurdjieff taught his followers at his Institute for the Harmonious Development of Man to value life and he pushed them physically to the edge of their endurance, often handing out tasks that taxed them to the limit. Only through this type of effort, he argued, could one overcome the slavery of robot-like existence that most people confuse with real life.

Ichazo similarly emphasised the need for spiritual awakening and claimed in an interview in *Psychology Today* that one of his major aims was to destroy ego-dominated thoughts. When the ego or a society of egos reap the full hell they have sown in their quest for false security and status, they come to a point of collapse and rebirth. The collapse comes at the moment when the ego games are completely exposed and understood: illusion is shattered, subjectivity is destroyed, karma is burned.

For Ichazo, the decline of society thus brings with it the first moment of enlightenment—its roles and 'programmes' are suspended. The only thing left is the *first Satori*—the *first enlightenment.*

Lilly had come to Ichazo for an alternative to current scientific conceptual frameworks, and it was Ichazo who provided Lilly with a structure of the positive and negative states of consciousness from *Satori* through to *anti-Satori.*

Following Gurdjieff's system, Ichazo had identified nine states of consciousness, beginning with the highest state—which was assigned a 'vibrational' number of 3, through to successive states, which were identified symbolically by doubling the number of the previous state:

3   6   12   24   48   96   192   384   768.

The last of these states in the Gurdjieff/Ichazo model was considered a type of hell state.

Lilly now redesigned the scale, assigning positive and negative values to states on either side of what he called 'the middle of the range', or 'normal reality (state 48). This made the nine-level spectrum of consciousness look quite different:

+3 +6 +12 +24 +48 and −48 −24 −12 −6 −3.

Lilly's sequence identified the highest state of awareness as +3 and the lowest as −3. In the composite framework presented in Lilly's book *The Centre of the Cyclone*, he identifies these states as follows (I have presented them in a simplified form here, for greater accessibility):

| State of Consciousness | Description |
|---|---|
| +3 *Dharma-Megha/Samadhi* <br> Classical satori | Death of the ego. <br> Fusion with the Universal Mind. Union with the Godhead. |
| +6 *Sasmita-nir bija* <br> Buddha Consciousness | A point source of consciousness, energy, light and love. Communication at the level of essence. |
| +12 *Sananda* <br> Christ Consciousness | A state of cosmic love and divine grace. Highest state of bodily awareness. |
| +24 *Vicara* <br> Basic satori | Control of the human biocomputer. Ability to act knowledgeably and freely. |

| State of Consciousness | Description |
|---|---|
| +48 *Vitarka* | |
| Normal human consciousness | |
| −48 Openness to new ideas | |
| −24 | Pain, guilt and fear. |
| −12 | Extremely negative bodily state. Consciousness dominated by pain. |
| −6 | A purgatory-like situation. A sense of meaningless is prominent. |
| −3 | The 'quintessence of evil, the deepest hell of which one can conceive'. |

The Lilly/Ichazo/Gurdjieff model also allows for comparisons with the *chakras* in Kundalini yoga and the *sephiroth* in the Kabbalah, both of these latter systems conceiving of various symbolic 'energy' levels between normal waking consciousness and the more transcendental states of being.

Interestingly, in a more recent memoir—*John Lilly, So Far . . .*, published in 1990—Lilly mentions that while his initial relationship with Ichazo was one of 'immediate rapport', they soon came to a major hurdle over the issue of ego. Ichazo's philosophy focused on reducing ego while, as Lilly himself puts it, his role 'wasn't to get rid of ego but rather to spend as much time as possible near the top end of the scale'.[13] Lilly meanwhile became gradually disenchanted by what he perceived as Ichazo's unwillingness to entertain any belief systems other than those which he had developed through the Gurdjieff work. Lilly acknowledges that his six-month stay in Arica helped him to find his own centre—'the eye of his storm of Being'—but by the end of 1970 their paths were diverging. Intent on pursuing complete freedom of spiritual belief, Lilly realised that he could not confine himself to the restrictions of spiritual organisations—even those based on Gurdjieff and the Arica mystery school teachings.[14] Since then he has gone his own way, looking for truth as he finds it. There are now few answers he takes for granted. Instead, he says, he is looking 'for a few good questions'—new scientific ideas to stretch his mind.[15]

## KEN WILBER'S MODEL OF THE SPECTRUM OF CONSCIOUSNESS

Few minds dominate the New Spirituality of the 1990s more than Ken Wilber's. For a man only now entering his fiftieth year

Wilber has earned extravagant praise for his work. Psychologist Daniel Goleman was moved to write in *The New York Times* that Wilber has joined 'the ranks of the grand theorists of human consciousness like Ernst Cassirer, Mircea Eliade and Gregory Bateson', and Dr Roger Walsh of the University of California Medical School at Irvine has called him 'the foremost writer on consciousness and transpersonal psychology in the world today'. Wilber started young, writing his first book, *The Spectrum of Consciousness*, in the winter of 1973 when he was still finishing graduate studies. He has now produced over a dozen substantial volumes on the history and development of consciousness, including *No Boundary*, *Up from Eden* and *Sex, Ecology and Spirituality*.

Ken Wilber studied at Duke University and later at graduate school in Nebraska, pursuing degrees in chemistry and biology. However, he was also extremely interested in psychotherapy, philosophy and religion. Eventually he began to perceive a major gulf between Freudian psychology, which emphasised the strength of the ego, and the Buddhist concept of surrendering the ego in an act of transcendence. He came gradually to the view that there is a hierarchy, or spectrum, of levels of consciousness, with each part of the spectrum comparatively valid and apparently 'real' on its own level. For Wilber the different levels are rather like boxes within larger boxes, each potentially more all-encompassing than the others. 'Just as Newtonian physics is a subset of Einsteinian physics', he maintains, 'so existentialism is a smaller box—correct as far as it goes—which is encompassed by the larger box of the transcendentalists'.[16]

Wilber himself has been substantially influenced by Theosophy, by the teachings of Krishnamurti, and by such figures as Philip Kapleau, Eido Roshi and Da Free John. His own meditative practices derive from the *Vajrayana* Tibetan Buddhist tradition, which consists of oral instructions and secret teachings intended to develop wisdom and compassion; his principal teachers have been Kalu Rinpoche and Trungpa Rinpoche. However, Wilber's spectrum model derives not so much from his meditative experience as from his remarkably far-ranging scholarly review of the 'Perennial Philosophy'—the wisdom tradition of both East and West. According to Wilber:

> Human personality is a multi-levelled manifestation or expression of a single Consciousness, just as in physics the electro-magnetic

spectrum is viewed as a multi-banded expression of a single, characteristic electro-magnetic wave . . . each level of the Spectrum is marked by a different and easily recognised sense of individual identity, which ranges from the Supreme Identity of cosmic-consciousness through several gradations or bands to the drastically narrowed sense of identity associated with egoic consciousness.[17]

Wilber believes that 'man's "innermost" consciousness is identical to the absolute and ultimate reality of the Universe known variously as Brahman, Tao, Dharmakaya, Allah, the God-head—to name but a few'. He refers to these collectively as 'Mind' for, according to the Perennial Philosophy, this is all that exists in the ultimate sense. However, a problem arises because humans usually operate in a dualistic state of consciousness—characterised, for example, by the distinction between 'subject' and 'object'—and each of us tend to lose sight of this overriding One-ness. As Wilber notes in *The Spectrum of Consciousness*, dualism gives rise to psychological boundaries which are perceived as real. 'We divide reality', he writes, 'forget that we have divided it, and then forget that we have forgotten it'.[18] So each level of mind below the level of Unity Consciousness represents a progressive distortion of Mind's truly unified reality. These levels of consciousness (or illusion) represent the different states of perception which all human beings must pass through in their quest for self-knowledge.

According to Wilber's model, the levels below the state of Unity Consciousness are like bands in a spectrum:

The 'lowest' level of Wilber's spectrum is a stage of consciousness he calls the 'Shadow', where individuals identify with an impoverished self-image and have repressed part of their psyche as 'alien', 'evil' or 'undesirable'. To this extent Wilber follows Carl Jung quite closely.

On the next level of 'Ego', the individual identifies with a mental image of himself but perceives himself to exist '*in* his body and not *as* his body'. This, for Wilber, is a substantially intellectual level of reality.

At the next level in Wilber's hierarchy—the existential level—individuals identify with the 'total psycho-physical organism'. Wilber would say that here there has been a profound development towards individual integration because the person now accepts all facets of his or her total organism. He quotes Gestalt therapist Fritz Perls: 'Lose your mind and come to your senses!'

Wilber recognises, though, that beyond the individual level of psychophysical awareness and at a higher existential level of consciousness may be found what he calls 'biosocial bands'. Here we are considering the individual in the context of society. But social patterns channel our capacity for feeling and perceiving into culturally accepted modes and so distort or restrict consciousness. All societies consist of people in a web of relationships which require a certain amount of social cohesion and stability. However, as a consequence, human consciousness is prevented from attaining complete self-realisation.

At the transpersonal levels of the spectrum we come to a perceptual domain where consciousness is able to transcend the individual level. However even here, as Wilber puts it, transpersonal awareness may not yet be 'completely identified with the All'. The transpersonal levels of consciousness have been associated by some theorists with the level of the Jungian archetypes and the Collective Unconscious—the realm of mythic, primordial consciousness. Jung himself defined mystical experience as the 'experience of archetypes'.[19] However, Wilber has recently made it clear, in his somewhat grandly titled *A Brief History of Everything*, that he disagrees with Jung on this point. For Wilber,

> . . . the *collective* is not necessarily *transpersonal*. Most of the Jungian archetypes . . . are simply archaic images lying in the *magic* and *mythic* structures . . . There is nothing transrational or transpersonal about them . . . they are not themselves the source of a transpersonal or genuinely spiritual awareness.[20]

Many commentators though, myself included, would disagree with Wilber on this point, and such a view demarcates Wilber strongly from those within the consciousness movement—figures like Jean Houston and Jean Shinoda Bolen, among many others—who, in continuing the work of scholars like Joseph Campbell, have sought to enrich the exploration of mystical consciousness with a great mix of mythic diversity. In the final analysis, though, it may come down to how one defines magic and myth. For Wilber, these elements are pre-rational and therefore regressive, whereas for others such archetypes enliven what would otherwise be a comparatively sterile collective psyche. It is also of interest that in his experiential work, as we have seen, Stanislav Grof has confirmed the existence of archetypal levels of mythic awareness at profoundly transpersonal levels of consciousness and feels they have a defining rather than regressive role.

For Wilber, nevertheless—and few transpersonal theorists would disagree on this point—the supreme level is reached only when Mind alone exists; when there is no distinction whatsoever between subject and object. Wilber reminds us, for example, that there is still a hint of dualism when the mystic feels he is *witnessing* something beyond himself. The truth of Unity Consciousness is only realised, says Wilber, when 'the witness and the witnessed are one and the same'.[21]

In the final analysis, Wilber's spectrum model embraces the essentially non-dualist position of Vedanta and Mahayana Buddhism, and the breadth of his study, as I have mentioned, has been widely acclaimed. However, it has to be said that some have found Wilber's tendency to categorise and label different religious, psychological and philosophical traditions—a necessary approach if one is considering 'boxes within boxes'—in itself a limiting process. Also, at times his approach in defining levels of human consciousness seems too cerebral in its construction to be completely convincing. Somehow the dynamism—the sheer awesomeness of metaphysical consciousness and the rich poetic tapestry of archetypal imagery—is diminished by highly structured models like this. I myself share some of these concerns, for structures tend to imply their own sense of certainty, and when we embrace them we tend to forget that, after all, models and maps of mystical and visionary consciousness are only that: they draw finally on metaphors and symbols and allusions. Nevertheless, Ken Wilber's spectrum model remains one of the most all-encompassing approaches to spiritual consciousness that has yet been devised. Together with Stanislav Grof's framework of perinatal and transpersonal levels, and John Lilly's model of positive and negative mystical states, the Wilber model has helped define transpersonal development as we move towards the new millennium.

Others within the New Spirituality, though, have been drawn more to mythic and archetypal expressions of the sacred than to formal models of analysis. Concerned more with process than with structure, they have sought to embody some of the divine magic of the ancient gods and goddesses and have made it their aim to re-ignite archaic mystical realities within the context of a highly desacralised urban society. For these individuals the sacred mystery lies not only in the paradox of transcendence but also in celebratory dance, in the transcendental drama of ritual enactment, and in the archetypal potency of myth. These people, too, make up a substantial undercurrent within the new spiritual stream, and we must consider them as well.

## THE MYTHIC REVIVAL

There can be no doubting the enormous influence of the American scholar of comparative religion and mythology, Joseph Campbell—a man of whom Sam Keen has said: '. . . he was the encyclopedia—all by himself. None of us had as much data as he did. I don't think even Eliade rivalled him.'[22]

During his productive life as a teacher and writer, Campbell produced a number of authoritative but accessible studies on oriental, indigenous and Western mythology, and many insightful essays on metaphor and symbol in comparative religion, culminating in a fine series of television interviews with Bill Moyers, 'The Power of Myth', which explored the universality of myth and brought his wisdom and articulate thought to literally millions of viewers across the world. However Campbell remained primarily a scholar and a teacher during his long career and probably would not have considered himself part of the 'personal growth movement' or the transpersonal perspective—even though he knew many of its key figures. And yet one aspect of Joseph Campbell's credo has had enormous impact and is widely quoted in alternative mystical circles: 'Follow your bliss'. In saying this Campbell was endorsing the idea that we should all follow a 'path with heart', a path that defines our place in the cosmos and on this earth. Campbell was not alone in articulating this view but he helped endorse it, and since his time there has been a substantial resurgence of interest in the role mythology can play in contemporary human life.

Several key figures in the transpersonal movement, among them Jean Shinoda Bolen, Jean Houston, David Feinstein and Stanley Krippner, have been prominent in exploring practical and inspirational ways of introducing archetypal mythic realities into everyday consciousness.

Dr Bolen is a Jungian psychiatrist and author of such works as *Goddesses in Everywoman*, *Gods in Everyman* and *The Tao of Psychology*. For many years she has been advocating that each of us can apply the archetypal energies of the gods and goddesses in our lives.

Bolen trained as a doctor, was strongly influenced by the women's movement in the 1960s and taught a course on the psychology of women at the University of California's San Francisco campus. She is now Clinical Professor of Psychiatry at the University of California Medical Center.

Bolen believes, like Jung, that myths are a path to the deeper levels of the mind:

> Myth is a form of metaphor. It's the metaphor that's truly empowering for people. It allows us to see our ordinary lives from a different perspective, to get an intuitive sense of who we are and what is important to us . . . Myths are the bridge to the collective unconscious. They tap images, symbols, feelings, possibilitites and patterns—inherent, inherited human potential that we all hold in common.[23]

While, for some, myths may perhaps have an archaic, distant quality that hardly seems relevant in the everyday world, Bolen takes the opposite view. For her, mythic or archetypal awareness can provide a real sense of meaning in day-to-day life:

> If you live from your own depths—that is, if there is an archetypal basis for what you're doing—then there's a meaningful level to it that otherwise might be missing . . . When people 'follow their bliss' as Joseph Campbell says, their heart is absorbed in what they're doing. People who work in an involved, deep way are doing something that matters to them just to be doing it, not for the paycheck, not for someone saying to them: 'What a good job you're doing'.[24]

In her own life, and despite her Japanese ancestry, Jean Shinoda Bolen has identified, like Margot Adler, with the Greek goddesses. She told interviewer Mirka Knaster that, for her, the goddesses who had most influence in her life were Artemis, Athena and Hestia—all of whom represented the 'independent, self-sufficient qualities in women'. Artemis, Goddess of the Hunt, seemed to embody her Japanese family's frequent moves around the United States in the 1940s, to avoid being detained in an American concentration camp; Athena, Goddess of Wisdom, seemed present in her decision to train as a medical doctor; and Hestia, Goddess of the Hearth, epitomised her present love of 'comfort in solitude'.

However in her role as a writer and lecturer she has also felt drawn to Hermes as an archetype of communication, and she has emphasised that we can all embody both the gods *and* goddesses in our lives, not just the archetypes of our own gender. Significantly, she sees such mythic attunement as opening out into greater, planetary awareness. Echoing the sentiments of both Margot Adler and Starhawk, she says:

> The current need is a return to earth as the source of sacred energy. I have a concept that I share with others that we're evolving into looking out for the earth and our connection with everybody on it. Women seem more attuned to it, but increasingly more men are too. I believe that the human psyche changes collectively, when enough individuals change. Basically, the point of life is to survive and evolve. To do both requires that we recognise our planetary community and be aware that we cannot do anything negative to our enemies without harming ourselves. I think that we may be evolving—but then, I'm an optimistic soul.[25]

Dr Jean Houston, also a leading advocate of Goddess psychology, takes much the same position and is similarly attuned to the new 'Gaia consciousness'. 'The Earth is a living system,' she says.

> That is why women are now being released from the exclusivity of a child-bearing, child-rearing role. This is also a time when the Earth desperately needs the ways of thinking and being that women have developed through thousands of years.

Jean Houston is the former president for the Association of Humanistic Psychology and a director of the Foundation for Mind Research in Pomona, New York, but her talents also extend into many forms of creative expression. An award-winning actress in Off-Broadway theatre, she has developed numerous training programmes in spiritual studies which include the enactment of themes from the ancient Mystery traditions. Her many methods include visualisation, chanting, storytelling and rituals. Now a prominent exponent of sacred psychology, she believes strongly that myths can shape and transform consciousness. In an interview published in *Magical Blend* she explained her own role in this process: 'My task is to evoke people into that place of identifying the god or goddess or archetype that is personal to them and allowing that being to speak for them . . .'.[26]

Houston is personally interested in a broad range of myths, especially those which describe sacred journeys of transformation. She is also fascinated by archetypal figures like Parsifal and the Holy Grail, St Francis of Assisi, Odysseus, Christ, Isis and Osiris—for all of these are examples of how we may undertake a quest of spiritual renewal. For Houston, myths and archetypes are of central concern in our daily lives:

> Myths may be the most fundamental patterns in human existence. They're source patterns, I think, originating from beneath us, behind us, in the transpersonal realm . . . yet they are the key to our personal and historical existence. That's why I often say they're the DNA of the human psyche . . .[27]

Houston believes that not only mythologically, but also quite literally, our origins are in the cosmos:

> Earlier peoples saw archetypes in Nature and in the starry Heavens—in the Sun, the Moon, the Earth, the vast oceans—implicitly realising our descent from these primal entities. Everyone and everything derives from the stars—those fiery solar generators of the primary elements of beingness. The sediments of Earth make up our cells, and the briny oceans flow through our veins and tissues. Our ancestors storied this deep knowing into tales of the community of Nature: the marriage of Heaven and Earth; the churning of the ocean to create the nectar of life; the action of the wind upon the waters to bring form out of chaos. In these mythic tellings, our forerunners located higher reality and its values in the larger community—in the things of this world, shining reflections of the community of archetypes. They clearly perceived that the pattern connecting both world and archetype was the essential weave that sustains all life.[28]

And it is precisely because myths and archetypes are so primal, and because they help define our relationship with the cosmos, that they are of such vital importance today. For Houston our present era—a time on the planet when many feel gripped by a sense of existential crisis—is characterised not simply by a sense of 'paradigm shift' but by a 'whole system transition, a shift in reality itself'. We live in a time of a 'radically changing story', and sacred psychology—with its lessons of transformation and renewal—will play a vital role in this transition. For Jean Houston the characteristic hallmarks of the age are an increasing sense of 'planetisation', the rebirth of the feminine, the emergence of new forms of science, new understandings of the potential for extending human capacities and the 'ecology of consciousness', and an emergence, overall, of a global spiritual sensibility.[29]

During the early 1980s Houston used a variety of experiential techniques to take participants into mythic states of being. One of these was to invite participants to learn 'shape-shiftings' by relaxing and identifying with different god and goddess identities, thereby helping them to acquire archetypal perceptions. This could involve, for example, meditating on such figures as the Great Mother, the Wise Old King, the Young Redeemer, the Trickster or the Divine Child. Houston now believes that visualisations in themselves, while helpful, are not enough. It may well be that some sense of personal conflict is required to spur one on in the spiritual quest. Personal growth, she feels, can often grow from a sense of being 'wounded'—expressed, perhaps, in the feeling of being abandoned or hurt in some way. 'God,' she says, 'may reach us through our affliction . . . we can be ennobled and extended by looking at this wounding in such a way that we move from the personal particular to the personal universal.'[30]

Houston likes best to work in groups rather than one-to-one. Experientially, this helps awaken in each person a sense of participating in a mythic reality:

> We need the symbiosis with others. That's why I like to work in groups . . . there's more to share, more images. There are more aspects and alternatives, so more can happen. Group energy helps us grow . . . The Story is larger than you or the group, so you can find a relatively open space within it to discover what in the Story speaks directly to you and your unique life experience. The Story frees us.[31]

A comparable approach, endorsed both by Jean Houston and Joseph Campbell, has been developed by Dr David Feinstein and Dr Stanley Krippner, authors of the influential book *Personal Mythology: The Psychology of Your Evolving Self*. This book had its origins in a research project at the Johns Hopkins University School of Medicine that began by comparing several emerging 'personal growth' therapies with a number of traditional therapies. Feinstein arrived at the conclusion that each therapy, in its own way, helped people construct an understanding of themselves and where they stood in relation to the world as a whole, and he used the term 'personal mythology' to describe what he calls the 'evolving construction of inner reality'. All human constructions of reality, in a sense, are mythologies.

Dr Krippner, meanwhile, brought to the project an extensive knowledge of dreams, spiritual healing and altered states of consciousness. Over a period of several years Feinstein and Krippner held workshops to help people become aware of the mythologies that have guided them in their past. The task soon became one of helping group participants develop rituals and spiritual practices that would guide them in their daily lives.

Feinstein and Krippner have divided their work with personal mythology into five stages. In the first stage the individual is asked to recognise and define their own personal myth and to question whether this myth remains an 'ally' or not. Stage Two involves identifying an 'opposing' personal myth—one that would create conflict within the person's psyche. Such conflicting myths are then explored to see how they are connected to experiences from the subject's past. Stage Three, meanwhile, is a period of synthesis and unified vision. Here the original myth and the conflicting myth are brought into confrontation and then to a point of resolution—obstacles to unity in this sense are envisioned as opportunities for personal growth and self-realisation. In Stage Four, the therapeutic focus ends and individuals are asked to make a commitment to the new emergent vision, while in Stage Five they are encouraged to weave their personal mythologies into their daily lives.

For Feinstein and Krippner—as for Jean Houston—the approach is essentially one of applying the principles of mythological thought to individual experience, of grounding an authentic mythic awareness in the here and now. As Feinstein and Krippner confirm:

> Each of us is challenged to direct our strength and wisdom toward creating mythological harmonies wihin ourselves. Within our families. Within our organisations. Within our Nation. Within the world. And as we reconcile our logic with our intuition, our egos with our shadows, our old myths with our new ones, and our personal needs with those of our community, we also pave the way for a world steeped in contradictions to move forward in greater peace and creative harmony.[32]

It is appropriate, though, to leave the final word to Joseph Campbell, who had, perhaps, already anticipated these sentiments in his book *Myths to Live By*:

> If you really want to help this world, what you will have to teach is how to live in it. And that no-one can do who has not himself

learned how to live in it in the joyful sorrow and the sorrowful joy of the knowledge of life as it is. That is the meaning of the monstrous Kirttimukha, 'Face of Glory', over the entrances to the sanctuaries of the god of yoga, whose bride is the goddess of life. No-one can know this god and goddess who will not bow to that mask in reverence and pass humbly through.[33]

# Shamanism and the Sacred Earth

6

*Holy Mother Earth, the trees and all Nature are the witnesses
of your thoughts and deeds*
—Winnebago saying

*Speak to the earth and it shall teach thee*
—Job 12:18

There is a widespread recognition today that indigenous peoples
live their lives more closely and qualitatively attuned to the
cycles of Nature than those of us who live in urban settings.
And it is the native mythology of the earth and sky, of the
cosmos and the founding ancestors—associated in turn with a
more innate understanding of the archetypal forces that shape
our world—that endears devotees of the New Spirituality to the
indigenous peoples who remain scattered across the surface of
the planet. Rightly or wrongly, and perhaps at times romanti-
cally, a perception has arisen of an ancient native wisdom—an
authentic way of living—that we have lost and that we could,
perhaps, regain. A sense of this is captured in the following
Navajo song:

> The thoughts of earth are my thoughts
> The voice of earth is my voice
> All that belongs to the earth belongs to me
> All that surrounds the earth surrounds me
> It is lovely indeed; it is lovely indeed.

This type of holistic consciousness is also found in the
account of the Oglala Sioux medicine man, Black Elk, who stood

on the summit of Harney Peak in the Black Hills of South Dakota and experienced a vision of the universe uplifted by a profound sense of harmony and balance:

> . . . I was standing on the highest mountain of them all, and round about me was the whole hoop of the world and while I stood there I saw more than I can tell and I understood more than I saw, for I was seeing in a sacred manner the shapes of things in the spirit, and the shape of all shapes as they must live together like one being. And I saw that the sacred hoop of my people was one of many hoops that made one circle, wide as daylight and as starlight, and in the centre grew one mighty flowering tree to shelter all the children of one mother and one father. And I saw that it was holy.[1]

Similarly, Galarrwuy Yunupingu, a Yolngu Aboriginal from the Yirrkala community in north-east Arnhem Land, has expressed his deep love of the earth:

> The land is my backbone . . . I only stand straight, happy, proud and not ashamed about my colour because I still have land. I can paint, dance, create and sing as my ancestors did before me. I think of land as the history of my nation. It tells of how we came into being and what system we live . . . My land is mine only because I came in spirit from that land and so did my ancestors of the same land . . . My land is my foundation.[2]

It is this rediscovery of the bond that native peoples feel with the sacred earth that has led many associated with the New Spirituality to explore indigenous mythic belief systems and the most ancient spiritual tradition of all: *shamanism*.

## THE ANCIENT TRADITION OF SHAMANISM

Shamanism is not only the earliest but is also the most widespread spiritual tradition in human culture and extends back to the Paleolithic era. Remnants of it are still found scattered through Siberia, the United States, Mexico, Central and South America, Japan, Tibet, Indonesia, Nepal and Aboriginal Australia.

Anthropologists and archaeologists associate the first dawnings of human spiritual awareness with Neanderthal cave sites in Europe and Central Asia. In a cave at Le Moustier in France the bones of a dead youth were discovered, surrounded by a selection of tools and animal bones—suggesting a belief that such implements and companions could assist the youth in his life after death. Similarly, in a grave in Uzbekistan a circle of Ibex horns had been placed reverently around the body of a dead child.

But it is at other locations like the Franco-Cantabrian cave of Les Trois-Frères that the shamanic bond with Nature can be seen more clearly. Here, cave art dating back some 15 000 years reveals the quite specific figure of the hunter–shaman armed with a bow and disguised as a bison in the midst of a herd of wild animals. From earliest times, shamans have mimicked birds and animals in their rituals, revered sacred plants, and developed what we in the twentieth century now call a 'holistic' relationship with the cosmos.

Shamanism, though, is more than just imitative magic. It can be regarded as an animistic approach to Nature and the cosmos that utilises visionary states of consciousness as a means of contacting the denizens of the spirit world. The shaman—who can be a man or a woman, depending on cultural determinants—is essentially a magical practitioner who, through an act of will, can enter into a state of trance, and then journey to the land of the gods or perhaps, closer to home, divines by visionary means the causes of sickness and malaise.

Underlying all forms of shamanism is the notion that the universe is alive with gods and spirits. The shaman's role is to divine the presence of harmful or malicious spirits that are causing individual illness or 'cursing' members of the tribal group. The healer–shaman is thus an intermediary between the natural and metaphysical worlds, meeting the spirits on their own territory.

A classic example of shamanic journeying is found in the following account of shamans in Siberia, one of the areas of the world in which shamanism has been extensively practised until recent times. The anthropologist A. A. Popov recorded trance journeys among the Nanay people of the Tungus region in the 1920s. Here, in a state of trance, the shaman would descend to the 'lower world' and would meet magical animals—for example, an ermine or a mouse—that would act as spirit guides.

During an initiatory visionary journey, the Nanay shaman would be suckled by a cosmic deity known as the Mistress of the Water and then, with his animal guides, would be shown a community of spirits responsible for sickness in the world. Later the shaman would 'fly' in spirit form to the top of an enormous tree that would explain to him: 'I am the tree that makes all people capable of living'. The tree spirit would then provide the shaman with a branch with three shoots that could be used in the construction of three special drums: one for performing shamanic rituals over women in childbirth, the second for treating the sick, and the third for aiding those who were dying. In Siberia the drum itself had a special role because it was on the rhythmic drumbeat that the shaman would 'ride' into a state of ecstasy. And the idea of shamanism as a 'journey' into the metaphysical world is a feature not only of Nanay cosmology, but of shamanic cultures generally.

It therefore comes as no surprise that among the Jivaro of Eastern Ecuador, for example, the normal everyday world is considered to be false or a 'lie', while the truth about the real nature of things is to be found only by entering the 'supernatural' world.[3] Undertaking this vision quest, clearly, is the role of the shaman.

## Becoming a Shaman

Shamanism is a magical vocation. Some shamans adopt their role in society as part of an ancestral lineage, while others are called to the path through dreams or spirit-visions. The Chukchee of Siberia say that future shamans have a certain look in their eyes which indicates that they can see beyond the domain of everday reality to the realm of spirit which lies beyond. And perhaps because this visionary capacity is restricted to just a few, shamans have often found themselves somewhat on the edge of society—rather like visionary eccentrics. Often introverted and sometimes smitten themselves by disease or misfortune, potential shamans function in parallel mental universes and, as a result, some psychiatrists have compared them to schizophrenics. There is, however, a crucial difference between shamans and schizophrenics. Schizophrenics move in and out of different mental states continually and without control, thus dwelling in a world of experiential chaos, while shamans have to learn to integrate their visionary capacities and subject them to the individual will. For this reason, the noted scholar of comparative religion, Mircea Eliade, has referred to the shaman or medicine man as one 'who has succeeded in curing himself'. With this self-mastery comes the ability to undertake spirit-journeys, to drive away evil spirits, and to cure the sick.

Often during the initiatory process of becoming a shaman there are special revelations. The North American Gitksan Indian Isaac Tens began falling into trance states when he was 30 and frequently experienced terrifying visions.

On one occasion, animal spirits and snake-like trees seemed to be chasing him and an owl tried to attack him and lift him up. Later, on a hunting trip, Tens again saw an owl and shot it, but was unable to locate its body. He fell into a trance. His body began to 'boil' and 'quiver' and he found he was singing spontaneously:

> A chant was coming out of me without my being able to do anything to stop it. Many things appeared to me presently: huge birds and other animals. They were calling me. I saw a *meskyawawderh* (a kind of bird) and a *mesqagweeuk* (bullhead fish). These were visible only to me, not to the others in my house. Such visions happen when a man is about to become a *halaait* (shaman); they occur of their own accord. The songs force themselves out, complete, without any attempt to compose them. But I learned and memorised these songs by repeating them.[4]

Similarly, the Paviotso shaman Dick Mahwee had his first shamanic visions while dreaming in a cave. Aged around 50, Mahwee was in a state of 'conscious sleep' and had a mystical encounter with a tall, thin Indian holding an eagle tail-feather. The Indian instructed him in ways of curing sickness and as a consequence Mahwee now knew that he must enter a trance state in order to perform shamanic healing:

> I smoke before I go into the trance. While I am in the trance no-one makes any noise. I go out to see what will happen to the patient. When I see a whirlwind I know that it causes the sickness. If I see the patient walking on grass and flowers it means that he will get well; he will soon be up and walking. When I see the patient among fresh flowers and he picks them it means that he will recover. If the flowers are withered or look as if frost had killed them, I know that the patient will die. Sometimes in a trance I see the patient walking on the ground. If he leaves footprints I know that he will live, but if there are no tracks, I cannot cure him.[5]

### Regalia and Rituals

As noted earlier, the shaman has been traditionally perceived as a master of ecstasy; the shaman's role has always been to fly in the spirit vision to where the gods were, for it was here that the revelations were received. And since the shaman was able to travel from one dimension of perceptual reality to another, it was understandable that his rituals and clothing would embody all that was sacred or mythically relevant within the given culture.

Sometimes shamans would decorate their clothing with motifs relating to their magical animal allies, or with important symbols from their mythology. Traditional Japanese shamans, for example, wore caps of eagle and owl feathers and their cloaks were adorned with stuffed snakes. Siberian Yakut shamans wore kaftans embellished with a solar disc—thought to be the opening through the earth leading to the Underworld—while Goldi shamans wore coats depicting the Cosmic Tree and magical animals like bears and leopards. Buryats wore costumes laden with iron implements, symbolising the iron bones of immortality, and also incorporated motifs representing the bears, serpents and lizards they had befriended as their helper spirits.

Shamans, as we have already noted, imitate birds and animals in their dances. Yakuts could imitate the lapwing, falcon, eagle and cuckoo, while Kirghiz shamans learned not only bird songs but also how to imitate the sounds of their wings in flight. Zuni Pueblo Indians still summon their Beast Gods in ceremonies involving dancing, rattling and drumming. Wearing ritual masks, they work themselves into a state of frenzy where they feel they are becoming the animals themselves through an act of ritual identification. According to anthropologist Dr Michael Harner, who has observed them, the Zuni dancers are doing much more than simply impersonating animal forms. Transported into an altered state of consciousness by the dancing, drumming, rattling and whirr of bull-roarers, the shaman 'becomes for the time being the actual embodiment of the spirit which is believed to reside in the mask'.[6]

As one can see from accounts like this, the drum plays a vital role in shamanic practice: it is literally the 'vehicle' that carries the shaman into the magical world. The rhythmic sound of the drumbeat acts as a focusing device for the shaman, enabling him to enter the trance state in a controlled way. Some shamans also embellish their drums in ways that are symbolically significant. Lapp shamans decorate their drums with motifs like the Cosmic Tree, the sun, the moon, or a rainbow, while Evenks traditionally fashion their drum rims from sacred larchwood.

## Sacred Plants and Helper Spirits

In divining the origins of sickness, some healer–shamans have frequent recourse to sacred mind-altering plants and helper spirits—or 'familiars'.

The Mazatec Indians of Mexico, who have female shamans as their healers, make use of sacred psilocybe mushrooms; the shamans actually use the altered state of consciousness induced by the mushrooms to determine the cause of the sickness or affliction. Among the Mazatecs, both the patient and the shaman take the sacred mushrooms so that the sick person may hear the healing words that issue forth from the spirit world, and thereby participate directly in the cure.

When the adventurer and former banker R. Gordon Wasson visited the Sierra Mazateca in 1955, he made contact with the renowned shaman Maria Sabina. Maria had become well known in the town of Huatla for assisting people who were either ill, had suffered some sort of loss or theft, or wished to recover from the effects of an accident. Wasson obtained permission to attend a *velada*, or all-night healing vigil. During the *velada* Maria took thirteen pairs of mushrooms while the other participants took five or six pairs each, the idea being that the mushrooms would eventually 'speak' through the voice of the shaman. The spirits of the sacred mushroom were invoked and, at a special point during the evening, divinatory pronouncements were made. As Maria Sabina explained to Gordon Wasson: 'I see the Word[s] fall, come down from above, as though they were little luminous objects falling from heaven. The Word[s] fall on the Holy Table, on my body: with my hand I catch them. Word by Word.'[7]

A similar use of sacred psychedelic plants is found in the ceremonies of Peruvian shaman Eduardo Calderon. Like Maria Sabina, Calderon blends Christianity and native Indian traditions. Born in 1930, he grew up in a Spanish-speaking, Roman Catholic family but at the age of 24 began an apprenticeship with a *curandero* who was his second wife's uncle. This native healer made ritual use of the psychedelic San Pedro cactus and also had an altar, or *mesa*, containing various magical 'power objects'. After successfully treating a sick person through his newly-learned shamanic techniques Calderon became a *curandero* in his own right.

According to Calderon, the visionary cactus enables him to contact healing energies in the cosmos and allows him to interpret the magical influences afflicting his patients. Calderon's *mesa* includes symbolic zones pertaining to the polarities of good and evil, and also has a middle zone where the opposing forces are held in balance. The left zone is ruled by Satan, the right by Jesus Christ, and various artefacts and images of the saints are used in the divinatory ritual.

During a healing session Calderon drinks a San Pedro infusion and in due course this 'activates' the artefacts on the magical altar, enabling him to 'see' the cause of witchcraft or bad luck affecting his patient. Once diagnosed, such evil influences can be ritually exorcised. Well educated as he is, Calderon was able to describe the process to anthropologist Douglas Sharon in terms familiar to the Western mind:

> The subconscious is a superior part [of a person] . . . a kind of bag where the individual has stored all his memories . . . By means of the magical plants and the chants and the search for the roots of the problem, the subconscious of the individual is opened like a flower.[8]

If sacred plants are often a vital ingredient in shamanic healing rituals, so too are magical helper spirits or 'allies'. There are many different terms for these entities—they are variously known as 'familiars', 'guardian spirits', 'dream healers' or 'power animals'—but it is generally agreed by scholars of comparative religion that healer–shamans need spirit guides of one form or another in their divinatory practices. As Michael Harner has observed, 'A shaman may be defined as a man or woman who is in direct contact with the spirit world through a trance state and has one or more spirits at his command to carry out his bidding for good or evil.'[9]

These allies appear to the shaman in dreams and visions and in some circumstances can be inherited from other shamans or family elders. Allies can be summoned into action through songs and dances and often require ritualistic offerings. Some shamans have even claimed to be married to their spirit guides!

The divinatory functions of helper spirits are diverse. They might be sent by the shaman into the patient's body in order to detect the cause of sickness, or they might be despatched in order to locate missing objects. And, as we have seen, healer spirits may also accompany the shaman on the visionary journey to the magical world.

The Yurok Indians of north-western California still practise shamanic healing using spirit guides. Yurok healer Tela Lake describes the shaman as 'a holistic healer who uses the physical and spiritual forces of Nature to effect a cure'. She believes that the soul is the very essence of a human being and that the body, mind and soul are held together by a force-field of power or spirit. It is this energy field that can be treated by the shaman through spirit divination.

Patients abstain from drugs, sex and alcohol for four days prior to a healing cermony with Tela Lake: they are then considered 'clean'. After the patient arrives, Tela goes outside to consult with her familiar spirits and then accepts or rejects the patient for the healing ceremony (refusal usually occurs only when the patient has contravened the spiritual laws of the Yurok in some way). Immediately before the actual ceremony, all participants are required to bathe, and various plants and herbal medicines are used to purify the patient.

As the ceremony begins, the shaman, facing east, sits in front of her patient and invokes her spirits through song and prayer. According to Tela, the spirits will feel welcome if the area is 'clean' and they will assist her in identifying the cause of the patient's problems. She says that some spirits can fly backwards in time to seek the origins of disease, while other 'interpreter' spirits can divine and translate information received magically in different languages. Included among Tela's helper spirits are a woodpecker (who can remove pain from the patient's body) and a hummingbird (who can suck out poison). She also summons bear and wolf 'allies' to fight off sickness and a spirit-fish to eat away at illness, as the need arises.[10]

The Shoshoni medicine-man, Tudy Roberts, on the other hand, told Professor Ake Hultkrantz that he had spirit helpers of both animal and human appearance. Once he had a dream-vision where he saw three bear spirits, one of which claimed to be immune to bullets and offered one of his ears to the shaman as a protection. Later Roberts found a dead bear, cut off its ear, and began to wear it during the important Sun Dance ceremony performed by the Shoshoni as a thanksgiving to the Supreme Being.

Roberts also had contact with three humanoid spirit beings after performing a Sun Dance and then falling asleep in the foothills of Fort Washakie. These spirits looked like Indians but wore feathers in their hats and had 'very clean clothes'. Roberts learned that they were lightning spirits and that they would help him in his healing practices. The spirits showed him how to perform shamanic divination using the wing and tail feathers of an eagle, and he subsequently gained the power to treat colds, measles and paralysis. However Roberts never sought to cure anybody unless he received instructions from his helper spirits in shamanic dream-vision.[11]

## SHAMANISM AND THE NEW SPIRITUALITY

While New Age shamanic interpreters are now legion and 'shamanic wisdom' has become a metaphysical product alongside many others, there can be no doubting the considerable, if controversial, impact of Carlos Casteneda. Castaneda and his 'teacher', Yaqui shaman don Juan Matus, were for many in the American counter-culture a first point of contact with the figure of the shaman, and Castaneda's influence continues today alongside that of his equally controversial female counterpart, Lynn Andrews. While Casteneda's later works are now regarded as substantially 'fiction', his early writings did appear to be grounded in more solid shamanic research and their core authenticity has been affirmed by anthropologist Dr Michael Harner, who helped Castaneda get his first book published by the University of California Press in 1968.

Until his recent death, Castaneda remained a highly private person and only sketchy details of his personal history are known. However it has been established that between 1959 and 1973 he undertook a series of degree courses in anthropology at the University of Califoria, Los Angeles. Although his real name was Carlos Arana, or Carlos Aranha, and he came from either Lima, Sao Paulo or Buenos Aires, he adopted the name Carlos Castaneda when he acquired United States citizenship in 1959. The following year, having commenced his studies, he apparently travelled to the American southwest to explore the Indian use of medicinal plants. As the story goes, a friend introduced him to an old Yaqui Indian who was said to be an expert on the hallucinogen peyote.

The Indian, don Juan Matus, said he was a *brujo*, a term which connotes a sorcerer, or one who cures by means of magical techniques. Born in Sonora, Mexico, in 1891, he spoke Spanish 'remarkably well' but appeared at the first meeting to be unimpressed with Castaneda's self-confidence. He indicated, however, that Castaneda could come to see him subseqently, and an increasingly warm relationship developed as the young academic entered into an 'apprenticeship' in shamanic magic.

Carlos Castaneda found many of don Juan's ideas and techniques strange and irrational. The world of the sorcerer contained mysterious, inexplicable forces that he was obliged not to question, but had to accept as a fact of life. The apprentice sorcerer would begin to 'see' whereas previously he had merely 'looked'. Eventually he would become a 'man of knowledge'.

According to Castaneda's exposition of don Juan's ideas, the world that we believe to be 'out there' is only one of a number of worlds. It is in reality a description of the relationship between objects that we have learned to recognise as significant from birth, and which has been reinforced by language and the communication of mutually acceptable concepts. This world is not the same as the world of the sorcerer, for while ours tends to be based on the confidence of perception, the *brujo*'s involves many intangibles. His universe is a vast and continuing mystery which cannot be contained within rational categories and frameworks.

In order to transform one's perception from ordinary to magical reality, an 'unlearning' process has to occur. The apprentice must learn how to 'not do' what he has previously 'done'. He must learn how to transcend his previous frameworks and conceptual categories and for a moment freeze himself between the two universes, the 'real' and the 'magically real'. To use don Juan's expression he must 'stop the world'. From this point he may begin to *see*, to acquire a knowledge and mastery of the mysterious forces operating in the environment which most people close off from their everyday perception.

'Seeing', said don Juan, was a means of perception which could be brought about often, although not necessarily, by hallucinogenic drugs—among them *mescalito* (peyote), *yerba del diablo* (Jimson weed, or datura) and *humito* (psilocybe mushrooms). Through these, the *brujo* could acquire a magical ally, who could in turn grant further power and the ability to enter more readily into 'states of non-ordinary reality'. The *brujo* would become able to see the 'fibres of light' and energy patterns emanating from people and other living organisms, encounter the forces within the wind and sacred water-hole, and isolate as visionary experiences—as if on film—the incidents of one's earlier life and their influence on the development of the personality. Such knowledge would enable the *brujo* to tighten his defences as a 'warrior'. He would know himself, and have complete command over his physical vehicle. He would also be able to project his consciousness from his body into images of birds and animals, thereby transforming into a myriad of magical forms and shapes while travelling in the spirit-vision.[12]

While Castaneda's books have been attacked by critics like Weston La Barre and Richard de Mille for containing fanciful and possibly concocted elements it is likely that the early volumes in particular are based substantially on shamanic tradition—even if some of the material has been borrowed from elsewhere. For example there are parallels between the shamanic figure don Genaro, a friend of don Juan, and the famous Huichol shaman Ramon Medina.

One of Castaneda's friends, the anthropologist Barbara Myerhoff, was studying the Huichol Indians at the same time that Castaneda was claiming to be studying Yaqui sorcery, and Myerhoff introduced Ramon Medina to Castaneda. It may be that Castaneda borrowed an incident in A *Separate Reality*—where don Genaro leaps across a precipitous waterfall clinging to it by magical 'tentacles of power'—from an actual Huichol occurrence.

Myerhoff and another noted anthropologist, Peter Furst, watched Ramon Medina leaping like a bird across a waterfall which cascaded three hundred metres below over slippery rocks. Medina was exhibiting the balance of the shaman in 'crossing the narrow bridge to the other world'. Myerhoff told Richard de Mille how pleased she felt, in terms of validation, when Castaneda related to her how the sorcerer don Genaro could also do similar things. It now seems, she feels, that Castaneda was like a mirror—his own accounts reflecting borrowed data from all sorts of sources, including her own. The rapid mystical running known as 'the gait of power', for example, was likely to have come from accounts of Tibetan mysticism and there were definite parallels between don Juan's abilities and statements in other anthropological, psychedelic and occult sources.[13]

However, if Castaneda succeeded in capturing the popular imagination with his accounts of the magical world of don Juan there have been others who have also bridged the gulf between traditional shamanism and the contemporary world. These include the Native American figures Sun Bear and Brooke Medicine Eagle.

## Sun Bear and Brooke Medicine Eagle

Sun Bear, or Gheezis Mokwa, was born in 1929 on the White Earth Reservation in northern Minnesota, and died in 1991. A medicine-man of Chippewa descent, he headed a communal organisation consisting mainly of non-Native Americans, and through his extensive workshops and vision quests became a popular figure in New Age circles.

As a young child Sun Bear had a vision of a large black bear sheathed in a vivid array of rainbow colours. The bear looked steadfastly at him, stood on its hind legs and gently touched him on the head. It was in this way that he got his name. Sun Bear learned native medicine from his uncles and his brothers on the reservation but didn't practise the medicine path until he was 25 years old.

In 1961 Sun Bear began publishing a magazine called *Many Smokes*, which was intended as a forum for Native American writers and as a means of assisting the ecological cause of Earth awareness. The magazine changed its name to *Wildfire* in 1983 and began publishing a broader range of articles encompassing holistic health, vision quests, wilderness studies, herbalism and New Age philosophy. In this way Sun Bear became a bridging figure linking Native Americans with urban Americans interested in alternative spiritual paths—an influence that continues to this day.

After working for the Intertribal Council of Nevada as an economic development specialist, Sun Bear assisted in a Native Studies programme sponsored by the University of California at Davis, north of San Francisco. It was here, in 1970, that he founded the Bear Tribe. Most of the members were former students from the Davis campus. Sun Bear maintained that he selected the name because the bear is 'one of the few animals that heals its own wounds' and he had in mind an organisation whose members 'could join together to help with the healing of the earth'.

For a time the Bear Tribe was based outside Placerville, California, before relocating to a 100-acre farm close to Vision Mountain, near Spokane in Washington state. The Spokane community soon became self-sufficient, growing its own food, maintaining an extensive range of livestock, and also running an extensive programme of workshops.

Sun Bear believed that it was no longer appropriate to restrict Native American teachings only to his own people and much of his time was spent spreading this philosophy. To this end he produced several books—among them *The Medicine Wheel*, co-authored with his wife Wabun—and lectured in a number of countries, including Germany, Holland, England, India and Australia. His message was essentially *global*: that we should all 'walk in balance on the Earth Mother'. This quote from *The Medicine Wheel* captures this feeling very effectively: 'We all share the same Earth Mother, regardless of race or country of origin, so let us learn the ways of love, peace and harmony and seek the good paths in life.'[14]

Drawing strongly on Native American tradition, Sun Bear taught members of his community and visiting group participants how to undertake a vision-quest—this included fasting, prayers and ritual cleansing in a sweat lodge: 'a symbolic act of entering the womb of the Mother to be reborn'. He also showed how, in selecting sites for periods of visionary isolation, one could draw on the vitality of those locations where the Earth Mother seemed strong, and where spirits might appear. For Sun Bear it was the presence of spirits, in dreams or in visions, that would provide an authentic sense of personal direction: 'Each medicine-man has to follow his own medicine and the dreams and visions that give him power.' And one would always know when the spirits were near . . .

> Sometimes it is just little whisperings, and sometimes a different energy, a change in the air that you feel. It is very recognisable . . . You feel and experience things as an energy that comes through the spirit forces at the time.[15]

Brooke Medicine Eagle has similarly become a bridge between two cultures, emphasising through her work how shamanism can link the old and the new. Her lineage and ancestry point back to the traditional ways of the American Indians but she has also been educated at a Western university and has utilised various holistic health approaches in formulating her world view.

Brooke Medicine Eagle is of Sioux and Nez Perce extraction although she was raised on the Crow reservation in Montana. The great-great-grandniece of a Nez Perce holy man, Grandfather Joseph, Brooke Medicine Eagle was brought up in very modest circumstances, living ten miles from the closest reservation village and nearly sixty miles over dirt roads from any major town. She says that the initial desire to be a healer–shaman came substantially from within her own experience.

Brooke set out on her shamanic vision quest with an 85-year-old Northern Cheyenne shamaness called The Woman Who Knows. Together with a younger medicine woman they journeyed to a place called Bear Butte, near the Black Hills of South Dakota. This region has been used for hundreds of years by the Sioux and Cheyenne as a location for the vision-quest.

Here Brooke Medicine Eagle underwent the traditional preparation of fasting and cleansing. She was expecting to spend up to four days and nights alone on a mountain-top, without food and water, praying for her initiatory vision.

After preparing a sage-bed, smoking a pipe and offering prayers, the women departed and Brooke Medicine Eagle was left alone. She recalls that in the evening, as she lay there peacefully, she suddenly became aware of the presence of another woman who had long black braided hair and was dressed in buckskin. She seemed to be imparting some sort of energy into her navel—the communication between them was not in words.

As clouds moved across the sky, allowing the moonlight to filter through, Brooke Medicine Eagle became aware of a 'flurry of rainbows' caused by hundreds of beads on the woman's dress. Now she could also hear drumming, and it seemed then that two circles of dancing women—'spirits of the land'—surrounded her, and that these circles were interweaving with each other. One circle included seven old grandmothers, 'women who are significant to me, powerful old women'.[16]

Then the circles disappeared and once again she was alone with the Rainbow Woman. The woman now told her that the land was in trouble—that it needed a new sense of balance and, specifically, more feminine, nurturing energy and less male aggression. She also said that all dwellers on the North American continent were 'children of the rainbow'—mixed bloods—and there could be a balancing between the old cultures and the new.

After they had spoken with each other in this way it was time for the Rainbow Woman to leave, and it now became abundantly clear that this being was a spirit teacher, not a physical human being:

> Her feet stayed where they were, but she shot out across the sky in a rainbow arc that covered the heavens, her head at the top of that

arc. And then the lights that formed that rainbow began to die out, almost like fireworks in the sky, died out from her feet and died out and died out. And she was gone.[17]

For Brooke Medicine Eagle the impact of the visitation was both personal and profound, for the communication touched on the crucial distinction between Native American and Western ways, and also indicated how she could be of service:

> The Indian people are the people of the heart. When the white man came to this land, what he was to bring was the intellect, that analytic, intellectual way of being. And the Indian people were to develop the heart, the feelings. And those two were to come together to build a new age, in balance, not one or the other . . .
>
> [The Rainbow Woman] felt that I would be a carrier of the message between the two cultures, across the rainbow bridge, from the old culture to the new, from the Indian culture to the dominant culture, and back again. And in a sense, all of us in this generation can be that. We can help bridge that gap, build that bridge into the new age of balance.[18]

This has become Brooke Medicine Eagle's particular path in shamanism, and one which she brings to her workshops and writings. It is a path she treads with a special conviction, believing as she does that the earth will benefit from more feminine energy and more caring. 'We need to allow, to be receptive, to surrender, to serve . . . The whole society, men and women, need[s] that balance to bring ourselves into balance.'

## Shamanism and the Transpersonal Perspective

In addition to Native American teachers like Sun Bear and Brooke Medicine Eagle, who have drawn primarily on their own individual tribal shamanic traditions, one of the most influential figures in the New Spirituality is former anthropologist Dr Michael Harner, a leading practitioner in the international transpersonal movement. Author of the highly regarded *The Way of the Shaman*, a practical guide to exploring shamanic awareness, Harner has gone to great lengths to make his anthropological research accessible to a Western audience interested in exploring trance states and mystical consciousness. Unlike most of the other shamanic teachers in the West, Harner's material and techniques are drawn from many regions and cultures. He was personally initiated into the use of the 'visionary vine', *ayahuasca*, by the Conibo Indians of the Peruvian Amazon, and has worked with the Jivaro in Ecuador, the Wintun and Pomo Indians in California, the Lakota Sioux of South Dakota and the Coast Salish in Washington State. The techniques of applied shamanism which he now teaches through the auspices of the Foundation for Shamanic Studies are a synthesis of many cultures, and yet are true to the core essence of the tradition. For Harner, shamanism takes the individual 'into the realms of myth and the Dreamtime . . . and in these experiences we are able to contact sources of power and use them in daily life'.

Harner usually holds his shamanic workshops in city tenement buildings or in large open lecture rooms on different university campus sites, and has also trained numerous shamanic facilitators to continue this work both within the United States and internationally. Most of his workshop participants are familiar with the concept of the shamanic visionary journey and the idea of 'riding' rhythmic drumming into a state of meditative trance.

Harner begins his sessions by shaking a gourd rattle to the four quarters in nearly total darkness, summoning the 'spirits' to participate in the shamanic working. He also encourages his group members to sing native shamanic chants and to enter into the process of engaging with the mythic world. His techniques include journeying in the mind's eye down the root system of an archetypal 'cosmic tree' or up imaginal smoke tunnels into the sky. As the group participants delve deeper into a state of trance, assisted all the time by the drumming, they enter the 'mythic dreamtime' of their own unconscious minds, frequently having visionary encounters with a variety of animal and humanoid beings and perhaps also exploring unfamiliar locales. They may also make contact with spirit-allies or 'power animals'. Harner's approach is to show his participants that they can discover an authentic mythic universe within the depths of their own being.

In the core shamanic model he utilises, humanity is said to dwell on Middle Earth and the two magical domains—the upper and lower universes—may then be accessed through the shamanic trance journey. Often the upper and lower worlds appear to merge into a single 'magical reality' which parallels the familiar world but which also seems invariably to extend beyond it. The shaman seeks his 'power animals' or spirit allies as a way of obtaining new sources of vitality and sacred knowledge. The core intent is one of personal growth and healing, with many individual participants feeling that they have extended the boundaries of their awareness and their being. Sometimes one gains a sense of the extraordinary range of mythological images which become available through the shamanic process. One woman in a Harner workshop ventured to the upper world and had a remarkable 'rebirth' experience:

> I was flying. I went up into black sky—there were so many stars—and then I went into an area that was like a whirlwind. I could still see the stars and I was turning a lot, and my power animals were with me. Then I came up through a layer of clouds and met my teacher—she was a woman I'd seen before. She was dressed in a long, long gown and I wanted to ask her how I could continue with my shamanic work, how to make it more a part of my daily life. Then she took me into her, into her belly. I could feel her get pregnant with me and felt her belly stretching. I felt myself inside her. I also felt her put her hands on top of her belly and how large it was! She told me that I should stop breathing, that I should take my nourishment from her, and I could actually feel myself stop breathing. I felt a lot of warmth in my belly, as if it were coming into me, and then she stretched further and actually broke apart. Her belly broke apart and I came out of her, and I took it to mean that I needed to use less will in my work, and that I needed to trust her more and let that enter into my daily life. That was the end of my journey—the drum stopped and I came back at that point.[19]

Harner believes that mythic experiences of this sort are common during the shamanic journey and reveal a dimension of consciousness rarely accessed in daily life:

> Simply by using the technique of drumming, people from time immemorial have been able to pass into these realms which are normally reserved for those approaching death, or for saints. These are the realms of the upper and lower world where one can get information to puzzling questions. This is the Dreamtime of the Australian Aboriginal, the 'mythic time' of the shaman. In this area, a person can obtain knowledge that rarely comes to other people.[20]

This of course begs the question of whether the shaman's journey is just imagination. Is the mythic experience *really* real? Harner's reply is persuasive:

> Imagination is a modern western concept that is outside the realm of shamanism. 'Imagination' already pre-judges what is happening. I don't think it is imagination as we ordinarily understand it. I

think we are entering something which, surprisingly, is universal—
regardless of culture. Certainly people are influenced by their own
history, their cultural and individual history. But we are beginning
to discover a map of the upper and lower world, regardless of
culture. For the shaman, what one sees—that's *real*. What one reads
out of a book is secondhand information. But just like the scientist,
the shaman depends upon first-hand observation to decide what's
real. If you can't trust what you see yourself, then what can you
trust?[21]

Harner is now deeply committed to shamanic research and
is engaged in training native tribal peoples in shamanic techniques that have disappeared from their own indigenous cultures.
Several groups, including the Sami (formerly known as Lapps)
and the Inuit (formerly known as Eskimo) have approached him
to help them rediscover sacred knowledge lost as a result of
missionary activity or Western colonisation. Harner and his
colleagues at the Foundation for Shamanic Studies have been
able to help them with what he calls 'core shamanism'—general
methods consistent with those once used by their ancestors. In
this way, he believes, 'members of these tribal societies can
elaborate and integrate the practices on their own terms in the
context of their traditional cultures'.

Finally, in any overview that links native shamanism with
the New Spirituality, mention must be made of the unique and
potentially revolutionary vision of Terence McKenna. One of
the most controversial and illuminating figures to have emerged
from the counter-culture, and arguably the most obvious spiritual
successor to Timothy Leary, McKenna is renowned for his gift
of eloquent dialogue. In any of his lectures or media appearances
he will, more likely than not, amaze his audience with eclectic
references to shamanism, visionary literature, psychedelics,
UFOs, alchemy and the mystical traditions. But shamanism itself
is central to his contribution to contemporary transpersonal
perspectives.

McKenna believes that the shamanic model of the universe is
not only the most archaic but also the most accurate we have, and
that we should heed shamanic traditions and practices in our efforts
to map the psyche. He also believes that since research into
psychedelics has been banned by governmental authorities—a consequence both of the recklessness of the counter-culture as well as
the power politics of the establishment—valuable insights into the

potentials of consciousness are in danger of being overlooked at a crucial time in our history.

McKenna's original interest was in central Asian shamanism. During the late 1960s he went to Nepal to learn the Tibetan language and also to study indigenous Bon-Po shamanism. He then lived for a time in both India and the Seychelles before deciding to visit those regions of the world where shamanism was still being practised as a living tradition. This took him to several islands in Indonesia—Sumatra, Sumba, Flores, the Moluccas and Ceram—and later to South America, where he observed native shamanic practices first-hand.

In the upper Amazon basin of Colombia, Peru and Ecuador shamans make extensive use of *ayahuasca*, a psychedelic beverage made from the tree-climbing forest vine known botanically as *Banisteriopsis caapi*. Taking this beverage allows the shaman to enter the supernatural realm, to have initiatory visions, and to make contact with ancestors and helper-spirits.

The hallucinogenic qualities of *Banisteriopsis* derive from the presence of the harmala alkaloids, harmaline and harmine—formerly known collectively as 'telepathine' because of their apparent capacity to stimulate extra-sensory perception. The drug certainly produces in many subjects intensely coloured, dramatic visions and often results in the sensation of the 'flight of the soul'. The Conibo Indians say that *ayahuasca* helps them see demons in the air, while Jivaro shamans drinking this beverage have visions of giant anacondas and jaguars rolling over and over through the rainforest. Little wonder, then, that *ayahuasca* is the pre-eminent shamanic sacrament in South America.

McKenna was interested in the fact that, biochemically, *ayahuasca* appeared to resemble psilocybin, the active principle in the sacred psilocybe mushrooms used by shamans in the highlands of central Mexico. He also believes—and this is where he enters the realm of anthropological controversy—that the intake of psilocybin by primates living in the African grasslands prior to the last Ice Age may have led to the origins of human language itself. Psilocybe mushrooms produce a state of consciousness where the soul 'speaks' to the mind. These mushrooms also grow prolifically in cattle dung and McKenna argues that the entry of psilocybin into the food chain in Africa between fifteen and twenty thousand years ago and the subsequent domestication of cattle may have led to the establishment of the first paleolithic religion—that of the Great

Horned Goddess.[22] More specifically still, he maintains that psilo-cybin itself has a unique role to play in human culture because of its role as an inspirational guiding agent. As we saw in the case of Mazatec shaman Maria Sabina, who used these mushrooms in her healing ceremonies, the voice of psilocybin emerges from the cosmos itself. It is, says McKenna, quite literally the *Logos* of the planet. During an interview I conducted with him, he ex-plained the significance of this concept—both in relation to shamanism but also with regard to the origins of the western philosophical tradition:

> Under the influence of psilocybin there is an experience of con-tacting a speaking entity—an interiorised voice that I call the *Logos*. If we don't go back to Hellenistic Greek terminology then we are left with only the vocabulary of psychopathology. In modern times to hear 'voices' is to be seriously deviant: there is no other way to deal with this. And yet if we go back to the Classical literature the whole goal of Hellenistic esotericism was to gain access to this thing called the *Logos*. The Logos spoke the Truth—an incontrovertible Truth. Socrates had what he called his *daimon*—his informing 'Other'. And the ease with which psilocybin induces this phenom-enon makes it, from the viewpoint of a materialist or reductionist rooted in the scientific tradition, almost miraculous.[23]

For Terence McKenna the psilocybin experience is central to understanding the origins of spiritual awareness on our planet, and is also linked to the development of ancient religious struc-tures:

> What I think happened is that in the world of prehistory all religion was experiential and it was based on the pursuit of ecstasy through plants. And at some time, very early, a group interposed itself between people and the direct experience of the 'Other'. This created hierarchies, priesthoods, theological systems, castes, rituals, taboos. Shamanism, on the other hand, is an experiential science which deals with an area where we know nothing . . . So the important part of the Human Potential Movement and the New Age, I believe, is the re-empowerment of ritual, the rediscovery of shamanism, the recognition of psychedelics and the importance of the Goddess.[24]

Extending this still further, McKenna maintains that, as with those South American and Mexican shamans who use visionary sacraments respectfully, psychedelics like psilocybin put the indi-vidual literally in touch with the 'mind' of the planet:

This is the Oversoul of all life on Earth. It's the real thing. The Gaia Hypothesis which began by proposing that the entire planet is a self-regulating system has now been brought to the level where some people are saying it's almost alive. But I would go much further than that. Not only is it alive, but 'minded'.

I take very seriously the idea that the *Logos* is real, that there is a guiding Mind—an Oversoul—that inhabits the biome of the planet, and that human balance, dignity and religiosity depend on having direct contact with this realm. That's what shamanism is providing. It was available in the West until the fall of Eleusis and the Mystery traditions—to some people—but then was stamped out by barbarians who didn't realise what they had destroyed.

The soul of the planet is not neutral about the emerging direction of human history . . . We are tearing the Earth to pieces, we are spewing out toxins—and the entire planet is reacting. Psychedelics are going to play a major role in helping people to become aware of what is *really* happening . . .[25]

Such, then, is the significance of shamanism for Terence McKenna. For him, shamanism is nothing less than the best map we have of consciousness in the modern era, a map which allows us awe-inspiring access to the very core of our being and to the soul of the planet itself. From his perspective, nothing could be more profound or significant than that.

7

# Science and Spirituality

*Form is emptiness, emptiness is form.*
*Form is form, emptiness is emptiness*
—Gautama Buddha

*What we have come to know as objects and events are really*
*patterns in a universal, cosmic process*
—Ronald S. Valle

When we consider possible points of connection between the
world of science and the world of spirit, the so-called 'Gaia
Hypothesis' is one which comes readily to mind. As we have
seen in exploring the appeal of shamanism within the New
Spirituality—especially with regard to the concepts proposed by
Terence McKenna—the primal idea of a holistic bond with
Nature flows from the idea that the planet itself is a living
system: a concept reinforced by the Gaia Hypothesis.

Gaia was the ancient Greek 'Earth Mother', and from a
mythic perspective she is one of the many personifications of
Mother Nature—herself an archetype of renewal and abundance.
However the Gaia Hypothesis is not only a spiritual metaphor
but also a scientific proposition that was put forward by the
British chemist Dr James Lovelock, a former consultant to the
California Institute of Technology who at one time worked on
the scientific investigation of life on Mars.

While Lovelock concluded on the basis of his study of the
relatively static Martian atmosphere that no life existed on that
planet, he became intrigued by the dynamics of Earth's atmosphere. He found, for example, that Earth's atmosphere differed

greatly from the levels anticipated by physical chemistry. The concentration of atmospheric oxygen is around 21 per cent, and yet in theory—since oxygen is a very reactive gas—it should be almost completely absorbed, resulting in an atmospheric level close to zero. Lovelock was also fascinated by the fact that the Earth's atmosphere was able to retain a composition suitable for the continuation of life on the planet. His conclusion was that the Earth's atmosphere was affected by a wide range of living processes on the Earth itself, all of which helped maintain the atmosphere and the surface temperature: in short, that the Earth was a type of organically interrelated 'whole'. Gaia became Lovelock's metaphor for Earth's total biosystem, including the atmosphere, oceans and landforms, and all of Earth's plants, animals and fungi. This biosystem contributed to a state of homeostasis appropriate for the conditions of life.

Lovelock collected an extensive body of evidence for planetary homeostasis and presented it in his influential book *Gaia: A New Look at Life on Earth*. Included in his overview were details of such comparatively 'constant' factors as Earth's surface temperature (which seems to have remained within a tolerable range for many millions of years, thus enabling life to continue); the salt content of the oceans (around 3.4 per cent); the oxygen concentration in the atmosphere (21 per cent); the amount of atmospheric ammonia (allowing rain and soil to have the right degree of acidity to support life); and the continued existence of the ozone layer in the upper atmosphere.

The Gaia model thus appears to be a 'self-regulating, self-sustaining system, continually adjusting its chemical, physical and biological processes in order to maintain the optimum conditions for life and its continued evolution'.[1] And while Lovelock himself has resisted identifying the biosphere as a single living organism, the Gaia Hypothesis has nevertheless become a powerful metaphor for global environmental awareness. For many advocates of the New Spirituality the Earth itself is seen as having consciousness—*it is alive*.

This idea, of course, is reflected in the animistic beliefs of indigenous peoples across the planet. For the American Indians the planet is the Mother of all living beings—animals, plants, rocks and human beings all have life and are all interrelated—and Mother Earth herself needs to be honoured and nourished. As Sun Bear once said, 'The whole earth is sacred . . . Many parts of the sacred earth are hungry right now. They need people to go to them and feed them with prayers and thanksgiving . . .'[2] And as the Aboriginal writer Miriam-Rose Ungunmerr of the Ngangikurungkurr people has expressed it:

> In our view the Earth is sacred. It is a living entity in which other living entities have [their] origin and destiny. It is where our identity comes from, where our spirituality begins, where our Dreaming comes from; it is where our stewardship begins. We are bound to the Earth in our spirit. By means of our involvement in the natural world we can ensure our well-being.[3]

For the dominant Western cultures, though, Nature is a domain to be exploited and ravaged for her economic resources. Quite apart from feeling any sense of intrinsic respect or reverence for the natural environment, and failing to see—as indigenous people everywhere see—that to rape and ravage Nature is also to destroy ourselves, we in the West are actually at war with Mother Earth. We are everywhere engaged in a tragic, ongoing process of exterminating natural species, drastically reducing regions of native forests and grasslands, poisoning the water and making economic decisions for short-term gain, irrespective of our grudging acknowledgement that the planet's resources are finite and still have to fill the needs of the human generations yet to come. Ralph Metzner, a leading figure in the transpersonal movement, calls this process *ecocide* and sees it as arising through the loss of holistic consciousness:

> The metaphor of man against Nature, at war with Nature and the elements, is one that many people have formulated. It has a kind of religious world-view rationale in certain aspects of the Christian technological civilisation of Europe and North America. It represents the shadow side of our obsession with individual separateness and power. At the same time there are concepts and attitudes of the mystics, or shamanic cultures and contemporary formulations of ecologically holistic world-views that promise a way out of the self-created dilemmas of humankind.[4]

For Metzner, the Gaia model is aligned with the thinking of native peoples and we would be wise to heed it, for it points us back in the direction of interconnectedness:

> Once we recognise our inescapable embeddedness in the living, organic ecosystem and our mutual interdependence with all other co-existing species, our sense of separate identity, so strenuously acquired and desperately maintained, recedes more into the background, and the *relationships*, whether balanced or imbalanced,

become the foreground and focus of concern. This is the perceptual basis for the new and ancient points of view of the Gaian scientists and artists: it is holistic and comprehensive, and it is inevitably accompanied by a sense of wonder and reverence.[5]

So we appear to have a clear dichotomy between the holistic, indigenous world-view of a living planet whose residents and natural species are united through infinite webs of interrelatedness, and the modern industrial perspective dominated by notions of power and the exploitation of resources. But how could such a divide in human consciousness come about? Is it just a matter of world views and belief systems? And does this mean that the world of science and the world of spirit can never really meet because, essentially, they reflect different ways of thinking—different ways of evaluating and responding to the natural world? These are indeed fascinating questions, and deserve a considered answer. However, before such answers can even be attempted another issue must be settled in the first instance, and that has to do with the nature of science itself.

Most of us equate the world of science with measurement and objectivity, reflected in turn by the highly quantifiable world of technology. But how substantial is substance? How specific and distinct are material objects? The intangibles within science itself are issues to be resolved, in and of themselves, before we can even begin to consider the relationship of science and technology to the spiritual dimension. And paradoxically, even though the perceptual divide between indigenous and industrial cultures would appear to be vast, the apparent gulf between science and spirit may not be so insurmountable. In fact, as several commentators have observed, the closer we look at the paradigms and world-views proposed by mystics and shamans, the closer they appear to come to our ever-developing scientific understanding of the dynamics of the physical world. Much of this has to do with the nature of scientific world-views themselves, and with the implications of the New Physics and quantum theory.

## THE DISAPPEARING UNIVERSE

Many of us, in drawing on the apparent evidence of our senses, continue to hold to the so-called Newtonian–Cartesian model of the universe, based on the ideas of Isaac Newton and René Descartes. In this model the basic elements of the material universe are solid and ultimately indestructible. The fundamental building blocks of matter—atoms—are subject to gravity and the laws of cause and effect, and matter itself is mediated through the passage of time. Descartes believed that mind and matter were intrinsically separate: that matter was inert, and that the universe was objectively real—independent of the process of observation.

However, this model of the universe began to be challenged with the scientific analysis of light, when it became evident that light itself appeared at certain times to consist of particles while at other times it displayed the characteristics of waves. Einstein then proposed that perhaps space was not three- but four-dimensional. Time was not separate from the physical world but intimately connected with it: together they formed a four-dimensional space–time continuum. Einstein also believed that time was relative, because separate observers would perceive and construct events differently in time if these observers moved with different velocities relative to the events they were observing. This in turn suggested that space and time are mental constructs, not absolutes. As Ronald Valle has observed, 'both are merely elements of the language a particular observer uses for his or her description of phenomena'.[6]

The paradox of whether light consists of waves or particles began to move towards resolution when Max Planck discovered that heat radiation was not continuous but was emitted in energy packets he called 'quanta'. Planck believed that light could similarly be regarded in terms of electromagnetic waves and *quanta*; the latter are now known as photons—particles devoid of mass travelling at the speed of light. However the Newtonian three-dimensional model was rendered completely obsolete by another discovery—that, at the subatomic level, matter does not exist with certainty in any fixed location but only shows a 'tendency to exist'. Heisenberg's 'uncertainty principle' affirms that it is not possible to determine with absolute precision both the position and momentum of any given subatomic particle. According to Heisenberg's uncertainty principle, the wave and particle descriptions of being preclude one another. While *both* are necessary to get a full grasp of what being is, only *one* is available at any given time. We can never measure an electron's exact position (when it expresses itself as a particle) or its momentum (when it expresses itself as a wave) at the same time.[7] As a consequence of this discovery Heisenberg came to the view

that at a fundamental level 'reality' itself was essentially inde-
terminate: one could no longer rest in the security of a fixed
vantage point. The entire universe was characterised by flux and
change, by probabilities rather than certainties.

Heisenberg's findings have had an enduring impact on scientific perception. Indeed, Stanislav Grof believes that the very
authority of mechanistic science has been eroded because the
myth of solid and indestructible matter—its central dogma—dis-
integrated once scientists began to understand that atoms, far
from being solid, were essentially empty:

> Subatomic particles showed the same paradoxical nature as light,
> manifesting either particle properties or wave properties depending
> on the arrangement of the experiment. The world of substance was
> replaced by that of process, event and relation. In subatomic an-
> alysis, solid Newtonian matter disappeared. What remained were
> activity, form, abstract order and pattern. In the words of the famous
> mathematician and physicist Sir James Jeans, the universe began to
> look less like a machine and more like a thought system.[8]

While quantum theory led to a completely new way of
viewing matter, it also had profound implications for the study
of consciousness. As transpersonal physicist Dr Fritjof Capra
writes in *The Tao of Physics*:

> Quantum theory has . . . demolished the classical concepts of solid
> objects and of strictly deterministic laws of Nature. At the sub-
> atomic level, the solid material objects of classical physics dissolve
> into wavelike patterns of probabilities, and these patterns, ulti-
> mately, do not represent probabilities of things, but rather
> probabilities of interconnections. A careful analysis of the process
> of observation in atomic physics has shown that the subatomic
> particles have no meaning as isolated entities, but can only be
> understood as interconnections between the preparation of an
> experiment and the subsequent measurement. Quantum theory thus
> reveals the basic oneness of the universe. It shows that we cannot
> decompose the world into independently existing smallest units. As
> we penetrate into matter, Nature does not show us any isolated
> 'basic building blocks' but rather appears as a complicated web of
> relations between the various parts of the whole.[9]

## The Holistic Perspective of David Bohm

More recently the quantum physicist David Bohm, who worked
formerly with Einstein, developed a theory of quantum physics
which treats the whole of existence, including matter and con-

sciousness, as an unbroken whole. In his seminal work *Wholeness and the Implicate Order*, Bohm proposed that the 'unbroken wholeness of the totality of existence [be] seen as an individed flowing movement without borders'.[10] Bohm conceived of an *implicate order* within which the totality of existence is enfolded. This implicate order includes space, time and matter but can only be inferred through observing its manifestations. As in a number of mystical cosmologies—including the Kabbalah and various emanationist models in Gnosticism—the implicate order 'unfolds' into the world of manifestation. Then, what has been enfolded in the implicate order is unfolded in the explicate order—somewhat parallel to the Gnostic model of spirit—or 'potentiality'—taking form in matter. Using the reductionist methods of modern science prevents us from grasping that all things owe their existence to the unbroken wholeness—an unending process of constant flux Bohm termed the 'holomovement'. Bohm believed instead that the universe is more like a total organism in which the parts only make sense in relation to the whole. He also believed that in the final analysis there can be no distinction between mind and matter:

> The mental and the material are two sides of one overall process that are (like form and content) separated only in thought and not in actuality. Rather, there is one energy that is the basis of all reality . . . There is never any real division between mental and material sides at any stage of the overall process.[11]

Psychologist June Singer, meanwhile, has compared Bohm's perspective with that of Carl Jung:

> We experience the explicate order when we perceive realities with our senses. Our familiar world is one of separate objects subject to various physical forces like gravity etc. We can see that certain things may be in relationship to each other, and in this explicate world of things and thoughts, we can hope to integrate the various disparate parts. Wholeness appears to us as an ideal state of being . . . For Jung, the collective unconscious was the fundamental reality, with human consciousness deriving from it. In a similar way, Bohm sees the implicate order as the fundamental reality, with the explicate order and all its manifestations as derivative.[12]

### The Observer and the Observed

In quantum theory the very act of observation involves an interaction with what is observed, and Nature and the observer are not separate and distinct as we have always assumed. Scientific psychology, on the other hand, is based on the principle that if perceptions of the physical world are to be accepted as real, separate observers must be able to agree on, and 'validate', the innate characteristics of what is observed—that there is a clear need for 'objectivity', or an ability to stand apart from what is being observed. Clearly quantum theory and scientific psychology reflect two essentially different perspectives—and in this instance quantum physics appears to favour the mystics. Eastern mysticism and quantum theory are essentially holistic while scientific psychology is innately reductionist—focusing on discrete and tangible 'facts'. Quantum theory supports the position of the Eastern mystical tradition in affirming that the observed and the observer are essentially one. As Gary Zukav notes in his influential book *The Dancing Wu Li Masters: An Overview of the New Physics*:

> According to quantum mechanics there is no such thing as objectivity. We cannot eliminate ourselves from the picture. We are a part of Nature, and when we study Nature there is no way around the fact that Nature is studying itself.[13]

However while quantum theory proposes a holistic view of the physical universe the entire foundations of Western science are still based substantially on Newtonian–Cartesian principles. Scientific psychology continues to be strongly influenced by behaviourism which insists that the observer or experimenter be treated as separate and distinct in relation to the behaviour being observed and measured. Matter is considered to be innately inert, and human consciousness and intelligence are seen as byproducts of matter. Mental processes are derived from prior sensory input stored in the brain. This leaves no room whatever for a spiritual component in life because as Grof points out:

> In the reductionist view, human intelligence, creativity, art, religion, ethics and science itself are all byproducts of material processes in the brain. There is no place for mysticism or religion, and spirituality is seen as a sign of primitive superstition, intellectual and emotional immaturity, or even severe psychopathology that science will one day explain in terms of deviant biochemical processes in the brain.[14]

So is there a way out of the impasse? Are there any ways of bridging the divide between mainstream science and the quantum/transpersonal/mystical perspectives of the universe that are now emerging? The answer seems to lie in applying quantum theory perspectives to the study of human consciousness itself and also in recognising that dominant scientific paradigms are themselves subject to change with time. In the same way that the New Spirituality is seeking to dissolve the boundaries which restrict religious models of spiritual reality, the New Physics is similarly intent on transforming the reductionist Newtonian–Cartesian model which persists in mainstream scientific consciousness.

## QUANTUM PSYCHOLOGY: TOWARDS A HOLISTIC VIEW OF CONSCIOUSNESS

All of us, as human beings, live in what David Bohm called the *explicate* order—the world of manifested appearances. So how do we know what is real? Clearly our perceptions involve a dramatic filtering process. For example, the eye transmits less than one trillionth of the information reaching its surface so there is a massive difference between the available sensory data impinging on the eyeball and that which the brain subsequently constructs as 'reality'. Our senses clearly operate within a given spectrum and we see the way we do, and agree on the 'consensus reality' of everyday appearances substantially because, as human beings, we have all evolved with comparable faculties. As psychologist Dr Robert Ornstein notes:

> Personal consciousness is outward oriented [and] seems to have evolved for the primary purpose of ensuring individual biological survival . . . We first select the sensory modalities of personal consciousness from the mass of information reaching us. This is done by a multi-level process of filtration, for the most part sorting out survival-related stimuli. We are then able to construct a stable consciousness from the filtered output.[15]

This selectivity of perception—the filtering of data to produce a modified 'reality'—has also intrigued Yale neurosurgeon Karl Pribram. According to Pribram we use our mental equipment to 'tune in' to a specific reality:

> It is possible to think of the brain cortex as being like a piano sounding board where each cell, when stimulated, resonates maximally to a particular frequency with its broad band tuning at

approximately one octave. The only difference is that in vision the frequencies are spatial.[16]

Pribram is a leading advocate of the view that the brain in many ways resembles a hologram. Pribram was fascinated by the fact that many stroke and head-injury victims whose cases he was familiar with did not lose specific memory traces and that memory seemed to be distributed across the brain as a whole, even when large parts of the brain were missing. Pribram subsequently proposed the Holographic Hypothesis of Brain Function in which he suggested that holography might provide a useful way of looking at brain physiology.

A hologram is a type of three-dimensional lens-less photograph. The technique of holography was developed by Dennis Gabor, whose research earned him the Nobel Prize in 1971. A hologram is created photographically when a beam of light that has encountered an object crosses, and thus interferes with, another beam of light that has not encountered that object. The hologram produces a three-dimensional record of the interference pattern, while a normal photograph is only a two-dimensional image of an object seen from a single perspective.

In his experimental work Pribram undertook extensive tests on the brains of monkeys, using implanted electrodes, and these tests suggested that visual information is radically modified prior to reaching the visual cortex. It seemed to him that incoming information 'collided', as it were, with stored memories and expectations—producing an 'interference pattern' comparable to that found in a hologram. Also of interest to Pribram was the fact that a small fragment of a hologram retains all the characteristics of the whole image. In the same way, any given section of the brain could have potential access to the total content of one's individual memory.

Pribram has compared the 'interference patterns' referred to above with what happens in the brain generally, and here again he is using a musical analogy:

> Ripples are vibrations, waves, and the evidence is that individual cells in the brain cortex encode the frequency of waves within a certain band width. Just as the strings of a musical instrument resonate to a specific range of frequency, so do the cells of the brain cortex.[17]

But Pribram sees an important connection between his model of brain functioning and the model of the implicate and explicate order proposed by David Bohm. For Bohm individual consciousness is necessarily part of the universal consciousness because intelligence at its most profound level is grounded in the holomovement. However for Bohm because the scientific method depends on lenses and other optical equipment geared to scientific measurement and evaluation, we have developed a science that focuses on specific aspects of the universe—details of the explicate order—rather than the greater reality of the holomovement itself.

Pribram, meanwhile, notes that in the same way that holograms are produced without lenses, it is similarly important to ask what 'reality' would look like if we did not utilise the lenses in our eyes. Lenses, he argues, produce a reality of their own: they filter through into consciousness a specific type of perception. In his essay 'The Holographic Hypothesis of Brain Function' Pribram writes:

> The importance of holonomic reality is that it constitutes what David Bohm calls an 'enfolded', or 'implicate order' which . . . is also a distributed order. Everything is enfolded into everything else and distributed all over the system. What we do with our sense organs and telescopes—lenses in general—is to explicate, to unfold that enfolded order. Our telescopes and microscopes are even called 'objectives'. That is how we explicate things: we make objects out of them with the lenses in our senses. Not only the eye, but also the skin and the ear are lens-like structures. We owe to David Bohm the conceptualisation that there is an order in the universe—the enfolded order—which is spaceless and timeless in the sense that both space and time are enfolded in it. We now find that an important aspect of brain function is also accomplished in the holonomic domain . . . But this holonomic order is not empty: it is a boundariless plenum filling and flowing. Discovery of these characteristics of the holonomic order in physics and the brain sciences has intrigued mystics and scholars steeped in the esoteric traditions of East and West: for is not this just what they have been experiencing all along?[18]

Another important contribution to quantum psychology is provided by the American physicist Danah Zohar, who relates the principles of quantum mechanics directly to an understanding of the human condition.

Zohar is concerned with issues like the nature of individual identity and its relationship to the universe as a whole. On a physical level our physical being is subject to continual change—

it is an intriguing fact, for example, that the neurones in the brain and the cells of the body change over entirely every seven years—so where does this leave our sense of self and individuality? Indeed, she asks, if individual people are real, what is it that holds them together? Each of us is an organism made up from billions of cells, with each cell in some sense possessing a life of its own. Within our brains alone some ten thousand million neurones contribute to the rich tapestry of our mental life. And yet if our brains consist of all those myriad neurones, how does the idea of a 'person' actually emerge and how tangible is that person's existence?

Zohar's conclusion is that people, like subatomic matter, exhibit the same wave–particle duality identified in Heisenberg's Uncertainty Principle. Our individuality, our apparent separateness, is equivalent to the specificity of a particle whereas the way we interrelate with others, and with the world as a whole, has more of the characteristic of a wave. If we consider the human being from the perspective of quantum theory—as a *quantum self*—both aspects emerge. Seen this way, 'the quantum self is simply a more fluid self, changing and evolving at every moment, now separating into sub-selves, now reuniting into a larger self. It ebbs and flows, but always in some sense being itself . . .'[19]

Zohar rejects computer-based models of consciousness because they are essentially impersonal and offer no insights into the continuity of individual identity and the nature of human relationships. All computer models of the brain assume that the brain itself functions like a giant computer but, assuming that to be the case, where do we find the 'central committee of neurones' overseeing the whole process that provides us with our sense of individuality and the will to make spontaneous decisions? Clearly, without a sense of wholeness, as distinct from a myriad variety of brain functions, there is no sense of self. And yet we all know from our own experience that human consciousness is characterised by a sense of unbroken wholeness and continuity that provides cohesion in daily life:

> The whole corpus of classical physics and the technology that rests on it (including computer technology), is about the separateness of things, about constituent parts and how they influence each other across their separateness, as the separate neurones in the brain act on one another across the synapses. If there were no other good reasons to reject the computer model of the brain, the argument

pointing towards the unity of consciousness would be the most damning.[20]

Zohar believes that, in the final analysis, quantum theory leads us towards the realisation that either consciousness is a property of matter or else consciousness and matter arise together from the same source. And, inevitably, all sentient beings are ultimately connected and share a common destiny on the planet:

> On a quantum view of the person, it is impossible *not* to love my neighbour as myself, because my neighbour *is* myself . . . In a quantum psychology, there are no isolated persons. Individuals do exist, do have an identity, a meaning and a purpose, but, like particles, each of them is a brief manifestation of a particularity . . . Each of us, because of our integral relationship with others, with Nature, and with the world of values, has the capacity to beautify or to taint the waters of eternity.[21]

The implications of the New Physics and the approaches presented by Pribram, Bohm and Zohar are far-reaching. We begin to understand that at a core level everything in the universe would seem to be interconnected; that totally separate and individual identity is ultimately an illusion; that what we know as 'individual' consciousness contains in essence all the potentials of universal consciousness; and that the 'reality' we are so convinced of represents perhaps one small part of a much larger spectrum that we cannot adequately tune into with the undoubtedly limited physical and mental apparatus available to us as human beings. It also becomes clear that 'reality' as such is not 'fixed' as we have always assumed, but is constructed by our brains so we can make sense of it.

Fritjof Capra similarly adopts the holistic perspective that the physical world is best considered not in terms of separate constituent objects, but rather as a complex web of relationships. For him there is a clear and fundamental distinction between the Cartesian, reductionist view of consciousness and the trans-personal/mystical view:

> The Western scientific view considers matter as primary and con-sciousness as a property of complex material patterns that emerge at certain stage of biological evolution. The other view of con-sciousness, the mystical view, regards consciousness as the primary reality and ground of all being. According to this view, conscious-ness in its purest form is nonmaterial, formless and void of all contents; it is often described as 'pure consciousness', 'ultimate

reality', 'suchness' and the like. This manifestation of consciousness is associated with the Divine in many spiritual traditions. It is said to be the essence of the universe and to manifest itself in all things. All forms of matter and all living beings are seen as patterns of divine consciousness.[22]

All of this, of course, comes close to the spiritual position we spoke of earlier in relation to the shamanic perspective of indigenous peoples: they too conceive of a holistic, interconnected universe that is alive with meaning and grounded in a reality more profound and sacred than the restricted domain of everyday awareness. From an animist view everything is alive, and consciousness—or spirit—is the very basis of life. For Capra, this type of awareness reinforces an ecological perspective which honours the planet and our place upon the Earth:

> The new vision of reality is ecological, but it goes far beyond immediate concerns with environmental protection. It is supported by modern science, but rooted in a perception of reality that reaches beyond the scientific framework to an intuitive awareness of the oneness of all life, the interdependence of its multiple manifestations, and its cycles of change and transformation. When the concept of the human spirit is understood in the transpersonal sense, as the mode of consciousness in which the individual feels connected to the cosmos as a whole, it becomes clear that ecological awareness is truly spiritual.[23]

### The Quest for a New Paradigm

Regrettably, Capra's holistic vision and also the quantum perspectives of David Bohm, Karl Pribram and Danah Zohar have made little impact so far on reductionist scientific models of reality and perception. A recently published work by the American philosopher Daniel C. Dennett, *Consciousness Explained*, makes no mention of any of these thinkers and neglects the transpersonal perspective altogether. But Dennett—who is himself an exponent of computer-based models of consciousness—has at least been bold and honest enough to assert: 'The prevailing wisdom . . . is *materialism*: there is only one sort of stuff, namely matter—the physical stuff of physics, chemistry and physiology—and the mind is somehow nothing but a physical phenomenon. In short, the mind is the brain.'[24]

Nevertheless, for many in the transpersonal movement it is just a matter of time before a sense of the larger perspective makes its presence felt. The groundswell supporting the new paradigm in physics is already underway and a change of perspective is inevitable—for even scientific paradigms are subject to the fashions of the times. As Grof has noted:

> One of the most important achievements of the Western philosophy of science is the recognition that scientific theories are but conceptual models organising the data about reality available at the time. As useful approximations to reality, they should not be mistaken for correct descriptions of reality itself. The relationship between theory and the reality which it describes is like that between a map and territory . . . to confuse the two represents a violation of scientific thinking.[25]

In fact, while it purports to be empirical, scientific enquiry is often highly subjective and value-laden, as Thomas Kuhn demonstrated in his influential book *The Structure of Scientific Revolutions*. Here Kuhn explained how scientific perspectives evolve, and in describing his concept of 'paradigm shift' he also explored the dynamics involved when one paradigm replaces another. Initially a dominant paradigm consolidates a body of scientific data, helps define various areas of research, provides methodology for experiments and also proposes acceptable criteria for evaluating the data collected. For a time the dominant paradigm will go unchallenged—and vocal critics may even be denounced as scientific heretics—but with time new data emerges that are incompatible with the prevailing view. Eventually an accumulation of such data challenges the prevailing paradigm and forces a revision of the dominant perspective. And so the process continues. According to Kuhn, all scientific revolutions are really paradigm shifts and perhaps one should consider both the New Spirituality and the New Physics in this light. In the realm of physics the gradual ascendancy of the quantum/transpersonal model, with its holistic implications, presents a clear challenge to the model of reductionist materialism that continues to prevail. Yet who can predict when a point of critical mass will be reached enabling the emergent paradigm to gain widespread currency? It is also true, as Ian Barbour points out in his interesting book *Myths, Models and Paradigms*, that while paradigms may help determine the way a scientist sees the world, it is also the case that 'scientists with rival paradigms may gather quite dissimilar sorts of data'.[26]

Hopefully, in the name of science, the most complete ideas will triumph in the end.

Meanwhile, if the emergent paradigm affirms the concept of a holistic universe grounded in a matrix of universal order, mind or consciousness, what does this say to us about the nature of death? All of us face the inevitable trauma of our own impending death and there are many deep and profound issues to consider. Does the death of the brain entail the extinguishment of our personal identity, as the reductionist model in science would imply? Is our sense of personal worth and individuality nothing more than a by-product of our human biochemistry? How significant are spiritual and religious beliefs in the dying process? Can they be evaluated in any meaningful way as models of experiential reality? And what happens when we die?

# 8
# The Challenge of Death

*Death is the highest high of all—that's why they keep it till last.*
—popular graffiti

*Dying is the most fascinating experience in life. You've got to approach dying the way you live your life—with curiosity, hope, experimentation, and with the help of your friends.*
—Timothy Leary

From a transpersonal perspective, exploring the experience of death is perhaps the greatest remaining challenge in the study of human consciousness. Knowing more about death would not only teach us more about what to expect as we die, but also how we should live our lives. Fortunately, the scientific and medical investigation of the near-death experience is beginning to provide useful insights into the possible nature of death itself. Thanatology—the study of death and the dying process—is now a major realm of enquiry within the international transpersonal movement and the emerging perspectives on death may yet challenge current concepts of the mind/body relationship.

## DEATH—THE FINAL STAGE OF GROWTH

This phrase belongs to Swiss psychiatrist Dr Elisabeth Kubler-Ross, who used it as the title of one of her many books on death and dying. What is so impressive about it, for me, is its essential optimism. Death, despite its sense of trauma and crisis, is no longer a tragedy so much as a challenge. There is an implicit sense that death is a culmination of all that has preceded it in life but also that death is yet another transitional state of consciousness. The final stage of growth, yes. The end of identity and awareness? Probably not . . .

We usually define death as the absence of all visible signs of life—there is no heartbeat or respiration and brain-wave activity has apparently ceased (that is, any EEG monitoring of electrical brain impulses would register as zero). To all intents and purposes such a person is clinically dead. The issues we are considering here relate to the experiences of people who have been pronounced clinically dead and yet have revived to recount their often mystical and visionary experiences. Because these people didn't finally die after all, their visionary episodes are referred to as *near-death experiences*, or NDEs. They nevertheless provide us with the best scientifically based data on what may happen to us when we die, and to that extent they represent a potential meeting ground between the worlds of science and spirituality.

## Exploring the Near Death Experience

The term 'near-death experience' is a recent one—it was coined in 1975 by the American philosopher and teacher, Dr Raymond Moody, author of the best-selling book *Life After Life*. Moody had begun collecting anecdotal accounts of near-death incidents in 1972 and his book was based on 150 accounts from people who contacted him as a result of articles he had written or lectures he had given on this topic.

By definition, the NDE involves the return from apparent clinical death to waking consciousness and as such can be considered a substantially contemporary phenomenon because it has been greatly assisted by advances in medical technology.[1] It is only because the techniques of medical resuscitation and life-support are now so sophisticated that we have a burgeoning literature which describes the accounts of people who have seemingly 'died' and yet lived to tell the tale. These accounts, and the scientific and medical commentaries accompanying them, provide a new focus for the philosophical issues of mind and body in the ongoing debate over the nature of human consciousness and the 'soul'.

Among the first modern accounts to anticipate the NDE studies was that of the Swiss geologist, Professor Albert Heim, who collected data on the experiences of people who had nearly died in mountain-climbing accidents or warfare. Heim's writings were translated in the 1970s by Russell Noyes and Ray Kletti, and included instances where people faced with the prospect of imminent death experienced a panoramic life-review or heard transcendental music.

Also preceding the more recent NDE literature were the findings of Dr Karlis Osis, a Latvian-born parapsychologist based in New York, who conducted a survey of death-bed visionary experiences. Osis despatched questionnaires to 10 000 physicians and nurses and received 540 responses. On the basis of these he published a book titled *Death-bed Observations by Physicians and Nurses* in 1961 and followed it with a more substantial volume, *At the Hour of Death*, in 1977. In these works Osis noted that terminal subjects often experienced periods of bliss and spiritual peace prior to death. Some also saw apparitions of deceased relatives or friends coming to greet them, and seemed to realise intuitively that these figures were about to help them through the transition of death itself.

However it was Raymond Moody's book, *Life After Life*, that became the principal catalyst and inspiration for others interested in NDEs, and there have been several systematic research studies of the phenomenon since then—in the United States, Britain and Australia. Among those who have played a prominent role in this work are Dr Kenneth Ring, Professor of Psychology at the University of Connecticut, his British colleague Dr Margot Grey, founder of the International Association for Near-Death Studies (IANDS) in the United Kingdom, world-famous thanatologist Dr Elisabeth Kubler-Ross, Dr Cherie Sutherland of the University of New South Wales, and Dr Michael Sabom of Emory University in Atlanta.

Kenneth Ring's *Life At Death*, published in 1980, was the first scientific study of NDEs and was based on over 100 interviews with medical subjects who had survived near-death. Ring followed this work in 1984 with *Heading Toward Omega*, a lucid overview of the spiritual implications of the NDE, and at the time of writing is currently researching cases of the NDE among blind people. The latter will be a major research project because if it can be established that blind people have vision restored to them during the NDE—and anecdotal data from Elisabeth Kubler-Ross supports this possibility—then the whole relationship between mind, body and consciousness will have to be reassessed.

Ring and his international colleagues have described the 'core' NDE in broadly the same way: an altered state of feeling (peace, joy, serenity, etc.); a sense of movement or separation from the body (an aerial perspective on the body, generally heightened awareness); a journey through a tunnel towards either a transcendent dimension or some other, more tangible realm (a celestial valley, garden or city), the experience of light and beauty; and encounters in the spirit world with deceased relatives, spirits, 'guides' or religious figures like Jesus or 'God'. They have also sought to evaluate the impact such visionary experiences have had on the lives of the NDE subjects themselves.

Ring, Grey and Sutherland have all come to the conclusion that the 'core' NDE is largely *invariant*, that it occurs in much the same form—though not with all the characteristics present in every individual case—irrespective of nationality, social class, age, sex, educational level or occupation. What is highly significant about this finding is that the core aspects of the NDE are comparatively constant irrespective of whether that person is a religious believer, atheist or agnostic: in other words, the NDE seems to be pointing towards characteristics of universal human consciousness rather than towards a wide variety of disjointed or divergent sensory experiences such as one might expect if the experience was purely hallucinatory. To this extent the NDE seems to be telling us about the process of dying itself and the various stages or transitions of human consciousness which might occur beyond bodily death.

Once again we have the difficult issue of body, mind and spirit to resolve: during a NDE, is the subject projecting consciousness beyond the confines of the physical body and, if so, how is such a thing possible? In Kenneth Ring's *Life at Death* survey, 97.4 per cent of core experiencers felt that their bodies were light or absent; 94.6 per cent found their sense of time either expanded or absent, and 81.8 per cent experienced space 'as either extended, infinite or absent'. As Ring noted: 'for most respondents, body, time and space simply disappear—or, to put it another way, they are no longer meaningful constructs'.[2]

Such aspects of the NDE, as one would expect, have proved problematic for reductionist researchers keen on explaining away the phenomenon as illusory or hallucinatory. For to admit the possiblity of consciousness extending beyond the physical organism would entail a total reformulation of currently held frameworks of human perception and consciousness.

Among the most commonly reported 'explanations' from this camp are that NDEs are either delusory experiences resulting from temporal lobe seizure or loss of oxygen as one approaches death; simply re-enactments of the birth process; caused by anaesthetic drugs; or that they are the symptoms of psychological factors related to the likely onset of death.

In fairness to these viewpoints, and especially in view of the important implications of the NDE phenomenon, here is a summary of these explanations, with comments on their relevance in each case.

*Hallucinations and delusions*: Dr Michael Sabom was particularly impressed in his medical survey by the ability of autoscopic (out-of-the-body/self-observing) NDE subjects to report details of actual events (medical equipment, surgical procedures, real conversations) from a detached and elevated position. 'The details of these perceptions were found to be accurate in all instances where corroborating evidence was available.' Sabom also reported that some NDE subjects also experienced hallucinations during their coma states and were able to distinguish clearly between the two categories of perception.[3]

*Temporal lobe seizure*: Seizures deriving from the temporal lobes (or non-motor portions) of the brain involve sensory distortions of the size or location of objects close by, and sometimes a feeling of detachment from the environment. They are also characterised by feelings of fear and loneliness and visual or auditory hallucinations. On the other hand, many NDE subjects report accurate, undistorted perceptual fields and may feel elated or relaxed about their dissociated condition.

*Loss of oxygen in the brain*: Under normal circumstances, if the oxygen supply to the brain is reduced, this produces in turn a state of mental confusion and cognitive dysfunction. This is certainly not characteristic of the core NDE, which is often described by subjects as profoundly real and perceptually coherent. Some subjects suffering from brain hypoxia (oxygen loss)—for example, mountain climbers who have trekked in rarefied atmospheres—find they experience an onset of laziness and irritability, and they may also find it difficult to remember what they were thinking or doing at the time. Many NDE subjects, on the other hand, are so awed by the clarity and detail of their experiences that they remember them for many years afterwards.

*Reliving the birth process*: If NDEs, which are characterised by feelings of passing through a tunnel towards light, are somehow related to the normal birth process, then people born by Caesarian section should not have them. Dr Susan Blackmore—a well known sceptic in relation to the NDE data—gave a questionnaire to 254 people, of whom 36 had been born by Caesarian section. 'Both groups reported the same proportion of out-of-the-body and tunnel experiences. It could be that the experiences are based on the *idea* of birth in general, but this drastically weakens the theory.'[4]

*Anaesthetic drugs*: There are several cases of NDE subjects who received no anaesthetic drugs during their hospitalisation, so this explanation, if indeed it is one at all, obviously would not apply in those instances. While it is true that some dissociative anaesthetics like ketamine hydrochloride (Ketalar) may produce an experience in which one's consciousness appears distinct from the body and there may also be an awareness of journeying through tunnels in space, Ketalar is not widely used in human medical treatment and is now for the most part restricted to veterinary practice. In general, drug-induced hallucinations seem to be markedly different from NDEs. Dr Sabom notes that drug experiences are 'highly variable and idiosyncratic' and 'markedly different from NDEs, which always show a remarkable degree of invariance'.

*Psychological factors*: One psychological view of NDEs is that the experience derives from 'depersonalisation'. This theory, advanced by Noyes and Kletti, argues that the ego has to protect itself from impending death and thus creates a perceptual scenario that supports the feeling of continuing mental integration. As Dr Noyes has said: 'As an adaptive pattern of the nervous system it alerts the organism to its threatening environment while holding potentially disorganising emotions in check'. Dr Sabom rejects this view as a blanket explanation of the NDE because there were subjects in his survey who had out-of-the-body NDEs without being aware psychologically of any likelihood of imminent death. Some of these were subjects who experienced loss of waking consciousness without warning, due to a stoppage of the heart. Also, as Dr Margot Grey has indi-cated, 'depersonalisation' is unable to account for NDE subjects who have claimed to have had meetings with relatives who had recently died but whom the NDE subject *did not know at the time* had died. Here the NDE subject would learn of the relative's actual death only after recovering from the NDE: the expec-tation prior to the NDE would be that the person concerned was still alive.

### What happens during a NDE?

It may be worthwhile at this point to quote a few brief but characteristic examples of what NDE subjects actually report, because their testimonies are our starting point and they provide insights into the processes that seem to be involved.

> I felt as though I was looking down at myself, as though I was way out here in space . . . I felt sort of separated. It was a wonderful feeling. It was marvellous. I felt very light and didn't know where I was . . . And then I thought that something was happening to me . . . This wasn't night. I wasn't dreaming . . . And then I felt a wonderful feeling as if I was out in space.

> I felt myself being separated: my soul drawing apart from the physical being, was drawn upward seemingly to leave the earth and to go upward where it reached a greater Spirit with whom there was a communion, producing a remarkable new relaxation and deep security.

> I went into this kind of feeling of ecstasy and just started moving outward energetically . . . and then I experienced a replay of all of my life . . . from my birth to the actual operation . . . it was like it was on a fast-forward video . . . people, places, everything . . . I could see a light—like a silver-white light . . . It was just massive darkness and then massive light. I felt myself, just my being, move toward that . . .

It is not uncommon for NDE subjects to report contact with deceased relatives or friends. In Dr Sabom's survey of 116 NDE subjects, 28 described encounters with other personages. One of Dr Sabom's case studies involved a seriously injured soldier, and his account of his deceased colleagues is intriguingly matter-of-fact:

> I came out of my body, and perceived me laying on the ground with three limbs gone . . . What makes this so real was that the thirteen guys that had been killed the day before, that I had put in plastic bags, were right there with me. And more than that, during the

course of that month of May, my regular company lost 42 dead. All 42 of those guys were there. They were not in the form we perceive the human body, and I can't tell you what form they were in because I don't know. But I know they were there. I felt their presence. We communicated without talking with our voices. There was no sympathy, no sorrow. They were already where they were. They didn't want to go back. That was the basic tone of our communication . . . that we were all happy right where we were.[5]

Other accounts take us further into metaphysical territory. One of these testimonies is provided by Dr George Ritchie, a practising psychiatrist. Ritchie nearly died from pneumonia while serving in the military towards the end of World War Two and had a NDE. It was a meeting with Ritchie that first stimulated Dr Raymond Moody's interest in NDEs.

Ritchie was pronounced clinically dead for a period of nine minutes and during his NDE had an experience in his 'spirit body' that took him into a bar. All of the patrons physically present had an 'aura' but there were other non-physical beings like himself, and some of these were trying to pick up glasses in order to have a drink. In this endeavour they were unsuccessful: 'Their hands just passed straight through the tumblers. It was obvious that none of the patrons could see or feel these thirsty, disembodied beings.'

The bar itself was a popular drinking place for sailors on service leave. Dr Ritchie continues:

One very intoxicated sailor rose unsteadily from his stool and then fell heavily to the floor, unconscious. I was staring in amazement as the bright cocoon around him simply opened up. It parted at the crown of his head and began peeling away. Instantly, quicker than I'd ever seen anyone move, one of the insubstantial beings who had been standing at the bar was on top of him. In the next instant, to my mystification, the springing figure had vanished. It all happened even before the two men beside him had dragged the unconscious body from under their feet. One minute I'd distinctly seen two beings like myself, yet, by the time they'd propped the sailor up against the wall there was only one.

Ritchie watched this happen again, twice, and went on to comment:

Presumably these substanceless creatures once had solid bodies as I myself had. Suppose that when they had been these bodies they had developed dependence on alcohol that went beyond the physical. That became mental. Spiritual even. Then when they lost that body, except when they briefly could take possession of another one, they would be cut off for all eternity from the thing they could never stop craving.[6]

Ritchie's NDE account provides a fascinating insight into a possible metaphysical mechanism behind some 'possession' cases—accessed only in an altered state of consciousness like a NDE—where discarnate beings endeavour to interact with the living.[7]

## Different Levels of the NDE

Let us consider now the different categories within the NDE. As indicated above, a number of the experiences involve a substantially physical frame of reference. Many subjects perceive themselves to be just slightly dissociated from the physical plane of events—perhaps observing their comatose bodies, before rising into the sky above their house or perhaps observing themselves being resuscitated by a doctor in a hospital. In such instances it is not uncommon for subjects to also hear and accurately report specific conversations which have taken place at that time.

At a more removed level, though—perhaps at a level that brings the subject closer to physical death—a different experiential domain reveals itself: one that the American parapsychologist D. Scott Rogo has referred to as 'eschatological'.

It is here that the NDE subject may have visionary, religious or spiritual experiences—usually shaped by cultural expectations or by the person's individual belief system. The visionary material itself can be of varying degrees of profundity, ranging from a dreamlike or surreal flow of imagery through to powerful archetypal experiences. In instances like these, subjects report encounters with celestial beings, superhuman beings from classical mythology or encounters with 'God'. And sometimes they even transcend these levels of imagery, experiencing a dissolving of personal boundaries as the ego melts into other beings or forms, or seems to unite with the entire manifested universe.

## Implications for an Afterlife

Many researchers believe that the NDE has profound implications for concepts of an afterlife, although there is widespread acknowledgement of the fact that all NDE subjects are, by their very nature, *survivors* of near death—they haven't actually fully experienced the one-way journey which is death itself. Never-theless, to the extent that NDE research challenges many reductionist ideas of the relationship between mind and body, and suggests that personal identity—one's essential sense of self—depends more on one's state of consciousness than on one's sense of physicality, there do appear to be important implications in near-death research for concepts of an after-life.

In recent years Dr Sukie Miller, Director of the Institute for the Study of the Afterdeath, has conducted a cross-cultural exploration of after-death beliefs, mapping the cosmologies of a number of indigenous peoples. Together with research affiliates in Nigeria, Benin, Brazil, India and Indonesia, she has co-ordinated interviews with shamans, priests, religious leaders and holy men and women in order to compare the different cultural perspectives on death and dying. Following this research Dr Miller has identified various stages of the after-death experience that she believes may be universally relevant. The first of these is the 'waiting place', a calm place of transition, that lies just across the border from waking reality. Then there is a place of judgement, that may involve presiding gods or spirits, or some sort of life review where one judges oneself—the latter a common feature of the near-death experience. The next phase involves entering a heavenly domain, although this varies greatly from culture to culture. And then, for many groups, there is a belief in rebirth—one must be reincarnated to continue the lessons learned in life. Dr Miller acknowledges, though, that she is dealing essentially with belief systems and that, in the final analysis, these are based on hope:

> Hope is nothing less than the fullest expression of life itself—life without borders, life after death, the infinite possibilities open to us as we prepare to journey beyond the existence we know. Like any travellers, we yearn for smooth passage for ourselves and each other and ardently wish each other well. We prepare as best we can for a destination whose name we cannot know—and whose true nature, from this side of death, we can only imagine.[8]

However while Dr Miller confines her research to a study of cross-cultural belief systems, and any belief by its very nature is hypothetical, Dr Elisabeth Kubler-Ross is personally convinced about the evidence for an afterlife.

Perhaps more than any other living person, Kubler-Ross has been associated with the process of death and dying. She acknowledges cultural variations with regard to the visionary episodes different individuals might anticipate after death, but maintains that there is substantial evidence for post-mortem survival. 'For me,' says Kubler-Ross, 'it is no longer a matter of belief, but rather a matter of knowing.'[9]

Kubler-Ross's medical work with dying patients predates scientific research into NDEs—it extends back some thirty years—although her contribution to thanatology is of course ongoing. Much of her original medical work and her earlier publications on the process of death and dying were concerned primarily with the various stages of engaging with death, including denial and self-questioning, the role of grief, and the idea of death as an integral part of human development. It is only comparatively recently that Kubler-Ross has expressed her ideas on the afterlife in any detail. A small volume titled *On Life After Death*, published in 1991, brought together Kubler-Ross's principal writings on the afterlife for the first time.

Kubler-Ross is well aware that many of her professional colleagues believe that she has now become too metaphysical to retain any credibility, but this has not deterred her from expressing her perspectives on this controversial topic. As she has put it, 'The opinion which other people have of you is their problem, not yours.'[10]

Kubler-Ross maintains that her views are based on a study of more than 20 000 people who have had near-death experiences although, unlike the Ring and Sabom studies, many of her references are anecdotal. In essence she believes that none of us dies alone, that those of our loved ones who have preceded us in death will be there to assist our transition through death, and that death, like life, is 'a birth into a different existence'.[11] Kubler-Ross says that she became convinced about the reality of meeting loved ones after death after researching family car accidents. In particular she was interested in the evidence from accidents where most, but not all, of the people had been killed. Seriously injured children involved in accidents of this sort were generally taken to trauma units in hospitals, and Kubler-Ross was able to visit them two or three days before they died. She found that children about to experience death in these circumstances were invariably calm and serene and were always somehow assured that others would be waiting for them after death. These children had not been advised by the medical staff that their parents or siblings had died because there was always a practice of keeping such information secret. It was thought that children in crisis would give up hope and not fight to stay alive if they knew that other members of their family had died. Nevertheless, says Kubler-Ross, 'In fifteen years I have not had a single child who did not somehow know when a family member had preceded them in death.'[12]

Many dying subjects experience a distinct separation of body and 'consciousness'—sometimes to the extent of looking down on their bodies in a hospital or at the scene of an accident—and Kubler-Ross says quite categorically that none of her patients who has ever had an out-of-body experience was ever again afraid to die. In her view, death may be considered as the discarding of one's physical form and a transition to a different state of conscious awareness:

> Death is simply a shedding of the physical body like the butterfly shedding its cocoon. It is a transition to a higher state of consciousness where you continue to perceive, to understand, to laugh, and to be able to grow. The only thing you lose is something that you don't need anymore, your physical body. It's like putting away your winter coat when spring comes. You know that the coat is shabby and you don't want to wear it anymore. That's virtually what death is about.[13]

Kubler-Ross agrees with Dr Sukie Miller that individual cultural or religious beliefs may shape the visionary and symbolic aspects of the after-death process. A dying Jewish child would not be likely to see Jesus, for example, because Jesus does not feature in the Jewish religious pantheon, but that child, in her view, would nevertheless be welcomed by supportive figures.

> We always get what we need the most. The ones we meet are the ones we loved the most and who preceded us in death. After we are met by those we have loved, after we are met by our own guides and guardian angels, we are passing through a symbolic transition often described as a tunnel. Some people experience it as a river, some as a gate; each one will choose what is most symbolically appropriate . . . This is culturally determined.

According to Kubler-Ross, this transitionary experience then opens out into a state of cosmic awareness:

> After we pass through this visually very beautiful and individually appropriate form of transition, say the tunnel, we are approaching a source of light that many of our patients describe and that I myself experienced in the form of an incredibly beautiful and unforgettable life-changing experience. This is called cosmic consciousness. In

the presence of this light, which most people in our western hemisphere call Christ or God, or love or light, we are surrounded by total and absolute unconditional love, understanding and compassion.[14]

Kubler-Ross's emphasis on the positive and loving aspects of the afterlife transition is also supported by Kenneth Ring's NDE data, although he does not draw the same final conclusion as she does. Ring believes that the almost universal occurrence of *positive* visionary states of consciousness experienced during a NDE (as distinct from negative, hell-like states) may simply be a mapping of one's initial contact with the Inner Light and may by no means represent the total spectrum of visionary after-death encounters. It may well be that works like the *Tibetan Book of the Dead* present a more complete picture, and that what Kubler-Ross is describing is simply the first stage of a much more extensive process. Considered in this context, if the *Tibetan Book of the Dead* is in any sense correct, at the point of physical death we will all encounter the Great Light and the positive deities— or archetypes of the psyche—first, and the negative images will emerge later. According to the Tibetan model of post-mortem consciousness, if we are unable to transcend these powerful visionary encounters we may then find ourselves being gradually drawn back into the more tangible dimensions of physical awareness prior to entering a new human incarnation.

## Addendum: A Celebratory View of Death

In May 1997 a satellite-bearing Pegasus rocket was launched above the Atlantic Ocean with a number of lipstick-sized containers strapped to one of its booster engines. Inside the containers were the cremated remains of Timothy Leary, Gene Roddenberry—creator of *Star Trek*—and twenty-two other posthumous space travellers. In what was to become the world's first space funeral, Pegasus soared into space and then jettisoned both its engines and the ashes, allowing them to fall into orbit. They will re-enter the Earth's atmosphere in a few years time—vaporising in a flash of light.

Carol Rosin, a close personal friend of Leary's, co-ordinated the mission to place his ashes into orbit. Rosin says that his message to her during the last phase of his life was that all of us are 'free to ride the light' on earth and into space. It is an optimistic message, and Leary both believed it and put it into practice. His approach to death was essentially celebratory. After being told by his doctors in January 1995 that he was terminally ill with an advanced cancer in his prostate gland, Leary decided to gather his friends around him, 'to reflect on the past, help plan and design my future death, and just plain hang out and have a good time'. For Leary there could be no morbidity—he simply wanted his friends around him in a spirit of joy and friendship. 'Instead of treating the last act in your life in terms of fear, weakness and helplessness', wrote Leary in his posthumously published book *Design for Dying*, 'think of it as a triumphant graduation'.[15]

Forever a showman and always intently hostile to the dictums of the status quo, Leary believed in the idea that you should live fully and joyously until you die. 'The house party is a wonderful way to deal with your divinity as you approach death', said Leary. 'I can't recommend it enough . . . Invite people to your house party who share your celestial ambitions.' No stranger to controversy, Leary was happy to flaunt contemporary taboos around death by maintaining a running commentary about his dying process on a home web-site.

Leary always maintained that death is a trip to higher realms of consciousness and he also emphasised that it is 'the single transcendent experience that *every* person will undergo'.[16] This makes death special. If we are to follow Timothy Leary's advice, it is something we should all plan for, and hope to do well when our time comes.

## WHERE TO FROM HERE?

What then, are the implications that flow from our exploration of mystical and spiritual consciousness? The first point one can make is that what we take to be our normal state of perceptual reality is clearly only one part of a much broader spectrum of awareness. When we explore the visionary terrain of inner space we open ourselves to the sacred images and archetypes that have inspired mythologies, religions and artistic endeavours in all parts of the world. At that time, too, we become increasingly familiar with the *polarities* of consciousness: the archetypal powers for good and evil which all visionaries and mystics acknowledge as integral to the spiritual terrain. As many have affirmed—from the authors of the *Tibetan Book of the Dead* through to Carl Jung, Timothy Leary, John Lilly and many others—it is only by acknowledging and amalgamating these forces within our being, and then transcending them, that we can be truly liberated.

Access to the sacred images of the psyche invariably evokes a profound sense of awe: one feels privileged to have encountered such potent, transformative energies. This is why prophets and shamans the world over sometimes embody a type of divine madness—they have glimpsed the Greater Mystery, they have been seized by its sacred power, and have then sought to communicate that feeling to others.

The transpersonal movement and, on a more general level, the New Spirituality, call us in a way that I believe has enduring implications for religious belief and doctrinal orthodoxy. The key message now is that we should all seek to be visionaries ourselves, to explore every way possible of expanding our spiritual horizons. Each of us will find that sacred source in different ways. It may be that some of us will embrace the infinite through some form of guru or spiritual teacher. Some will reach spiritual realms through meditation, shamanic journeying or devotional prayer, and others by wandering in wilderness regions, mountains or rainforests—opening their hearts and minds to the rhythms and harmonies of Nature.

Personally, I don't think that it is important any more to insist on the essential 'rightness' of any specific religious path, for what will open one person to the sacred and infinite might seem inappropriate to another. The question will surely be for each of us: is the path that I am following broad enough to embrace all the possibilities of mind and spirit that clearly exist? Are my frameworks of reality broad enough? Are the practices and teachings that I am following essentially liberating or restrictive? Do they encourage the possibilities for inner personal growth and connectedness with others—thus leading eventually to powerful possibilities for social transformation—or do they perpetuate an outdated and restrictive belief system? In the end each of us will have to decide this for ourselves.

We stand at a very interesting crossroads in spiritual history. We can either embrace the many approaches that lead towards spiritual realisation and use them to build new paradigms for human development, or we can retreat into the security of the formal doctrinal belief systems that have persisted for centuries as explanations of the perceived relationship between humanity and God.

All around us are signs that many are opting for the more secure doctrinal course, allowing their lives to be ruled by the dictates of fundamentalism. However the evidence of transpersonal research indicates that it is misleading for any spiritual leader or figurehead to claim exclusive access to transcendental realms of awareness—because these sacred realities are potentially available to all of us. The essential task is to remove the restrictive filters that confine our spectrum of awareness. As Gurdjieff said—we have to learn to wake up.

It also seems to me that we should do all we can to ensure that our belief systems are reinforced by personal experience of the deeper, inner realities. At the same time we may also need to remind ourselves that the path we have chosen for ourselves is but one of many possibilities—an essential attitude if we are to have any hope of engendering religious tolerance and feelings of personal humility.

Throughout human history the revelations and teachings of religious visionaries have been filtered and interpreted by people in positions of authority and political influence who have not adequately explored the sacred realms themselves. While mystical experience brings with it an intrinsic feeling of liberation and certainty—the 'This is IT' of Zen practitioner Alan Watts— the insistence on formal belief and practice, as advocated by the established religious institutions, often has a completely constricting effect on the consciousness of the devotee or follower. By way of contrast the New Spirituality proposes that we map our belief systems on the spectrum of transpersonal states of consciousness, evaluate for ourselves the perceptual possibilities accessed through different spiritual teachings, and make our religions 'accountable' as metaphors of transcendent realities. From the perspective of the New Spirituality we can now ask while following our chosen spiritual path or practice: will this work, will this take me in the direction I wish to go?

At this time in our cultural history and perhaps for the first time on a wide scale within our society, our belief systems and paradigms can be formulated on the basis of what we can *experience*, rather than what we have hoped for, or have been brought up to believe. In this way, our shared knowledge and cumulative experiential wisdom can become the crucial determinants of spiritual authenticity in the years which lie ahead.

# Glossary of Terms

*Acupuncture*: A Chinese system of medicine involving the inser-
tion of needles into the skin. Acupuncture utilises around a
thousand points on the human body, and these are said to
lie along twelve lines known as meridians. Six of these lines
are *yang* (positive) and six *yin* (negative), each of them
relating to a particular organ or health process in the body.

*Adam Kadmon*: Judaic concept of the archetypal man, the primordial human being formed in the creation of the universe.
Adam Kadmon is also, metaphorically, 'the body of God'.

*Ain Soph Aur*: Hebrew expression meaning 'the Limitless Light'.
In the Kabbalah it represents the source from which all else
comes forth.

*Allah*: The Supreme Being in Islam, proclaimed by Muhammad
to be the only true god.

*Altered State of Consciousness*: A state of consciousness different
from normal, everyday consciousness. Altered states exclude
or minimise the external world and include trance, out-of-
the-body experiences, hallucinations and some types of
dreams.

*Animism*: The belief, common in many indigenous societies, that
trees, mountains, rivers and other natural phenomena possess
an animating power or spirit.

*Archetype*: In the psychology of C. G. Jung, a primordial image
found in the collective unconscious. Archetypes are often
personifications of processes or events in Nature (for example, the sun-hero or the lunar goddess) or universal
expressions of familial figures (for example, the Great Father
or the Great Mother).

*Ascendant*: In astrology, the degree of the zodiac rising on the eastern horizon at the specific moment for which the horoscope is cast.

*Ashram*: The Hindu equivalent of a monastery. A place where a sadhu or guru is engaged in spiritual teaching with a group of devotees.

*Astral body*: The 'double' of the human body, sometimes regarded as its animating force—providing the body with 'consciousness'.

*Astral travel*: Sometimes known as the out-of-the-body experience, the apparent dissociation from the body in an altered state of consciousness—resulting in different qualities of perception.

*Astrology*: A system based on the belief that celestial bodies influence the character and lives of human beings. Astrologers claim that individuals are affected by the cosmic situation existing at the time of birth and plot a map of the heavens at the time—a horoscope—to identify and evaluate these particular influences.

*Aura*: In occult or psychic terminology, the energy field that is said to surround both animate and inanimate objects. Some believe that the halos depicted around the heads of saints are an example of mystically pure auras.

*Bardo*: In Tibetan Buddhism, the state between death and rebirth. According to the *Tibetan Book of the Dead*, the consciousness of deceased individuals passes through various *Bardo* visions that can be good or evil according to the nature of one's own personal karma.

*Bhakti*: Hindu term for total devotion to, and love for, God.

*Bodhi Tree*: The tree under which Gautama Buddha sat when he became enlightened.

*Bodhisattva*: In Buddhism, one who aspires to be like the Buddha but who has not quite attained this level of complete enlightenment.

*Brahma*: Hindu creator god in the trinity which also includes Vishnu (the preserver) and Shiva (the destroyer). Brahma was born from Narayana, the primeval egg.

*Brahman*: In Hinduism, the Supreme Reality—the eternal and ineffable Truth that transcends all boundaries and forms. Brahman is more than God, more than Spirit, and is totally beyond definition: the Absolute.

*Chakras*: In Kundalini Yoga, the spiritual nerve-centres that align with the central nervous column, or *Sushumna*. The yogi learns to arouse the Kundalini energy through each of the chakras in turn—from the base of the spine to the crown of the forehead.

*Channelling*: Contemporary term for spiritualism, in which a psychic medium, or 'channel', acts as the spokesperson for a spirit-being or 'guide'. This guide then provides advice from the spirit-realm.

*Chela*: Hindu term for the pupil of a guru, or spiritual teacher.

*Chi*: In Taoist mysticism and traditional Chinese medicine, the flow of energy or life-force in the body.

*Collective Unconscious*: Concept developed by C. G. Jung, who believed that certain primordial images in the unconscious mind were not individual in origin, but 'collective'—symbolic expressions of the 'constantly repeated experiences of humanity'. In Jung's view these collective images were mostly religious, and were acknowledged almost universally as significant, regardless of cultural differences.

*Concentration*: The act of focusing one's attention on a particular point, image or thought—a common feature of meditative disciplines requiring mind control.

*Consciousness*: From the Latin *conscire*, 'to know', the faculty of being aware, of feeling and perceiving. It is often equated with 'mind'.

*Contemplation*: The ability to hold an idea or image in one's mind without being distracted by outside influences. The contemplative life is associated with mystics and ascetics engaged in prayer and meditation.

*Cosmic consciousness*: Expression used by Richard Bucke (1837–1902) to describe the state of spiritual illumination—the 'momentary lightning flash of Brahmic Splendour'.

*Cosmic Mind*: Mystical term for the 'Universal Mind', or God.

*Coven*: A group of witches, or Wiccans, who gather together to perform magical ceremonies and invocations. Traditionally there are thirteen members in a coven.

*Curandero, Curandera*: In Mexico and South America, a shaman or shamaness who is skilled in summoning spirits to heal the sick.

*Deity*: From the Greek *deus*, a god or supreme being.

*Dharana*: In yoga, the act of meditative concentration.

*Dharma*: Sanskrit term for duty, virtue and law—ethical rules of conduct.

*Dhyana*: The meditative state where the yogi surrenders to the emptiness of space and transcends awareness of time altogether.

*Divination*: The act of foretelling the future, often by interpreting omens or through other psychic means.

*Dogma*: A religious belief or teaching accepted as true by devotees or followers of a church, sect or group.

*Dream*: An occurrence associated with the rapid eye movement (REM) period of sleep. Freud regarded dreams as expressions of wish-fulfilments or repressed desires in combination with memories and associations based on recent events. Jung proposed that while this was often true, dreams could also include archetypal symbols from the Collective Unconscious.

*Dreamtime*: In Aboriginal tradition, the period during the creation of the world when heroes and totemic animals roamed the earth, establishing links with sites now considered sacred. For tribal Aborigines the Dreamtime still continues and provides a sense of mythic identification and purpose.

*Ecstasy*: A state of rapture, joy or spiritual enlightenment in which a person feels lifted up into a state of visionary transcendence.

*Elements*: In some mystical traditions the manifested world is divided into elements. In Pythagorean mysticism and medieval alchemy, for example, all aspects of the physical world were said to consist of varying amounts of fire, earth, air and water while the fifth element—the quintessence—was Spirit. In the Hindu *tattvas*, the elements are symbolised by a red triangle (fire), a yellow square (earth), a blue circle (air), a silver crescent (water) and a black egg (spirit).

*Emanation*: A vibration that issues forth from a single source. In mysticism the world is sometimes considered to be the most physical, dense or 'gross' emanation of the Godhead.

*Enlightenment*: In various mystical traditions, the achievement of self-realisation through awakening the 'inner light' of spiritual knowledge.

*Esoteric*: Term applied to teachings that are secret and only for initiates of a group—something mysterious, occult or 'hidden'.

*Extrasensory perception*: General term used to describe phenomena that cannot be perceived through the normal senses. Sometimes known as ESP, this term refers to such faculties as mental telepathy, clairaudience, clairvoyance, precognition and certain forms of divination.

*Faith healing*: Ancient healing tradition in which an appeal is made to a spiritual source—a god or spirit—to participate in healing the sick.

*Feminine Principle*: In mystical cosmologies there is an interplay between masculine and feminine forces. The feminine principle is usally regarded as receptive (symbolising the womb from which the universe is born), lunar/negative (reflecting light rather than providing it) and intuitive rather than intellectual.

*Fundamentalist*: One who clings to the fundamental teachings or beliefs of a religious or mystical creed and interprets all facets of this belief as being literally true. Fundamentalists resist symbolic interpretations of their beliefs. The term is often used to describe Christians who insist that the Bible contains the absolute truth and the complete revelation of God.

*Gnostic*: One who believes in 'higher spiritual knowledge'. The term is also used to describe esoteric sects that emerged in the early Christian centuries and were regarded by the orthodox Church fathers as heretical.

*God*: The Supreme Being and Ruler of the Universe.

*Godhead*: The essential nature of God.

*Great Goddess*: The personification of fertility and the regenerative powers of Nature. She took many different forms in classical and ancient mythology. For example she was Cybele in Phrygia, Astarte in Phoenicia, Isis in Egypt, Demeter in the Greek mystery religion and Dana among the Celts.

*Guardian spirit*: A personal, protective spirit who overviews one's day-to-day activities and provides warnings of impending danger.

*Guide*: In spiritualism or channelling, a protective spirit that is able to offer advice and guidance through a psychic medium at a seance.

*Guided Imagery*: Technique used in psychotherapy whereby a subject is asked to visualise specific images in sequence. In this way the subject may be guided towards encountering images of personal or archetypal significance.

*Guru*: Hindu term for a spiritual teacher or leader who guides a pupil (or chela) towards self-knowledge and enlightenment.

*Hallucination*: A visual illusion or state of perception that is not compatible with familiar, everyday reality. Hallucinations may often be brought on through the actions of psychedelic drugs or states of sensory isolation.

*Hatha Yoga*: A form of yoga that teaches techniques related primarily to the physical control of the body. It makes use of various *asanas*, or body postures, and also employs aspects of *pranayama*, or breath-control.

*Heresy*: A religious teaching regarded as contrary to, or deviating from, the established and orthodox form of a doctrine or belief.

*Higher self*: One's spiritual self, realised fully through meditation as the divine essence that links one to God. See also *Cosmic consciousness*.

*Horoscope*: In astrology, a 360-degree map of the heavens that, for a specific moment in time, identifies the positions of the planets and the sun in different signs of the zodiac. A natal horoscope defines the moment when an individual first draws breath.

*Human Potential Movement*: Term given to the movement that arose in the late 1960s and early 1970s as humanistic psychologists and other social thinkers began to explore the potentials of human consciousness. This included research into the mind/body relationship, the study of peak experiences and creativity, and an exploration of visionary and mystical states of consciousness.

*Hypnosis*: A form of trance in which the subject's powers of concentration are mobilised and subconscious memories and perceptions brought to the surface. The hypnotherapist provides the subject with cues that allow the individual to overcome personal barriers and emotional blockages, and bring into consciousness abilities and memories formerly neglected.

*I Ching*: Chinese book of divination dating from at least 1000BC. Confucius and the Taoist sages valued it highly and in recent times it has become popular as a method of divination. Yarrow sticks are divided on the ground until the resulting pattern is interpreted as a line in one of the hexagrams from the *I Ching*. At the same time a personal question related to one's destiny or a proposed course of action is asked intuitively. When the hexagram is completed, its meaning can be read in the *I Ching* commentaries. The specific text for the given hexagram in this way provides spiritual guidance for the question which was asked.

*Illumination*: Mystical or spiritual enlightenment. When this level of consciousness is attained one is said to be an adept, a Master, a Buddha or a saint.

*Immanent*: Term used in mysticism to describe the idea that the essence of God pervades the universe in all its manifested forms. It is the opposite of *transcendent*, in which God is regarded as having an existence beyond the realms of ma-terial creation.

*Individuation*: In the psychology of C. G. Jung, the concept of 'making the self whole'. For Jung this process included harmonising the forces of one's external life with the events of both the personal unconscious and the collective uncon-scious.

*Isolation tank*: Mechanical device, developed by neurophysiologist Dr John Lilly, to assist the exploration of meditative states and 'inner space'. Lilly constructed the tank to eliminate external stimuli and to stimulate the unconscious mind to compensate for the loss of external input. In these conditions a person may enter visionary or intuitive states of awareness and explore aspects of their own personal and spiritual beliefs.

*Journey of the soul*: In shamanism, the trance 'journey' undertaken by the medicine-man or healer in order to recover the soul of a person who has been bewitched by the spirits of disease.

*Kabbalah*: The esoteric or mystical branch of Judaism. The Kabbalah presents a symbolic explanation of the origin of the universe, the relationship of human beings to the God-head, and an emanationist approach to Creation whereby the Infinite Light—*Ain Soph Aur*—manifests through the different spheres, or *sephiroth*, on the Tree of Life.

*Kali-yuga*: Sanskrit term denoting the present epoch. The Kali-yuga commenced with the death of Krishna and will last for 432 000 years.

*Karma*: Hindu concept of actions followed by consequences. A person who lives a virtuous life builds up good karma, while a person committed to wrongdoing builds bad karma. According to Hindu belief, the circumstances of one's pres-ent life are a consequence of karma established in a former incarnation. The development of good karma is central to the process of spiritual growth.

*Kundalini*: From a Sanskrit term meaning 'coil' or 'spiral', spiritual or psychic energy which may be aroused systematically through yoga, and which can be channelled through the chakras from the base of the spine to the crown of the forehead.

*Lama*: In Tibet, a high-ranking monk, especially one who heads a monastery.

*Logos*: Greek term meaning 'word' or 'thought', used in Gnostic terminology to convey the idea that deities or archetypal beings are associated with sacred utterances or meanings in the manifest universe. In the Kabbalah the world itself is created when the sacred name of God is proclaimed.

*LSD*: The general name for the psychedelic drug lysergic acid diethylamide, first synthesised by the Swiss pharmacologist Dr Albert Hofmann. Derived from ergot fungus, it is one of the most potent psychedelics yet discovered, and is capable of producing profound, and at times terrifying, visionary states of consciousness.

*Mahatma*: Sanskrit term meaning 'Great Spirit', 'Great Soul' or 'Master'—denoting one who has attained a state of universal knowledge and self-realisation.

*Mahayana Buddhism*: The so-called 'Great Vehicle' of Buddhism as distinct from the Hinayana or 'Small Vehicle'—these two schools being the great streams in Buddhist thought. Mahayana Buddhism emphasises that all people may become *bodhisattvas* if they follow Gautama Buddha's precepts and share their love with other people.

*Male Principle*: In mystical cosmologies there is an interplay between masculine and feminine forces. The male principle is usually regarded as positive, outward going, dynamic and solar (as distinct from lunar). It is also intellectual rather than intuitive.

*Mantra*: In Hinduism, a sacred utterance or sound, often intoned silently as part of one's meditation. In some traditions the mantra is a way of merging one's identity with that of a deity since the very essence of the god is contained within the vibrational qualities of the sacred name.

*Maya*: From a Sanskrit root, *ma*, meaning 'to form, or limit', the term *maya* is often used to describe the illusory nature of appearances. It is also used to denote physical existence.

*Meditation*: A technique of mind control intended to produce a feeling of inner calm and peacefulness, that may also result in profound experiences of self-realisation and transcendental awareness. Meditation is a discipline found in many of the world's leading religions, including Buddhism, Hinduism, Islam and Christianity.

*Medium*: In spiritualism, one who acts as an intermediary between the world of spirits and discarnate entities, and the everyday world of normal reality. In contemporary New Age circles the medium is now referred to as a 'channel'.

*Mescaline*: The psycho-active ingredient in the peyote cactus, a hallucinogenic plant which is used as a sacrament by the Huichol Indians in Mexico and among the Plains Indians of the southwest United States.

*Monism*: The mystical and religious belief that all is One, that a supreme and infinite Being encompasses all creation.

*Monotheism*: The belief in one and only one God. Monotheism may be contrasted with polytheism, in which a pantheon of gods is recognised and worshipped. Christianity and Islam are examples of monotheistic religions.

*Mukti*: Sanskrit term for liberation. It is used by Hindus to refer to the freedom from endless cycles of rebirth earned by one who has become enlightened and who therefore has no further need to incarnate.

*Mystic*: One who through contemplation, meditation or self-surrender seeks union with the Godhead and who believes in the attainment of universal wisdom, cosmic consciousness or spiritual transcendence.

*Myth*: A story or fable relating to a god or supernatural being. Myths may sometimes embody universal principles in Nature and the cosmos and often express the spiritual values of the culture in which they arise.

*Nature worship*: The worship of the life-sustaining forces in Nature, associated with the cycles of the seasons that inevitably result in the rebirth of spring and new life. Nature worship relates also to fertility and sexuality and is usually associated with deities of the Earth and Moon.

*Near-death experience* (NDE): State of consciousness experienced by subjects who have been declared medically dead but who have later revived. The NDE is associated with the out-of-the-body experience and may also involve visions of spirit-beings and the sensation of travelling through a tunnel towards a serene and welcoming light.

*New Age*: Term connoting the post-psychedelic Aquarian Age believed by some to herald a new era of mystical and spiritual enlightenment.

*Nibbana*: Buddhist equivalent of the Hindu term *Nirvana*. Buddhists do not place as much emphasis on the annihilation of the self, however, and refer to *Nibbana* as a state of consciousness in which greed, hatred and delusion—the three evils—are overcome. The mystic who attains *Nibbana* is liberated from illusion and therefore his or her work is complete.

*Nirvana*: In Hinduism and yoga, union with the supreme Godhead—Brahman. In this state the ego is transcended and the self merges with Brahman, thus extinguishing one's individual nature. The mystic who attains this level of consciousness has no further need for rebirth.

*Numinous*: Word used by Rudolf Otto to express the idea of the sacred and holy essence of the great religions.

*Occultism*: From the Latin *occulere*, 'to hide', a term used to suggest the secret and hidden tradition of esoteric knowledge. The word is sometimes used to describe the study of magic, Theosophy and spiritualism and may also be used with reference to secret societies.

*Om*: In yoga, a mantra, or sacred utterance, that symbolises the essence of the entire universe and the spirit of Brahman.

*Pagan*: One who is not a Christian, Jew or Moslem. The term has been used to describe the heathen, or 'non-believer', but has now assumed a new currency among practitioners of magic and witchcraft. In this context it refers to a person who worships the sacred aspects of Nature.

*Pantheism*: The religious and mystical belief that the whole universe is God and that every part of the universe is an aspect or manifestation of God.

*Peak experience*: Term used by the psychologist Abraham Maslow to describe the experience of sudden and profound joy, ecstasy and illumination.

*Polytheism*: The belief in, and worship of, more than one god.

*Power animal*: In shamanism, a creature that appears on the spirit-journey of the soul while the shaman is in a state of trance. The power animal may become a spirit-ally, assisting the shaman in times of need.

*Pranayama*: In yoga, the science of breathing. The exercises of *pranayama* involve cycles of rhythmic breathing and may be used to raise the Kundalini energy or stabilise the life-energy (*prana*) in the body.

*Psychedelic*: Term coined by the English psychiatrist Dr Humphry

Osmond to refer to drugs that help reveal the contents of
the unconscious mind. It is associated with drugs like LSD,
mescaline and psilocybin.

*Psychic*: One who possesses paranormal powers or extra sensory
perception. The term is sometimes used to describe someone
who claims contact with the spirit-world.

*Rebirth*: Mystical term which can refer either to reincarnation or
to the act of spiritual awakening.

*Reincarnation*: The belief that one's core identity or self survives
physical death and may be reborn in different physical
bodies, in a succession of future lives. Belief in reincarnation
is commonly associated with the concept of spiritual evolution.

*Religion*: A system of beliefs and practices relating to the worship
of supernatural beings, deities, spirits or God. See also *Monotheism* and *Polytheism*.

*Resurrection*: The religious belief that one may rise again from
the dead. It is associated with linear rather than cyclic
cosmologies, and belief in a Final Judgement.

*Ritual*: A prescribed form of religious or magical ceremony, often
designed to invoke or placate a deity.

*Sacred*: That which is holy, or dedicated to a god.

*Sadhu*: Hindu term for a holy man or ascetic who has renounced
the world in order to seek spiritual liberation.

*Saint*: One who is holy or possessed of God.

*Samadhi*: Hindu term, also used in Buddhism, referring to the
highest state of yogic meditation. In the *Bhagavad Gita* it is
referred to as that state of awareness when one is able to see
the self in all things, and all things in the self.

*Samsara*: In Hinduism, the cycle of birth, death and rebirth that
arises as a consequence of karma. When one attains a state
of spiritual self-realisation there is no further need to
reincarnate.

*Sannyasin*: In Hinduism, one who renounces one's former life in
society in order to seek spiritual liberation.

*Satori*: In Zen Buddhism, sudden enlightenment. This state of
mind is often attained when paradoxes and contradictions—
presented in Zen *koans*—are understood and one's 'inner
Buddha-nature' is realised.

*Self*: In mysticism and occult philosophy, the divine essence of
one's being. It may be contrasted to the ego, which mystics
regard as a transitory entity that disappears at death. The

self, on the other hand, contains the spark of Godhead and is regarded as the source of pure consciousness.

*Shaman/Shamaness* A sorcerer, magician or spirit-healer who is able to enter a trance state under will, and who serves as an intermediary between people and the realm of gods and spirits.

*Soul:* The eternal, immaterial, spiritual dimension of an organism that animates its physical form and gives it life. In some traditions animals, plants and inanimate objects like rocks can have souls, as well as humans. The soul is usually considered to be a part of God or directly connected to the spiritual realm.

*Spirit:* The divine spark or 'essence' within each person that, according to mystical belief, unites that person with the Godhead. It is the vital ingredient in life.

*Spirit-helper:* In shamanism, a discarnate spirit being that acts as a guide, guardian or familiar.

*Subconscious:* In modern analytic psychology, that part of the mind which lies below the threshold of consciousness.

*Sun sign:* In astrology, the sign of the zodiac through which the Sun is passing at the time of one's birth. It is also known as the 'birth sign'.

*Sunya:* In Hinduism, the Void, or Nothingness. Associated with the number zero it connotes Everything and Nothing and equates with Nirvana.

*Sunyata:* The term for the Universal Void in Mahayana Buddhism—the Supreme Reality.

*Swami:* A Hindu holy man, spiritual teacher or adept.

*Tai Chi Ch'uan:* A Taoist form of self-expression, resembling dance, in which the practitioner surrenders to the natural flow of energy in the universe. It explores the processes of mind and body through creative movement, and reflects the view expressed in the *I Ching* that 'Nature is always in motion'.

*Tantra:* A form of Kundalini yoga in which the divine female energy, or *Shakti*, is aroused through sexual union.

*Taoism:* Ancient mystical tradition, said to have been founded by the Chinese sage Lao Tzu. According to Taoism, each human being is a reflection of the entire universe—a microcosm within the macrocosm—and both the universe and its inhabitants are subject to the same divine law, the Law of the Tao. To live according to the Tao is to live in harmony with Nature, heeding the flow of *yin* and *yang* energies that are the very basis of life.

*Tarot cards*: A pack of 78 cards of medieval origin, regarded as the precursor of modern playing cards and commonly used in divination. The Tarot pack is divided into the Major Arcana (22 cards) and the Minor Arcana (56 cards)—the latter divided in turn into four suits: wands, swords, cups and pentacles. The cards of the Major Arcana are considered by many to have archetypal significance and have been corre- lated in western occult tradition with the paths on the Kabbalistic Tree of Life.

*Tattvas*: the Hindu elements: *prithivi* (a yellow square symbolic of earth); *apas* (a silver crescent symbolic of water); *tejas* (a red triangle symbolic of fire); *vayu* (a blue circle or hexagram symbolic of air); and *akasha* (a black egg symbolic of spirit).

*Telepathy*: The apparent ability of two people to communicate on a mind-to-mind basis, without recourse to speech or other normal channels of communication. Mental telepathy is one of the most widely accepted faculties of extra sensory perception.

*Theosophy*: From the Greek *theos*, 'a god' and *sophos*, 'wise', a term for divine wisdom. The Theosophical Society was founded in New York in 1875 by Madame Helena Blavatsky, Colonel H. S. Olcott and William Q. Judge and has been instrumental in influencing many contemporary esoteric and mystical beliefs.

*Transpersonal*: That which is beyond the ego. Transpersonal psychology was first formulated in 1970 by Abraham Maslow, Anthony Sutich and Stanislav Grof, as a development from humanistic psychology.

*Tree of Life*: In the Kabbalah, a multiple symbol consisting of ten spheres, or *sephiroth*, through which—according to mys- tical tradition—the creation of the world came about. The Tree is surmounted by the Infinite Light—*Ain Soph Aur*— and the different spheres represent different aspects of divine manifestation.

*Universal Mind*: In theosophy and mysticism, the mind of the Supreme Being, or God, that pervades the universe and gives meaning and order to all aspects of Creation.

*Void, The*: The supreme, transcendent Reality that lies beyond form and manifestation. Often regarded as the First Cause and sometimes identified with the Godhead, the Void is also characterised in some cosmologies as a state of formlessness or chaos. *Ain Soph Aur* is the 'Limitless Light' in the Kabbalah and *Sunyata* is the Void in Buddhism.

*Wheel of Life and Death*: Hindu concept, incorporating belief in karma and reincarnation, in which one undergoes a succession of births, deaths and rebirths until the lessons of life have been learned and spiritual liberation attained.

*Yang*: In Taoism, the aspect of the universal life force (*chi*) that is masculine, outward looking and dynamic. Heaven, fire and the season of summer are all *yang*.

*Yin*: In Taoism, the aspect of the universal life force (*chi*) that is feminine, inward looking and passive. Earth, moon, water and the season of winter are all *yin*.

*Yoga*: From the Sanskrit *yuj*, 'to bind together'. Hindu spiritual teachings and techniques related to the attainment of self-realisation and union with *Brahman*, the supreme reality. There are several branches of yoga, including Hatha Yoga, dealing primarily with physical bodywork processes, and Kundalini Yoga, focusing on the awakening of the kundalini-energy through the various chakras.

# Biographies

*Assagioli, Roberto* (1888–1974): Italian psychotherapist and founder of psychosynthesis, a consciousness-expanding process that includes will and active imagination. Psychosynthesis stresses the uniqueness of each individual but its sympathy to mysticism aligns it, to some extent, with Jungian thought. Among Assagioli's best known books are *Psychosynthesis* and *The Act of Will.*

*Blavatsky, Madame Helena Petrovna* (1831–1891): Russian mystic and adventurer who co-founded the Theosophical Society in 1875. Blavatsky travelled widely through Europe, America and Asia, and after journeying in India and Tibet claimed that she had been initiated by certain spiritual Masters into the secrets of esoteric mysticism. She believed these Masters helped her to write many of her major works, which include *Isis Unveiled, The Secret Doctrine* and *The Key to Theosophy.* Her main contribution to mystical thought and, by extension, the personal growth movement, was the manner in which she sought to synthesise Eastern and Western spiritual philosophies into a universal wisdom tradition.

*Bohm, David* (1917–1992): An American-born physicist, Bohm was a Professor at Birkbeck College in London for over twenty years, and then Emeritus Professor at the University of London. His work was mainly in the field of quantum theory and relativity, although he was also interested in the relationship of consciousness and matter. For Bohm, consciousness appeared to be inseparable from the material processes of the brain and nervous system, and it was this perspective that connected him with the New Spirituality.

Bohm is best known for his books *Wholeness and the Implicate Order* and *Quantum Theory*. He also co-authored *Science, Order and Creativity* with F. David Peat in 1987.

*Bolen, Jean Shinoda:* Best known for her popular book *Goddesses in Everywoman*, Bolen is a Jungian analyst and also Clinical Professor of Psychiatry at the University of California. Intrigued by what she has called 'the global return of the Goddess in different forms', Bolen has identified herself with a spiritual perspective which discards the dominance of the old patriarchal forms of religion. Bolen supports the concept that both men and women should live their lives archetypally, and believes that myth has a major role to play in this process. 'Myth,' she says, 'is a form of metaphor . . . it allows us to see our ordinary lives from a different perspective.'

*Campbell, Joseph* (1904–87): Internationally renowned as a scholar of comparative mythology, Campbell taught at Sarah Lawrence College in Bronxville, New York for 38 years. He was strongly influenced by Jung's concept of the Collective Unconscious and believed there were universal parallels between myths, dreams and art. In his four-volume series, *The Masks of God*, he presented his study of world mythologies, classifying them as primitive, oriental, occidental and creative. Campbell gained widespread popular recognition following his interview series *The Power of Myth*, conducted in 1985–86 with Bill Moyers. In addition to his *Masks of God* series, Campbell also wrote The *Hero With a Thousand Faces*, *Myths to Live By* and *The Inner Reaches of Outer Space*, as well as editing *A Portable Jung*. He has been a major influence on the personal growth movement, particularly among those seeking to explore the mythic and archetypal aspects of daily life.

*Capra, Fritjof:* Capra studied theoretical physics at the University of Vienna and has researched high energy physics at several European and American universities. Now a leading figure in the international transpersonal movement, he has written and lectured extensively on the holistic implications of the New Physics and he is also concerned with global environmental issues. Founder of the Elmwood Institute, he is the author of several influential books, including *The Tao of Physics*, *The Turning Point* and *Uncommon Wisdom*.

*Castaneda, Carlos* (1925–98): Peruvian-born writer on shamanism, whose real name was thought to be Carlos Arana.

Castaneda studied at the University of California in Los Angeles and claimed to have made the aquaintance of an old Yaqui Indian named don Juan Matus, who allowed him to become his apprentice in magic and sorcery. Several of Castaneda's books had a major impact on the counter-culture, including *The Teachings of Don Juan*, *A Separate Reality* and *Journey to Ixtlan*. It is thought that most, if not all, of Castaneda's works contain borrowed or fictitious elements, but for many readers they opened the way to an understanding of shamanism. To this extent they can be considered authentic fictions.

*Chopra, Deepak* (1947– ): Born in New Delhi, the son of a cardiologist, Chopra studied medicine, graduating from the All India Institute of Medical Sciences in 1968 before emigrating to the United States. Drawn to alternative medicine in the 1970s, Chopra used transcendental meditation to help himself stop smoking and then became an adherent of ayurvedic medicine. He has since blended holistic health, New Age philosophy and a self-help orientation into a series of highly successful publications. Gifted with a talent for self-promotion, Chopra has utilised the media and his connections with the Hollywood glitterati to achieve extraordinary wealth and success. His books include *Ageless Body, Timeless Mind*, *Perfect Health* and *The Seven Spiritual Laws of Success*.

*Eliade, Mircea* (1907–86): Romanian-born authority on comparative religion and mysticism who was Professor of the History of Religions at the University of Chicago for many years. A remarkably prolific author, he wrote authoritative books on shamanism, yoga, alchemy and the nature of religious experience. He was especially interested in the symbolism of the sacred, and patterns of initiation in different cultures.

*Evans-Wentz, W. Y.* (1878–1965): American scholar best known for editing and translating several important works of Tibetan mysticism, including *The Tibetan Book of the Dead* and *The Tibetan Book of the Great Liberation*. Evans-Wentz also produced a book on the Tibetan mystic Milarepa. Earlier in his academic career he researched Celtic beliefs and folk-legends associated with fairies and Nature spirits.

*Fox, Matthew* (1940– ): Author, priest and proponent of Creation Spirituality, Fox grew up in Madison, Wisconsin, and joined a Dominican order when he was nineteen. Fox maintains that he always sought to focus more on spirituality than on religion and his particular emphasis was not only on the contemplative experience but on justice in the wider world. Fox believes in the divinity of the earth and maintains that Jesus was a pantheist. In rejecting the more orthodox concept of theism—of a God separate from the world—Fox has adopted a perspective that takes him to the very edge of Christian orthodoxy, if not beyond it altogether. For Fox, Christianity should be experiential rather than constricted by doctrine. 'Our job,' he says, 'is to keep our hearts open and learn the new names for divinity . . . everything is in God and God is in everything.' Fox is a prolific author and lecturer. Among his many books are *The Coming of the Cosmic Christ*, *Original Blessing: A Primer in Creation Spirituality* and *Illuminations of Hildegard of Bingen*.

*Freud, Sigmund* (1856–1939): The founder of psychoanalysis, Freud remains one of the pioneering thinkers of the twentieth century. From the perspective of transpersonal psychology, Freud's model of the unconscious mind is now considered limited but his great contribution to the study of human perception was in his scientific exploration of the unconscious mind and his analysis of dreams. Freud derived many of his most creative inspirations from biology and emphasised sexual repression and infantile sexual trauma as the roots of neurosis. This alienated him from many of his colleagues, and some of his most notable students, including Carl Jung and Alfred Adler, broke away to establish their own schools of psychology. Nevertheless, Freudian perspectives continue to underpin western medical psychiatry. Among Freud's most influential books are *The Interpretation of Dreams*, *The Psychopathology of Everyday Life* and *Three Contributions to the Theory of Sexuality*.

*Grof, Stanislav* (1931– ): Czechoslovakian psychiatrist, now resident in the United States. A leading authority on visionary experiences, LSD and altered states of consciousness, Grof introduced the word 'transpersonal' in 1967 and is a leading figure in the international personal growth movement. He is now associated with the practice of Holotropic Breath Therapy, which he conducts with his wife Christina. His many books include *Realms of the Human Unconscious*, *Beyond the Brain* and *The Adventure of Self-Discovery*.

*Gurdjieff, George Ivanovitch* (1872–1949): A mystical teacher, Gurdjieff was born of Greek and Armenian parentage at Kars on the Russo-Turkish border. Fascinated by trance states and paranormal phenomena, Gurdjieff travelled widely in central Asia, Finland and Turkey before eventually establishing his Institute for the Harmonious Development of Man at Fontainebleau, south of Paris. Here he taught his followers to work hard to overcome the slavery of robot-like existence that most people confuse with real life. Gurdjieff was an important precursor of the contemporary personal growth movement.

*Halifax, Joan* (1942– ): American anthropologist and director of the Ojai Foundation in California. Halifax has worked with spiritual healers and shamans around the world and is actively seeking to promote Buddhism and indigenous traditions in the West. Her books include *Shamanic Voices, The Human Encounter with Death* (co-authored with Stanislav Grof), and *Shaman: The Wounded Healer*.

*Harner, Michael* (1929– ): American-born authority on shamanism who spent many years of field research in the Upper Amazon, Mexico and western North America learning about indigenous spiritual traditions. A former visiting professor at Columbia, Yale and the University of California, Harner has now modified traditional shamanic techniques, making them more accessible to a Western audience. His methods include a style of repetitive drumming which enables individuals to undertake a visionary 'spirit-journey' in a state of trance. Harner also teaches shamanic healing. His best known book—a guide to practical shamanism—is *The Way of the Shaman*, but he has also published two academic books, *The Jivaro* and *Hallucinogens and Shamanism*.

*Houston, Jean:* For nearly 30 years, American psychologist and philosopher Dr Jean Houston has lectured and conducted seminars around the world. Renowned for her work in exploring myth and transformation, her approach also encompasses music, meditation, visualisation, movement and dance. A past-president of the Association for Humanistic Psychology, Houston is Co-director of the Foundation for Mind Research in Pomona, New York. The author of numerous books, articles and instructional audiotapes, her principal publications include *The Possible Human, The Search for the Beloved* and *The Hero and the Goddess*. She also co-authored *Mind Games* and *Listening to the Body* with her husband, Robert Masters.

*Huxley, Aldous* (1894–1963): English novelist and essayist who, in the latter part of his life, became interested in altered states of consciousness, comparative religion and parapsychology. A major influence on the American counterculture, the forerunner of the personal growth movement, Huxley experimented with psychedelics and wrote lucidly about his experiences. His books include *The Doors of Perception, Heaven and Hell* and *Moksha.*

*Jung, Carl Gustav* (1875–1961): Founder of analytic psychology and a pioneer of the exploration of mythic symbolism as a function of human consciousness. Jung worked with Sigmund Freud for a number of years but began to differ in his interpretation of the functions of the unconscious mind. Jung believed in a stratum in the unconscious that included a vast source of images and symbols which transcended the individual experience, and this led him to formulate his concept of the Collective Unconscious. In later years he also explored Eastern and Gnostic spirituality, providing commentaries on the *I Ching* and alchemy. Among his most important books are *Symbols of Transformation, The Archetypes and the Collective Unconscious* and his autobiography, *Memories, Dreams, Reflections.*

*Krippner, Stanley* (1932– ): Noted American parapsychologist who has also explored indigenous spirituality and healing. Professor of psychology at Saybrook Institute, San Francisco, and a former Director of the Dream Laboratory at the Maimonides Medical Center in New York, Krippner became interested in telepathic dreams and links between technology and life energy. In recent years he has been conducting experiential workshops in 'personal' mythology with Dr David Feinstein.

*Krishnamurti, Jiddu* (1895–1986): Indian mystic who lived at Adyar, Madras, as a young boy and was noticed by the theosophist Rev. Charles Leadbeater because he had a remarkable 'aura'. Leadbeater and Dr Annie Besant, both leading figures in the Theosophical Society, subsequently proclaimed Krishnamurti to be a World teacher, a claim Krishnamurti rejected. While Krishnamurti avoided the role of the guru, he established himself as a leading yogic philosopher and spent much of his time lecturing internationally. His many books included *Commentaries on Living, The First and Last Freedom* and *The Urgency of Change.* A book of dialogues with noted physicist David Bohm was also published under the title *The Ending of Time*.

*Kubler-Ross, Elisabeth* (1926– ): A world-renowned authority on death and dying, Kubler-Ross received her medical degree from the University of Zurich in 1957. After conducting seminars on death she moved into the field of working therapeutically with the terminally ill. Over the last twenty years Dr Kubler-Ross has studied more than 20 000 people who have had near-death experiences. She now considers it important that death be considered as a transitionary state of consciousness leading to another kind of existence, rather than as a decline into oblivion. Kubler-Ross has given workshops and lectures on the dying process in many countries. Her many books include *On Death and Dying*, *Death—the Final Stage of Growth* and *On Life After Death*.

*Leary, Timothy* (1920–96): Controversial American psychologist and consciousness researcher who became a figurehead in the counter-culture and an advocate of the use of psychedelic drugs as tools of personal transformation. A former lecturer at Harvard, Leary supported the use of LSD in conjunction with spiritual manuals like the *Tibetan Book of the Dead* and the *I Ching*, and co-authored *The Psychedelic Experience* with Richard Alpert and Ralph Metzner as a practical guide to experiencing the *Bardo* visions. He later became interested in cyberspace technology, and towards the end of his life advocated what he called 'designer death'—consciously planning your own transition through death. His many books included *The Politics of Ecstasy*, *High Priest*, *Psychedelic Prayers*, *Chaos and Cyberculture*, and his autobiography *Flashbacks*.

*Lilly, John C.* (1915– ): American neurophysiologist who has been a major pioneer in the study of mystical states of consciousness and is also well known for his work on belief systems and communication with dolphins. Lilly explored visionary states of consciousness in specially constructed sensory isolation tanks and decided that these experiences related directly to programming patterns in the mind produced by religious beliefs and doctrines. In his book *Simulations of God* Lilly puts forth his view that religious beliefs often inhibit mystical illumination and impose a limit or constriction on the experience of transcendental reality. Lilly's other books include *The Mind of the Dolphin*, *The Centre of the Cyclone* and *The Deep Self*.

*Maharishi Mahesh Yogi:* Founder of the Transcendental Meditation (TM) movement. Originally trained as a physicist, the Maharishi turned to mysticism and became a disciple of Guru Dev. The Maharishi's approach to meditation focuses on the use of an individual mantra that has been given specifically to the disciple. The Maharishi believes that when the mind is attuned to the mantra, it acquires a more profound and transcendental power, helping the person to attain true self-knowledge. In due course, the mind is emptied of its contents and the experience of Pure Being remains. According to the tenets of TM this is the true nature of the mind, and attaining this state of awareness enhances one's sense of happiness and unity with life.

*Maslow, Abraham* (1908–70): American psychologist credited with establishing humanistic and transpersonal psychology. Maslow graduated with a PhD from the University of Wisconsin and became chairman of the psychology department at Brandeis University in 1951. Reacting against behaviourism, Maslow emphasised creativity, well-being and spirituality as important dimensions of human life and believed that we should all strive for self-actualisation or fulfilling our individual potentials as completely as possible. His exploration of peak experiences moved humanistic psychology closer to the terrain associated with mysticism, and to this extent Maslow continued an approach pioneered by Jung. Maslow became one of the conceptual founders of the personal growth movement. Together with Anthony Sutich, he defined the transpersonal perspective that is central to an understanding of the New Spirituality.

*Metzner, Ralph* (1935– ): Born in Germany, Metzner studied psychology at Oxford University and Harvard, receiving his doctorate in 1962. Two years earlier, he had joined the Harvard Psychedelic Drug Project as a colleague of Dr Timothy Leary and Dr Richard Alpert. For a time they were perceived as a renegade triumvirate, researching the furthest boundaries of psychedelic consciousness in the quest for psycho-spiritual transformation. Metzner became editor of the *Psychedelic Review* in 1963 and helped co-author *The Psychedelic Experience*—an experiential manual based on the *Tibetan Book of the Dead*. However, in more recent years, he has pursued a more philosophical approach to the exploration of transpersonal states of awareness and is now

Professor of Psychology at the California Institute of Integral Studies in San Francisco. His most recent book is *The Unfolding Self*, a reworking of his 1986 classic, *Opening to Inner Light*. Here Metzner focuses on the transformation of consciousness as expressed through metaphors that appear in religious, mythological and psychological writings—including such themes as the journey of the hero, death and rebirth, the restoration of wholeness and the homeward journey to the Source of All Being.

Muktananda, Swami (1908–82): Indian mystic and practitioner of Siddha Yoga. A devotee of the late Swami Niytananda, Muktananda attracted an international reputation as a teacher of Kundalini yoga and visited the United States and Australia on several occasions. Muktananda believed that the grace of the guru was essential to the spiritual awakening of the disciple. He maintained also that the *kundalini* energy could be aroused in a person as a direct thought-transmission from the guru, through the guru's touch, or spontaneously through the pupil's spiritual devotion to the master. Muktananda's work now continues through the auspices of the Siddha Yoga Foundation, headed by Gurumayi Chidvilasananda.

McKenna, Terence (1946– ): Considered by many as the natural successor to Timothy Leary, McKenna advocates a shamanic perspective that promotes the psilocybin experience as an important means of communicating with the World Soul. McKenna has spent nearly 30 years studying shamanism and the 'ethnopharmacology of spiritual transformation'. For many years he travelled in Asia and the Amazon, studying shamanism and native healing. He now directs Botanical Dimensions, a non-profit research botanical garden in Hawaii. His books include *Food of the Gods*, *True Hallucinations* and a book of essays and interviews, *The Archaic Revival*.

Ornstein, Robert: One of the first psychologists to write lucidly about the left and right hemispheres of the brain, Ornstein is a professor of human biology at Stanford University and President of the Institute for the Study of Human Knowledge. Committed to distinguishing the valuable aspects of the new spiritual paradigm from its more superficial New Age features, Ornstein produced *The Mind Field* in 1976—one of the first critical overviews of the new spiritual paradigm. Best known for his internationally acclaimed work *The Psychology of Consciousness*, he has also written a number of other books, including *Multimind* and *Psychology: the Study of Human Experience*.

**Rajneesh, Bhagwan Shree** (1931–90): Indian spiritual teacher and mystic who, at one time, headed large communities in Poona and Oregon. A former university academic, Rajneesh was recognised by some as an important spiritual philosopher whose discourses paralleled those of Krishnamurti. Rajneesh had particular appeal to a Western audience and attracted controversy for encouraging his followers, or *sannyasins*, to free themselves from constricting moral codes. While he was often typecast as the 'sex guru' by the popular media, this description undervalues his achievements. He was an illuminating speaker on Zen, Taoism, Tibetan Buddhism, Christianity and ancient Greek philosophy and was also an advocate of bioenergy and modern holistic bodywork therapies. His many publications include *The Book of Secrets*, *The Way of the White Clouds* and *The Orange Book*.

**Ram Dass, Baba** (1931– ): Spiritual name of former Harvard psychologist Richard Alpert, who became a colleague and friend of Timothy Leary and a key figure in the American counter-culture. Alpert's spiritual direction changed when he offered LSD to a *sadhu* called Neem Karoli Baba in the foothills of the Himalayas. This holy man was apparently unaffected by the dose he had been given, and Alpert became convinced that he had found a guru whose consciousness transcended biophysical stimulation. Alpert became a convert to Raja yoga and was given the name Baba Ram Dass by his guru. He now lectures widely on the Indian spiritual tradition, relating it in a popular but insightful way to aspects of modern Western life. He also provides help and support to the dying.

**Ring, Kenneth** (1935– ): American psychologist and researcher who is internationally regarded as one of the leading authorities on the near-death experience. Ring received his PhD from the University of Minnesota and has served as an editorial adviser for *ReVision*, a leading journal in transpersonal psychology. His main contribution to consciousness research has been in the field of near-death studies, and he is credited with producing the first scientific investigation of this phenomenon, the results of which were published in his first book *Life at Death* (1980). Since then he has produced two further volumes on this topic: *Heading Toward Omega* and *The Omega Project*.

*Roszak, Theodore:* American historian and philosopher who has written widely on alternative approaches to spirituality. A recipient of a Guggenheim Fellowship, Roszak teaches at California State University. Roszak coined the term 'counter-culture' and was among the first observers to discern a new spiritual force amidst the eclecticism and diverse metaphysical perspectives embraced by American youth. His most influential books include *The Making of a Counter Culture*, *Where the Wasteland Ends*, *Unfinished Animal* and *The Voice of the Earth*.

*Singer, June:* An influential American analyst now practising in California, Singer is widely regarded as one of the leading writers on Jungian psychology—especially with regard to male/female relationships and the application of Jungian thought to business and industry. Singer trained at the C. G. Jung Institute in Zurich and received her PhD from Northwestern University. Her many books include *Androgyny*, *Boundaries of the Soul*, *Love's Energies* and *Seeing Through the Visible World*.

*Spangler, David* (1945– ): American mystic and author who, during the early 1970s, was co-director of the Findhorn Community in Scotland. Spangler had several mystical experiences as a child and for a period in his twenties also channelled a discarnate being as a healing guide and inspirational source. He is now regarded as a leading spokesperson for the New Age. While his personal orientation is towards Christian mysticism, his perspective is essentially global and transcends denominational differences. His books include *Emergence: Rebirth of the Sacred* and *Towards a Planetary Vision*.

*Starhawk* (1951– ): The magical name of Miriam Simos, an influential contemporary witch who founded two covens in San Francisco and produced a definitive volume on contemporary neopagan practice, *The Spiral Dance*. According to Starhawk, 'for women, the Goddess is an image of personal strength and creative power; for men, she is the nurturing source within'. Starhawk worked for a time with Christian theologian Matthew Fox and is currently engaged in exploring the socio-political implications of witchcraft and neopaganism.

*Stevenson, Ian* (1918– ): Arguably the world's leading authority on cases of claimed reincarnation, Professor Stevenson is Chairman of the Department of Neurology and Psychiatry at the University of Virginia School of Medicine. Stevenson has spent many years investigating instances of reincarnation memory patterns in young children, where conscious or unconscious fraud would appear to be out of the question. Stevenson's research data is international in scope and is contained in several books and journals, including his important book *Twenty Cases Suggestive of Reincarnation*.

*Tart, Charles* (1937– ): Internationally respected for his scientific research into trance, dreams, out-of-body experiences and extrasensory perception, Professor Tart is one of a number of contemporary scientists who are endeavouring to close the gulf between science and mysticism. Tart has called for recognition of 'state-specific sciences'—scientific systems that recognise the existence of different states of consciousness, each with their distinct types of 'reality'. Tart has produced several important books, including *Altered States of Consciousness, Transpersonal Psychologies* and *Open Mind, Discriminating Mind*. He is now professor of consciousness studies at the University of Nevada in Las Vegas.

*Watts, Alan* (1915–73): British philosopher and lecturer on Zen Buddhism who became a leading figure in the American counter-culture. Watts emigrated to the United States in 1936, embraced Christianity, and was ordained as an Anglican priest in 1944. He served as the Episcopal chaplain at Northwestern University for six years but then left the Church to pursue an alternative lifestyle. Always interested in Zen Buddhism and Taoism, Watts sought to reconcile these Eastern perspectives with a Western context, while also experimenting with psychedelics like LSD. He became friendly with figures like Timothy Leary, Allen Ginsberg and Jack Kerouac and was a familiar figure on the campus lecture circuit. Watts believed that 'all doctrines of God are ultimately false and idolatrous, because doctrines are forms of words which can never be more than pointers to mystical vision'. He was, nevertheless, a prolific author himself. His books include *The Way of Zen, The Wisdom of Insecurity, The Joyous Cosmology* and *Two Hands of God*.

*Wilber, Ken* (1949– ): A practitioner of Zen meditation, American author and philosopher Ken Wilber is a leading transpersonal theorist and has been acclaimed by John White as 'the long-sought Einstein of consciousness research'. A prolific author and former editor-in-chief of *ReVision*, Wilber has sought to develop a unified field theory of consciousness, encompassing the world's great psychological, philosophical and spiritual traditions. His many books include *The Spectrum of Consciousness*, *No Boundary*, *The Holographic Paradigm*, *Sex, Ecology and Spirituality* and *A Brief History of Everything*.

Zohar, *Danah*: American author who has explored parapsychology and the relationship of quantum physics to personal growth and identity. Zohar graduated in physics and philosophy from Massachusetts Institute of Technology in 1966 and undertook further research in philosophy and religion at Harvard. She is now based in Britain and is the author of two influential books, *Through the Time Barrier* and *The Quantum Self*.

# Bibliography

Abraham, R., McKenna, T. and Sheldrake, R. *Trialogues at the Edge of the West: Chaos, Creativity and the Resacralization of the World*, Bear & Co, Santa Fe, 1992

Achterberg, J. *Imagery in Healing*, Shambhala, Boston, 1985

Adler, M. *Drawing Down the Moon*, Beacon Press, Boston, 1988

Anderson, W.T. *The Upstart Spring: Esalen and the American Awakening*, Addison Wesley, Reading, Mass., 1983

Anthony, D., Ecker, B. and Wilber, K. *Spiritual Choices*, Paragon House, New York, 1987

Barbour, I.G. *Myths, Models and Paradigms*, Harper & Row, New York, 1976

Bharati, A. *Light at the Center*, Ross-Erikson, Santa Barbara, 1976

Blackmore, S. *Dying to Live: Science and the Near-Death Experience*, Grafton, London, 1993

Blair-Ewart, A. (ed.) *Mindfire: Dialogues in the Other Future*, Somerville House, Toronto, 1995

Bliss, S. (ed.) *The New Holistic Health Workbook*, Viking Penguin, New York, 1985

Bohm, D. *Wholeness and the Implicate Order*, Routledge & Kegan Paul, London, 1985

Bohm, D. and Peat, F.D. *Science, Order and Creativity*, Bantam Books, New York, 1987

Bolen, J.S. *Goddesses in Everywoman*, Harper & Row, New York, 1985

Campbell. J. *The Hero with a Thousand Faces*, Pantheon, New York, 1949

——*Myths to Live By*, Viking Press, New York, 1972; Souvenir Press, London, 1973

——*The Inner Reaches of Outer Space: Metaphor as Myth and as Religion*, Harper & Row, New York, 1988

Capra, F. *The Tao of Physics*, Shambhala, Boulder, Colorado, 1975

——*The Turning Point*, Wildwood House, London, 1982

——*Uncommon Wisdom*, Simon & Schuster, New York, 1988

Castaneda, C. *The Teachings of Don Juan*, University of Caifornia Press, Berkeley, 1968

——*A Separate Reality*, Simon & Schuster, New York 1971

——*Journey to Ixtlan*, Simon & Schuster, New York, 1972

——*Tales of Power*, Simon & Schuster, New York, 1974

——*The Art of Dreaming*, HarperCollins, New York, 1993

Comstock, W.R. (ed.) *Religion and Man*, Harper & Row, New York, 1971

Cott, A. *Fasting: The Ultimate Diet*, Bantam Books, New York, 1975

Daab, R. 'An Interview with Jean Houston', *Magical Blend* issues 18, 19 and 20, Berkeley, 1988

Dalai Lama, The, *My Land and My People*, McGraw-Hill, New York, 1962

De Mille, R. *Castaneda's Journey*, Capra Press, Santa Barbara, 1976

——*The Don Juan Papers*, Ross-Erikson, Santa Barbara, 1980

Dennett, D.C. *Consciousness Explained*, Penguin Books, London, 1993

Dilman, I. *Freud and the Mind*, Basil Blackwell, Oxford, 1986

Doore, G. (ed.) *What Survives? Contemporary Explorations of Life After Death*, Tarcher, Los Angeles, 1990

Drury, N. (ed.) *Frontiers of Consciousness*, Greenhouse Publications, Melbourne, 1975

——*The Healing Power*, Muller, London, 1981

——*Healers, Quacks or Mystics?* Hale & Iremonger, Sydney, 1983

——(ed.) *Inner Health*, Harper & Row, Sydney, 1985

——*The Occult Experience*, Robert Hale, London, 1987

——*The Elements of Shamanism*, Element, Dorset, 1989

——*The Visionary Human*, Element, Dorset, 1991

——*Echoes from the Void: Writings on Magic, Visionary Art and the New Consciousness*, Prism Press, Dorset, 1994

Dutt, S. *The Buddha and Five After-Centuries*, Luzac & Co., London, 1957

Edinger, E. *Ego and Archetype*, Penguin, London, 1973

Elder, B. *And When I Die, Will I Be Dead?*, Australian Broadcasting Corporation, Sydney, 1987

Eliade, M. *Cosmos and History*, Harper & Row, New York, 1959
——*The Sacred and the Profane*, Harper & Row, New York, 1961
——*Yoga, Immortality and Freedom*, Princeton University Press, New Jersey, 1969
——*Shamanism*, Princeton University Press, New Jersey, 1972
Evans-Wentz, W.Y. (ed.) *The Tibetan Book of the Dead*, Oxford University Press, New York, 1960
Fadiman, J. and Frager, R. *Personality and Personal Growth*, Harper & Row, New York, 1976
Farrar, J. and Farrar, S. *The Witches' Way*, Hale, London, 1987
Feinstein, D. and Krippner, S. *Personal Mythology*, Tarcher, Los Angeles, 1988
Ferguson, D.S. (ed.) *New Age Spirituality*, Westminster/John Knox Press, Louisville, Kentucky, 1993
Freud, S. *New Introductory Lectures on Psychoanalysis*, Norton, New York, 1949
——*The Interpretation of Dreams*, Avon, New York, 1967
Fry, P. and Long, M. *Beyond the Mechanical Mind*, Australian Broadcasting Commission, Sydney, 1976
Furlong, M. *Genuine Fake: A Biography of Alan Watts*, Unwin Hyman, London, 1987
Furst, P.T. (ed.) *Flesh of the Gods*, Allen & Unwin, London, 1972
Goldwag, E. (ed.) *Inner Balance*, Prentice-Hall, Englewood Cliffs, New Jersey, 1979
Goleman, D. (ed.) *Consciousness: Brain, States of Awareness and Mysticism*, Harper & Row, New York, 1979
——*The Meditative Mind*, Tarcher, Los Angeles, 1988
Gottlieb, R.S. *A New Creation: America's Contemporary Spiritual Voices*, Crossroad, New York, 1990
Grey, M. *Return from Death: An Exploration of the Near-Death Experience*, Arkana, London, 1985
Grof, S. *Realms of the Human Unconscious*, Dutton, New York, 1976
——'Modern Consciousness Research and the Quest for a New Paradigm', *ReVision*, vol. 2, no.1, winter/spring 1979
——*LSD Psychotherapy*, Hunter House, Pomona, California, 1980
——(ed.) *Ancient Wisdom, Modern Science*, State University of New York Press, Albany, 1984
——*Beyond the Brain*, State University of New York Press, Albany, 1985

——*The Adventure of Self-Discovery*, State University of New York Press, Albany, 1988

——*The Holotropic Mind*, HarperCollins, San Francisco, 1992

Grof S. and Halifax J. *The Human Encounter with Death*, Dutton, New York, 1979

Guiley, R.E. *Encyclopedia of Mystical & Paranormal Experience*, HarperCollins, New York, 1991

Hagon, Z. *Channelling*, Prism Press, Dorset, 1989

Halifax, J. (ed.) *Shamanic Voices*, Arkana, New York, 1991

Harner, M. *The Way of the Shaman*, Harper & Row, San Francisco, 1980

——*The Jivaro*, University of California Press, Berkeley, 1984

Heelas, P. *The New Age Movement*, Blackwell, Oxford, 1996

Hoffman, E. *The Right to be Human: A Biography of Abraham Maslow*, Tarcher, Los Angeles, 1988

Houston, J. 'Myth and Pathos in Sacred Psychology', *Dromenon*, vol. 3, no. 2, spring 1981

——*The Possible Human*, Tarcher, Los Angeles, 1986

——*The Search for the Beloved*, Tarcher, Los Angeles, 1987

——*The Hero and the Goddess*, Ballantine, New York, 1992

Huxley, A., *The Perennial Philosophy*, Chatto & Windus, London, 1946

——*The Doors of Perception/Heaven and Hell*, Penguin, London, 1963

——*Moksha: Writings on Psychedelics and the Visionary Experience*, Stonehill, New York, 1977

Ingram, C. 'Ken Wilber: The Pundit of Transpersonal Psychology', *Yoga Journal*, September/October 1987

Jamal, M. *Shape Shifters*, Arkana, New York and London, 1987

Jeffrey, F. and Lilly, J.C. *John Lilly So Far . . .* Tarcher, Los Angeles, 1990

Johnston, C. (trans.) *The Crest Jewel of Wisdom*, Watkins, London, 1964

Jung, C.G. *Two Essays in Analytical Psychology*, Routledge & Kegan Paul, London, 1953

——*Symbols of Transformation*, Bollingen Foundation, New Jersey, 1956

——*Memories, Dreams, Reflections*, Random House, New York, 1961

——*Man and his Symbols*, Dell, New York, 1968

Kalweit, H. *Dreamtime and Inner Space*, Shambhala, Boston, 1988

Kaplan, A. *Meditation and Kabbalah*, Weiser, New York, 1982

Kaufmann, W. *Religions in Four Dimensions*, Reader's Digest Press/T.Y. Crowell, New York, 1976

Knaster, M. 'The Goddesses in Jean Shinoda Bolen', *East West*, March 1989

Knight, J.Z. *A State of Mind*, Warner Books, New York, 1987

Krishna, G. *Kundalini*, Robinson & Watkins, London, 1971

Kubler-Ross, E. *Death: The Final Stage of Growth*, Prentice-Hall, Englewood Cliffs, New Jersey, 1975

——On *Life After Death*, Celestial Arts, Berkeley, California, 1991

Kuhn, T. *The Structure of Scientific Revolutions*, 2nd edn, University of Chicago Press, Chicago, 1970

Larsen, S. *The Shaman's Doorway*, Harper & Row, New York, 1976

Larsen, S. and Larsen, R. *A Fire in the Mind: The Life of Joseph Campbell*, Doubleday, New York, 1991

Leary, T. (et al.) *The Psychedelic Experience*, University Books, New York, 1964

——*High Priest*, New American Library, New York, 1968

——*Flashbacks*, Tarcher, Los Angeles, 1983

Leary, T. and Sirius, R.U. *Design for Dying*, HarperCollins, San Francisco, 1997

Lehrman, F. (ed.) *The Sacred Landscape*, Celestial Arts, Berkeley, California, 1988

Lewis, J.R. and Melton, J.G. *Perspectives on the New Age*, State University Press of New York, Albany, 1992

Lilly, J. *The Centre of the Cyclone*, Calder and Boyars, London, 1973

——*The Human Biocomputer*, Abacus, London, 1974

——*Simulations of God*, Simon and Schuster, New York, 1975

——*The Deep Self: Profound Relaxation and the Tank Isolation Technique*, Simon and Schuster, New York, 1977

Lings, M. *Muhammad*, Allen & Unwin, London, 1983

Lovelock, J. *Gaia: A New Look at Life on Earth*, Oxford University Press, London and New York, 1979

Lowrey, R. *Dominance, Self-esteem, Self-actualisation*, Brooks Cole, Monterey, California, 1973

McDermot, V. *The Cult of the Seer in the Ancient Middle East*, University of California Press, Berkeley, 1971

McKenna, T. *The Archaic Revival*, HarperCollins, San Francisco, 1991

Mann, A.T. (ed.) *The Future of Astrology*, Unwin Hyman, London, 1988

Maslow, A. *Toward a Psychology of Being*, Van Nostrand, New York, 1968

——*Motivation and Personality*, Harper & Row, New York, 1970

——*The Farther Reaches of Human Nature*, Viking, New York, 1971

Masters, R. and Houston J. *The Varieties of Psychedelic Experience*, Holt Rinehart and Winston, New York, 1966

May, R. *Physicians of the Soul*, Amity Press, Warwick, New York, 1988

——*Cosmic Consciousness Revisited*, Element, Dorset, 1993

Meares, A. *Cancer—Another Way?*, Hill of Content, Melbourne, 1980

Metzner, R. *The Ecstatic Adventure*, Macmillan, New York, 1968

——*Maps of Consciousness*, Collier Macmillan, New York, 1971

——*Opening to Inner Light*, Tarcher, Los Angeles, 1986

——'Gaia's Alchemy: Ruin and Renewal of the Elements', in F. Lehrman (ed.) *The Sacred Landscape*, Celestial Arts, Berkeley, California, 1988

——*The Unfolding Self: Varieties of Transformative Experience*, Origin Press, Novato, California, 1998

Miller, S. *After Death: Mapping the Journey*, Simon & Schuster, New York, 1997

Millikan, D. and Drury, N. *Worlds Apart?: Christianity and the New Age*, Australian Broadcasting Corporation, Sydney, 1991

Moody, R. *Life After Life*, Bantam Books, New York, 1978

Murti, T.R.V. *The Central Philosophy of Buddhism*, Allen & Unwin, London 1972

Neihardt, J.G. *Black Elk Speaks*, Pocket Books, New York, 1972

Ornstein, R. *The Psychology of Consciousness*, Cape, London, 1975

Radha, S. *Kundalini Yoga for the West*, Shambhala, Boulder, Colorado, 1981

Rice, E. *Eastern Definitions*, Doubleday, New York, 1978

Ring, K. *Life at Death: A Scientific Investigation of the Near-Death Experience*, Coward McCann & Geoghegan, New York, 1980

——*Heading Towards Omega*, Morrow, New York, 1984

Rogo, D.S. *The Return from Silence: A Study of the Near-Death Experience*, Aquarian Press, Wellingborough, 1989

Roszak, T. *Unfinished Animal*, Harper & Row, New York, 1975

——*The Voice of the Earth*, Simon & Schuster, New York, 1992

Russell, P. *The Awakening Earth*, Ark/Routledge & Kegan Paul, London, 1982

Singer, J. *Seeing Through the Visible World*, HarperCollins, San Francisco, 1990

Spangler, D. *Emergence: Rebirth of the Sacred*, Dell, New York, 1984

——'The New Age: The Movement Towards the Divine', in D.S. Ferguson (ed.) *New Age Spirituality*, Westminster/John Knox Press, Louisville, Kentucky, 1993

Starhawk, *The Spiral Dance*, Harper & Row, New York, 1979

——*Dreaming the Dark*, Beacon Press, Boston, 1982

Stevens, J. *Storming Heaven: LSD and the American Dream*, Atlantic Monthly Press, New York, 1987

Stockton, E. *The Aboriginal Gift*, Millennium Books, Sydney, 1996

Sulloway, F. *Freud: Biologist of the Mind*, Basic Books, New York, 1979

Sun Bear and Wabun, *The Medicine Wheel*, Prentice-Hall, Englewood Cliffs, New Jersey, 1980

Sutherland, C., *Transformed by the Light: Life After Near-Death Experiences*, Bantam Books, Sydney, 1992

Sutich, A.J. 'The Emergence of the Transpersonal Orientation: a Personal Account', *Journal of Transpersonal Psychology*, vol. 8, no. 1, 1976

Tart, C. (ed.) *Altered States of Consciousness*, Wiley, New York, 1969

——(ed.) *Transpersonal Psychologies*, Harper & Row, New York, 1975

Trenoweth, S. *The Future of God: Personal Adventures in Spirituality with Thirteen of Today's Eminent Thinkers*, Millennium Books, Sydney, 1995

Valle, R.S. and von Eckartsberg, R. (eds) *The Metaphors of Consciousness*, Plenum Press, New York, 1981

Voigt, A. and Drury, N. *Wisdom from the Earth: The Living Legacy of the Aboriginal Dreamtime*, Simon & Schuster, Sydney, 1997; Shambhala, Boston, 1998

Walsh, R.N. and Vaughan, F. (eds) *Beyond Ego*, Tarcher, Los Angeles, 1980

Wasson, R.G. *The Wondrous Mushroom*, McGraw-Hill, New York, 1980

Watts, A. *This is It and Other Essays on Zen and Spiritual Experience*, Pantheon, New York, 1960

——*The Joyous Cosmology*, Vintage Books, New York, 1962

Webb, J. *The Occult Establishment*, Richard Drew Publishing, Glasgow, 1981

White, J. (ed.) *The Highest State of Consciousness*, Doubleday Anchor, New York, 1972

Wilber, K. *The Spectrum of Consciousness*, Quest Books, Wheaton, Illinois, 1977

——*The Atman Project*, Quest Books, Wheaton, Illinois, 1980

——'Psychologia Perennis: The Spectrum of Consciousness' in R.N. Walsh and F. Vaughan (eds) *Beyond Ego*, Tarcher, Los Angeles, 1980

——*Up from Eden*, Doubleday Anchor, New York, 1981

——*A Brief History of Everything*, Gill & Macmillan, Dublin, 1996

Williams, V. 'The Sacred Craft', *East West*, October 1984

Woods, R. (ed.) *Understanding Mysticism*, Image Books/Doubleday, New York, 1980

Zaleski, C. *Otherworld Journeys*, Oxford University Press, New York, 1987

Zimmer, H. *Myths and Symbols of Indian Art and Civilization*, Harper & Row, New York, 1962

Zohar, D. *The Quantum Self*, Flamingo/HarperCollins, London, 1991

Zukav, G. *The Dancing Wu Li Masters: An Overview of the New Physics*, Morrow, New York, 1979

# Notes

## CHAPTER 1

1   See Ilham Dilman, *Freud and the Mind*, Basil Blackwell, Oxford, 1986, p. 7
2   J. Fadiman and R. Frager, *Personality and Personal Growth*, Harper & Row, New York, 1976, p. 14
3   Gardner Murphy, *An Historical Introduction to Modern Psychology*, Routledge & Kegan Paul, London, 1967
4   See S. Freud, *New Introductory Lectures on Psychoanalysis*, vol. 22, Norton, New York, 1949, p. 80
5   J. Fadiman and R. Frager, op cit., p. 20
6   See Frank J. Sulloway, *Freud: Biologist of the Mind*, Basic Books, New York, 1979, p. 338
7   C.G. Jung, *Memories, Dreams, Reflections*, Random House, New York, 1961, pp. 168–9
8   C.G. Jung, *Man and His Symbols*, Dell, New York, 1968, p. 13
9   ibid., p. 18
10  ibid., pp. 41–2
11  C.G. Jung, *Two Essays in Analytical Psychology*, Routledge & Kegan Paul, London, 1953, p. 68
12  ibid., pp. 65–6
13  ibid., p. 70
14  C.G. Jung. 'The Relations Between the Ego and the Unconscious', in *Collected Works*, 1928, p. 176
15  See R. Lowrey (ed.) *Dominance, Self-Esteem, Self-Actualisation*, Brooks/Cole, Monterey, 1973

16  A. Maslow, *The Farther Reaches of Human Nature*, Viking, New York, 1971, p. 47

17  A. Maslow, *Motivation and Personality*, Harper & Row, New York, 1970, p. 176

18  ibid., p. 164

19  A. Maslow, *Toward a Psychology of Being*, Van Nostrand, New York, 1968, p. 173

20  ibid., p. 127

21  ibid., p. 129

22  ibid., p. 130

23  A. Sutich, 'The Founding Of Humanistic and Transpersonal Psychology: A Personal Account', dissertation presented to the Humanistic Psychology Institute, San Francisco, April 1976, p. 22

24  ibid., p. 29

25  ibid., p. 35

26  ibid., p. 114

27  ibid., p. 115

28  ibid., p. 155

29  ibid., p. 167

30  ibid., p. 172

31  A. Maslow, 'A Theory of Metamotivation: the Biological Rooting of the Value Life' in R.N. Walsh and F. Vaughan (eds), *Beyond Ego*, Tarcher, Los Angeles, 1980, p. 130

32  See A. Huxley, 'Wings That Shape Men's Minds', *Saturday Evening Post*, 18 October 1958, pp. 111–13

33  See Monica Furlong, *Genuine Fake: A Biography of Alan Watts*, Unwin Hyman, London, 1987, pp. 115–16

34  Extract from J. Beck, 'Paradise Now' in the *International Times*, London, 12–25 July, 1968. See also T. Roszak, *Unfinished Animal*, Harper & Row, New York, 1975, pp. 151–2

35  Quoted in James Webb, *The Occult Establishment*, Richard Drew Publishing, Glasgow, 1981, p. 462

36  *Psychology Today*, January 1975, p. 69

37  A. Watts, *The Joyous Cosmology*, Vintage Books, New York, 1962, p. 1

38  T. Leary and R.U. Sirius, *Design for Dying*, HarperCollins, San Francisco, 1997, p. 211

39  Quoted in Peter Fry and Malcolm Long, *Beyond the Mechanical Mind*, Australian Broadcasting Commission, Sydney, 1976, p. 122

40  ibid., p. 123

## CHAPTER 2

1  Sukumar Dutt, *The Buddha and Five After-Centuries*, Luzac & Co., London, 1957, p. 39
2  *Matthew* 1: 20–1
3  Richard Owen, 'Middle-class Jesus wore well-heeled sandals', *The Australian*, 13 November 1997 (original report from *The Times*, London)
4  *Mark* 1: 10–11
5  *Mark* 12: 28–31
6  See W. Kaufmann, *Religions in Four Dimensions*, p. 121
7  See Janet K. O'Dea and Thomas F. O'Dea, 'Christianity in Historical Perspective', in W. Richard Comstock (ed.), *Religion and Man*, Harper & Row, New York, 1971, p. 427
8  Quoted in Martin Lings, *Muhammad*, Allen & Unwin, London, 1983, p. 44
9  See John Lilly, *Simulations of God*, Simon & Schuster, New York, 1975, p. 84
10  ibid., pp. 146–7
11  See Allan Cott, *Fasting: The Ultimate Diet*, Bantam, New York, 1975, p. 121
12  See Violet McDermot, *The Cult of the Seer in the Ancient Middle East*, University of California Press, Berkeley, 1971, p. 41

## CHAPTER 3

1  See Mircea Eliade, *Cosmos and History: The Myth of the Eternal Return*, Harper & Row, New York, 1959, pp. 113 and 127
2  ibid., p. 129
3  H. Zimmer, *Myths and Symbols in Indian Art and Civilization*, Harper & Row, New York, 1962, p. 68
4  See W.Y. Evans-Wentz, *The Tibetan Book of the Dead*, Oxford University Press, New York, 1960, p. 232
5  According to T.R.V. Murti in his seminal work *The Central Philosophy of Buddhism* (Allen & Unwin, London, 1955, p. 67) the seven Abhidhamma treatises of the Pali Canon, though proposed as the word of Gautama Buddha, are in fact a Hinayana or Theraveda interpretation and synthesis of his

teachings, many of them formulated during the reign of Emperor Asoka.

6 See Timothy Leary et al., *The Psychedelic Experience*, University Books, New York, 1964
7 ibid., p. 48
8 See W.Y. Evans-Wentz, *The Tibetan Book of the Dead*, p. 32
9 Edward Rice, *Eastern Definitions*, Doubleday, New York, 1978, p. 215
10 ibid., p. 216
11 From K.T. Telang (trans.) in F. Max Muller, *Sacred Books of the East*, VIII, pp. 241–2
12 See C. Johnston (trans.) *The Crest Jewel of Wisdom*, John Watkins, London, 1964, p. 13
13 Extract from F. Max Muller (ed.), *Sacred Books of the Buddhists*, London, 1899, vol. II, p. 90
14 The Dalai Lama, My *Land and* My *People*, McGraw Hill, New York, 1962, pp. 50–2
15 See Christopher Magarey, 'Meditation: The Essence of Health' in N. Drury (ed.) *Inner Health*, Harper & Row, Sydney, 1985
16 See John Cooper's interview with the late Swami Muktananda, 'Swami Muktananda and the Yoga of Power' in N. Drury (ed.) *Frontiers of Consciousness*, Greenhouse Publications, Melbourne, 1975, p. 135
17 Quoted in Swami Sivananda Radha, *Kundalini Yoga for the West*, Shambhala, Boulder, Colorado, 1981, p. 25 et seq.
18 See H. Chandhuri, 'Yoga Psychology' in Charles Tart (ed.) *Transpersonal Psychologies*, Harper & Row, New York, 1975
19 See Agehananda Bharati, *Light at the Center*, Ross-Erikson, Santa Barbara 1976, p. 164. It may, perhaps, have been more accurate to use the word 'imaginal' rather than 'imaginary' since the raising of the Kundalini obviously has its own experiential 'reality'.
20 See Mircea Eliade, Yoga: *Immortality and Freedom*, Princeton University Press, New Jersey, 1969, p. 247
21 See Gopi Krishna, *Kundalini*, Robinson & Watkins, London, 1971, p. 66
22 See Christopher Magarey, 'Meditation: The Essence of Health', loc. cit., p. 143
23 Included in the press-kit for Sri Chinmoy's tour of Australia and New Zealand, November–December 1987
24 ibid.

25 'Ma Anand Sheela interview on Cable News Network', *The Rajneesh Times*, vol. 3 no. 5, 9 August 1985, p. 4
26 See Catherine Ingram, 'Ken Wilber: The Pundit of Transpersonal Psychology', *Yoga Journal*, September/October 1987, p. 49
27 See N. Drury, *Healers, Quacks or Mystics?*, Hale & Iremonger, Sydney, 1983, p. 96


## CHAPTER 4

1 For a full description of these initiations see Janet and Stewart Farrar, *The Witches' Way*, Robert Hale, London, 1984
2 See N. Drury, *The Occult Experience*, Robert Hale, London, 1987, p. 51
3 Quoted in Victoria Williams, 'The Sacred Craft', *East West*, October 1984
4 See N. Drury, *The Occult Experience*, loc. cit., p. 44
5 Quoted in Victoria Williams, loc. cit.
6 See Michel Gauquelin, 'Neo-astrology: Forty Years of Research', in A.T. Mann (ed.) *The Future of Astrology*, Unwin Hyman, London, 1988
7 See Bruno and Louise Huber, 'The Future of Astrology' in A.T. Mann, op. cit. pp. 162–3
8 See Dane Rudyar, 'Whence, Why and Whither', in A.T. Mann, op. cit., p. 8
9 Deborah Cameron, 'Satan and the Showgirl: The New Age Under Fire', in *Good Weekend*, Sydney, 11 March 1989, p. 20
10 ibid.
11 Advertisement in *Interface*, Boston, Fall 1997, p. 31—advertising workshops planned for October 1997
12 *Southern Crossings*, 6, 1, Sydney, August 1985, p. 7
13 Mark Chipperfield, 'New Age Inc.', *The Australian Magazine*, Sydney, 10 December 1988


## CHAPTER 5

1 See Stanislav Grof, *Realms of the Human Unconscious*, Dutton, New York, 1976, p. 49 et seq.

2   Interview with the author of the Esalen Institute, Big Sur, December 1984

3   Richard T. Tarnas, *LSD, Psychoanalysis and Spiritual Rebirth*, unpublished manuscript, Esalen Institute, Big Sur, California, 1976, p. 37

4   See Stanislav Grof, *Realms of the Human Unconsciousness*, 1976, loc. cit., p. 107

5   See Stanislav Grof, *LSD Psychotherapy*, Hunter House, Pomona, California, 1980, p. 76 and also Stanislav Grof, *The Holotropic Mind*, HarperCollins, San Francisco, 1992, pp. 45–56

6   See Grof, 1976, loc. cit., p. 132

7   ibid., p. 142

8   See Stanislav Grof, 'Modern Consciousness Research and the Quest for a New Paradigm', *Re-Vision*, 2, 1, Winter/Spring 1979, pp. 42–3

9   See Grof, 1992, loc. cit., p. 83

10  ibid., p. 84

11  Interview with the author at Esalen Institute, Big Sur, December 1984

12  For additional background information, see John Lilly, *The Centre of the Cyclone*, Calder & Boyars, London, 1973, and *The Human Biocomputer*, Abacus, London, 1974

13  See Francis Jeffrey and John C. Lilly, *John Lilly, So Far . . .*, Tarcher, Los Angeles, 1990, p. 172

14  John Lilly's parting with Oscar Ichazo was clearly based, in part, on a clash of wills. Lilly acknowledges that he has always had a problem with ego. When I met him in Sydney in May 1988, I asked him to inscribe my copy of *The Centre of the Cyclone*. He wrote: 'Out of the centre, into whirling egos: mine is bigger than yours!'

15  See Francis Jeffrey and John C. Lilly, *John Lilly, So Far . . .*, loc. cit., p. 272

16  See Catherine Ingram, 'Ken Wilber: The Pundit of Transpersonal Psychology', *Yoga Journal*, September/October 1987, p. 44

17  Ken Wilber, 'Psychologia Perennis: The Spectrum of Consciousness' in Roger N. Walsh and Frances Vaughan (eds) *Beyond Ego*, Tarcher, Los Angeles, 1980, pp. 74–5

18  Ken Wilber, *The Spectrum of Consciousness*, Quest Books, Wheaton, Illinois, 1977, p. 241

19 C.G. Jung, *Analytical Psychology: Its Theory and Practice*, Vintage Books, New York, 1968, p. 110
20 Ken Wilber, *A Brief History of Everything*, Gill & Macmillan, Dublin, 1996, p. 214
21 Ken Wilber, 'Psychologia Perennis: The Spectrum of Consciousness' in Roger N. Walsh and Frances Vaughan (eds) *Beyond Ego*, loc. cit., p. 83
22 Quoted in Stephen and Robin Larsen, *A Fire in the Mind: The Life of Joseph Campbell*, Doubleday, New York, 1991
23 See Mirka Knaster, 'The Goddesses in Jean Shinoda Bolen', *East West*, March 1989, p. 45. An interesting interview with Bolen is also included in Alexander Blair-Ewart, *Mindfire: Dialogues in the Other Future*, Somerville House, Toronto, 1995
24 ibid., p. 44
25 ibid., p. 73
26 Richard Daab and Silma Smith, 'Midwife of the Possible: An Interview with Jean Houston', Part 3, *Magical Blend*, Fall 1988, p. 22
27 Alexander Blair-Ewart, interview with Jean Houston in *Mindfire: Dialogues in the Other Future*, Somerville House, Toronto, 1995, p.111
28 Jean Houston, *The Hero and the Goddess*, Ballantine, New York, 1992, p. 10
29 Jean Houston, *The Search for the Beloved: Journeys in Sacred Psychology*, Crucible, Wellingborough, UK, 1990, p. 13
30 Jean Houston, 'Myth and Pathos in Sacred Psychology', *Dromenon*, 3, 2, Spring 1981, p. 33
31 Richard Daab and Silma Smith, op. cit., pp. 23–4
32 David Feinstein and Stanley Krippner, *Personal Mythology: The Psychology of Your Evolving Self*, Tarcher, Los Angeles, 1988, p. 231
33 Joseph Campbell, *Myths to Live By*, Condor Books/Souvenir Press, London, 1973, p. 104

### CHAPTER 6

1 See John G. Neihardt, *Black Elk Speaks*, Pocket Books, New York, 1972, p. 36 (first edition William Morrow, New York, 1932)

2   Quoted in Eugene Stockton, *The Aboriginal Gift*, Millennium Books, Sydney, 1995, p. 82

3   For further information see Michael Harner, *The Jivaro*, University of California Press, Berkeley, 1984

4   Quoted in Joan Halifax (ed.), *Shamanic Voices*, Arkana, New York, 1991, p. 185

5   ibid., p. 183

6   See Michael Harner, *The Way of the Shaman*, Harper & Row, San Francisco, 1980, p. 62 (revised edition 1990)

7   Quoted in R. Gordon Wasson, *The Wondrous Mushroom*, McGraw-Hill, New York, 1980, p. 13

8   See Douglas Sharon, 'The San Pedro Cactus in Peruvian Folk Healing', in Peter T. First, *Flesh of the Gods: The Ritual Use of Hallucinogens*, Allen & Unwin, London, 1972, p. 131

9   See Michael Harner, op. cit., p. 20

10  See Robert G. Lake, 'Tela Donahue Lake: Traditional Yurok "Doctor"', *Shaman's Drum*, 15, Mid-winter 1989, p. 47 et seq.

11  See Ake Hultkrantz, 'The Wind River Shoshoni Sun Dance and Curing Practices' in *Shaman's Drum*, 17, Mid-summer 1989, p. 17 et seq.

12  Castaneda's first four books have been his most influential: *The Teachings of Don Juan, A Separate Reality, Journey to Ixtlan* and *Tales of Power*

13  See Richard de Mille's interview with Barbara Myerhoff in his fascinating book *The Don Juan Papers: Further Castaneda Controversies*, Ross-Erikson, Santa Barbara, 1980, p. 336 et seq.

14  See Sun Bear and Wabun, *The Medicine Wheel*, Prentice-Hall, Englewood Cliffs, New Jersey, 1980, p. xiii

15  Ron Boyer, 'The Vision Quest', *The Laughing Man*, 2, 4, p. 63

16  Quoted in Joan Halifax (ed.), *Shamanic Voices*, Arkana, New York, 1991, p. 68

17  Quoted in Michele Jamal, *Shape Shifters*, Arkana, London, 1987, pp. 89–90

18  ibid.

19  Personal communication during filming for the Cinetel Productions documentary *The Occult Experience*, New York, November 1984—in which I was involved as interviewer. This documentary, screened in Australia by Channel 10 and released in the United States through Sony Home Video,

included a lengthy segment on this particular shamanic drumming workshop.
20 See Nevill Drury, *The Occult Experience*, Robert Hale, London, 1987, p. 145
21 ibid.
22 See 'Magic Plants and the *Logos*: Terence McKenna in conversation with Alexander Blair-Ewart' in Alexander Blair-Ewart, *Mindfire: Dialogues in the Other Future*, Somerville House, Toronto, 1995, p. 60 et seq.
23 See 'Sacred Plants and Mystic Realities: an Interview with Terence McKenna' in Nevill Drury, *Echoes from the Void: Writings on Magic, Visionary Art and the New Consciousness*, Prism Press, Dorset, 1994, p. 158. This interview also appeared in Terence McKenna's anthology *The Archaic Revival*, HarperCollins, San Francisco, 1991.
24 ibid., pp. 159–60 and 166
25 ibid., p. 166

## CHAPTER 7

1 See Peter Russell, *The Awakening Earth*, Ark Books, London, 1982, p. 12
2 See Sun Bear, 'Honouring Sacred Places' in Fredric Lehrman (ed.), *The Sacred Landscape*, Celestial Arts Publishing, Berkeley, 1988, pp. 139–40
3 Quoted in Anna Voigt and Nevill Drury, *Wisdom from the Earth: The Living Legacy of the Aboriginal Dreamtime*, Simon & Schuster, Sydney, 1997, p. 66
4 See Ralph Metzner, 'Gaia's Alchemy: Ruin and Renewal of the Elements' in Fredric Lehrman (ed.), *The Sacred Landscape*, loc. cit., pp. 118–19
5 ibid.
6 See Ronald Valle, 'Relativistic Quantum Psychology' in Ronald S. Valle and Rolf von Eckarstberg (eds), *Metaphors of Consciousness*, Plenum, New York, 1981, p. 424
7 See Danah Zohar, *The Quantum Self*, Flamingo/HarperCollins, London, 1991, p. 5
8 See Stanislav Grof (ed.), *Ancient Wisdom and Modern Science*, State University of New York Press, Albany, 1984, p. 10
9 See Fritjof Capra, *The Tao of Physics*, Shambhala, Boulder, 1975, pp. 56–7

10 See David Bohm, *Wholeness and the Implicate Order*, Routledge & Kegan Paul, London, 1980, p. 172

11 See David Bohm, 'A New Theory of the Relationship of Mind and Matter' in *The Journal of the American Society of Psychical Research*, 1986, vol. 80, no. 2, p. 126

12 See June Singer, *Seeing Through the Visibile World: Jung, Gnosis and Chaos*, HarperCollins, San Francisco, 1980, p. 66

13 See Gary Zukav, *The Dancing Wu Li Masters: An Overview of the New Physics*, Flamingo, London, 1980, p. 55

14 See Stanislav Grof (ed.), *Ancient Wisdom and Modern Science*, op. cit., p. 9

15 See Robert Ornstein, *The Psychology of Consciousness*, Cape, London, 1975, p. 17

16 See Karl Pribram, 'The Holographic Hypothesis of Brain Functioning' in Stanislav Grof (ed.), *Ancient Wisdom and Modern Science*, op. cit., pp. 174–5

17 See Karl Pribram, 'Behaviorism, Phenomenology and Holism' in Ronald Valle and Rolf von Eckartsberg (eds) *The Metaphors of Consciousness*, op. cit., p. 148

18 See Karl Pribram in Grof, op. cit., pp. 178–9

19 See Danah Zohar, loc. cit., p. 106

20 ibid., p. 51

21 ibid., p. 151

22 See Fritjof Capra, 'The New Vision of Reality' in Grof, op. cit. pp. 144–5

23 ibid., p. 136

24 See Daniel C. Dennett, *Consciousness Explained*, Penguin Books, London, 1993, p. 33

25 See Stanislav Grof, loc. cit., p. 5

26 See Ian G. Barbour, *Myths, Models and Paradigms*, Harper & Row, New York, 1974, p. 105

## CHAPTER 8

1 Nevertheless, there are a significant number of historical cases that could also be considered as NDEs. Interested readers are referred to Carol Zaleski's fascinating book *Otherworld Journeys: Accounts of Near-Death Experience in Medieval and Modern Times*, Oxford University Press, New York, 1987

2  See Kenneth Ring, *Life at Death*, Coward McCann and Geoghegan, New York, 1980, pp. 96–7

3  See Michael Sabom, *Recollections of Death*, Corgi Books, London, 1982, pp. 70–1

4  Susan Blackmore, 'Visions of the World Beyond', *The Australian*, 14 May 1988 (reprinted from *The New Scientist*)

5  See Michael Sabom, op cit., pp. 70–1

6  From George Ritchie, 'Return from Tomorrow', quoted in Zoe Hagon, *Channelling*, Prism Press, Dorset, 1989, p. 97

7  This is by no means an isolated case. See also the case of Allan Lewis, reported in Bruce Elder, *And When I Die, Will I Be Dead?*, Australian Broadcasting Corporation, Sydney, 1987

8  See Sukie Miller, *After Death: Mapping the Journey*, Simon & Schuster, New York, 1997, p. 166

9  See Elisabeth Kubler-Ross, *On Life After Death*, Celestial Arts, Berkeley, California, p. 10

10  ibid., p. 9

11  ibid., p. 10

12  See interview with Elisabeth Kubler-Ross in Alexander Blair-Ewart (ed.), *Mindfire: Dialogues in the Other Future*, Somerville House, Toronto, 1995, p. 223

13  Elisabeth Kubler-Ross, *On Life After Death*, loc. cit., pp. 30–1

14  ibid., pp. 60–1

15  See Timothy Leary and R.U. Sirius, *Design for Dying*, HarperCollins, San Francisco, 1997, p. 99

16  ibid., p. 132

# Index

# Index